Hooked!

Hooked!

Buddhist Writings on Greed, Desire, and the Urge to Consume

EDITED BY

Stephanie Kaza

FOREWORD BY

PAUL HAWKEN

Shambhala

Boston & London ■ 2005

Shambhala Publications, Inc.
Horticultural Hall
300 Massachusetts Avenue
Boston, Massachusetts 02115
www.shambhala.com

9 8 7 6 5 4 3 2 1

First Edition

Printed in the United States of America

♾ This edition is printed on acid-free paper that meets the American
National Standards Institute z39.48 Standard.

Distributed in the United States by Random House, Inc., and in Canada
by Random House of Canada Ltd

Interior design and composition: Greta D. Sibley & Associates

Library of Congress Cataloging-in-Publication Data
Hooked!: Buddhist writings on greed, desire, and the urge to consume/edited
by Stephanie Kaza.—1st ed.
p.   cm.
Includes bibliographical references.
ISBN 1-59030-172-2 (pbk.: alk. paper)
1. Desire—Religious aspects—Buddhism. 2. Buddhism—Doctrines. I. Kaza,
Stephanie.
BQ4430.D47H66 2005
294.3´444—DC22
2004016053

Contents

Foreword

FOR PART OF MY CHILDHOOD, I was raised on a farm belonging to my Swedish grandmother and Scottish grandfather. Nothing was thrown away. Every other plate was chipped, but the china never left the dinner table with food on it. Gravy and juices were mopped up by homemade bread, vegetable peelings went to the chickens, the eggs were eaten at breakfast, the eggshells were put into the coffee grounds, the coffee grounds were placed into the compost, the compost was tilled into the garden, the beans and corn from the garden were canned into glass jars that joined the jams and jellies lining cool, dark basement walls. Paper lunch bags were brought back from school and neatly folded for the next day. Our idea of play included capturing horned toads and pretending they were dinosaurs or lying face up in the irrigation ditch, the tiny fry tickling our toes, and imagining we were floating down a great Amazonian river. Our only toy was a tire swing. Had my grandparents been from Chile, Korea, or Kerala, it essentially would have been the same. Nothing would have been wasted.

Until recently, most cultures and religions honored frugality and cautioned against excess. No longer. Western consumer society, the de facto global culture, is unique in all of history because underlying it is the highly developed consumption-based "science" called economics. It could even be called a science of voraciousness because at its roots is the belief that in order for nations to prosper, our desires must expand without limit. And grown they have. In the U.S. there are 45,000 shopping malls employing 10.7 million people. The average American family of four metabolizes four million pounds of material every year to support their lifestyle. That's 11,000 lbs. a day, 7.5 lbs. a minute. This keeps us busy, yet we are heedless because we don't see most of that consumption. It is offshore, and in mines, stockyards, slag heaps, landfills, and wastewater treatment plants. Billowing gases migrate to the stratosphere and double glaze the planet on behalf of us all. This constant expansion of desire and material goods forms our current definition of a healthy economy. Economists who take seriously the idea of steady-state production and consumption are marginalized or ignored by their peers although the deleterious effects of unquenchable desires are omnipresent. The consequences are studied by police, psychiatrists, physicians, sociologists, environmentalists, and biologists. But not economists.

In the Buddhist canon, there are six mind-states or realms, one of which is called the hungry ghost, depicted as a craven figure with a protuberant stomach and long pencil neck, a maundering wraith unable to satisfy its insatiable desires. In this realm, attempts to avoid pain by seeking satisfaction cause more pain for oneself and others. It is a useful metaphor reminding us of the compulsive shopper, the sports addict, the speculator, the megalithic global corporation hooking poor children around the world on fast food and hip-hop. In medieval times, the specter of the hungry ghost was a repugnant reminder of greed. Today the hungry ghost stars in movies and is the host on shopping channels. The women are svelte, tucked, and toothy; the men have private jets and new designer wives. At a private high school near my home, eighteen-year-olds hunger for today's car du jour, a Porsche Cayenne SUV.

It is tempting to see the problem of consumption as something other people do. People with SUVs should cut back and buy smaller cars, get more exercise, and use a bicycle. But this wonderfully edited volume shows us that it is more relevant and poignant to look at our own lives. A Buddhist perspective on consumption offers understanding of oneself. The quotidian ways in which we rob the earth are pathways to genuine insight. And in the awareness of self arises compassion for others, especially those who are weighed down so heavily by material desire. It is fair to say that people are overwhelmed by this world we share and live in. Alleviating people's sense of isolation and fear can do more than any recycling program. As Buddhist teachers so aptly point out, we can reduce our and others' desires by being generous and kind. It is hard to be grasping when we are reaching out.

Of course, we need to do everything in our power to lessen the harm to nature caused by this blowout sale of the earth's resources. More importantly, we must attend to the suffering this destruction visits upon people, rich and poor, everywhere. To live in this time and to attend to the suffering of others are gifts that we have received. All wars are wars of consumption, and every war starts with self. If we are borrowing resources from our grandchildren, which is an unpayable debt, we can also write checks of restoration to them. We can honor our veterans by not making more of them. We can honor an overpopulated world by welcoming and caring for every new child. We can honor resources by caring for everything that has already been made. We can begin to examine, mindfully and patiently, our every act and object, one by one, in order to understand how our lives affect others. We can use consumption, as is done in this book, as a means to know who and where we are. We can create lovely practices that remind us of the fragility of this earth and the joy of being able to reside here.

I have a friend who has, count them, six hundred objects in his home. That includes everything, even teaspoons. At one time he was officer of one of the world's largest banks. When he wants to buy something, or receives a gift, he selects something to give away. This is not a zero sum game. As the years have gone by, his home has become more nuanced and lovely. Every object has meaning; nothing is retained unnecessarily. His home is like a small temple. He needs very little money to live on, which means he spends most of this time helping others. He is utterly alive, elfish, bright-eyed and present.

We are human. We will always consume. The big question is how.

—Paul Hawken

Hooked!

Introduction

Stephanie Kaza

IN 1997 the film *Affluenza* premiered to audiences around the United States, offering a diagnosis for what ails the planet. It spoke to people of all political persuasions, receiving high ratings in both conservative and liberal cities. The virus at loose seemed to be infecting every member of society and, as the film's producer, John de Graaf, said, "threatening our wallets, our friendships, our families, our communities, and our environment."[1] In coining the term, he defined affluenza as "a painful, contagious, socially transmitted condition of overload, debt, anxiety, and waste resulting from the dogged pursuit of more."

The film received tremendous response. Finally someone was making an effort to confront the high-impact habits of the consumer society. How was it possible that Americans spend more for trash bags than 90 of the world's 210 countries spend for everything? Could it really be true that we have twice as many shopping malls as high schools? That we consume our average body weight—120 pounds—every day in extracted and processed materials? That humans take 40 percent of the earth's entire plant productivity for themselves?

These dramatic figures caught my attention. As a professor and student of environmental studies, I have been following the accelerating decline of the earth's resources for thirty years. For the most part, it is very

1

discouraging. To engage this information with students is often heart-breaking work. Species extinction, dying lakes, contaminated oceans, nuclear accidents, oil spills—the degradation of virtually every aspect of life is hard news to swallow. Even harder is the realization that human actions are responsible for much of the decline. The film *Affluenza* pointed out the obvious: the current rates of consumption are not sustainable. Life-support systems are giving out.

To deal with my own despair around these issues, I developed a course called "Unlearning Consumerism." Each week the students undertook a lab exercise to evaluate some aspect of their consumption habits. One of our first exercises was "the property list." The students had to make a list of *all* of their belongings, from underwear to electric guitars. The group also took up analyses of energy use, transportation habits, and food consumed. Students assessed their diets not in calories but in estimated energy expense to the planet. To break the grip of everyday consumption, I assigned a three-day technology fast. The students had to give up the Internet, the car, the television, or another technology of their choice and then evaluate the impact it carried in their lives.

This class and the students' enthusiastic response got me started in pursuing the links between consumption and environmental degradation. For too long economic development has focused mostly on technological improvement and population issues in Third World countries. Examining our own levels of consumption has been virtually off the table. "The American way of life is not up for negotiation," said President George H. W. Bush at the 1992 Earth Summit in Brazil. Fortunately this cloak of silence has been lifted by excellent research. In 1999 the Union for Concerned Scientists analyzed in detail the impact of U.S. energy use, transportation, food production, and housing on ecosystem health.[2] They sorted through consumer dilemmas such as paper versus plastic bags and concluded it was the big-ticket items—housing and vehicle use—that need our greatest attention. In 2004 the Worldwatch Institute focused its entire *State of the World* report on the consumer society, presenting current figures on global rates of resource use and generation of waste. The authors argued that it is not only possible but essential to move toward a less consumptive society.[3]

But there are other reasons to study this topic. Philosopher David Loy shows how "the Market" has become a world religion, replacing traditional religions in determining our reigning worldview and values. The two unshakable and unchallengeable statements of faith in this religion are (1) that growth and enhanced world trade will benefit everyone, and (2) that growth will not be constrained by the inherent limits of a finite planet. From a religious perspective, the power of this worldview lies in its extremely effective conversion techniques. The seductive appeal of product after product captures the masses, replacing other approaches to meaning and satisfaction. Loy points out that a significant flaw of economic religion is that it depletes "moral capital." Though the market requires character traits such as trust in order to be efficient, it simultaneously tends to erode personal responsibility for other people. Just as the market depends on the biosphere to regenerate natural capital, it also depends on the human community to regenerate moral capital. To confront the impact of consumerism is to confront this moral deterioration.[4]

My own concern is that consumer identity is crowding out or displacing ecological identity. Our sense of place, ecological concerns, and environmental values (such as respect, compassion, and reverence for life) make up our ecological identity. These all influence how we relate to the earth and to what degree we make environmentally conscious choices. Consumer identity, in contrast, is based on brand-name preferences, material possessions, class status, social group, and market desires. Just as ecological identity is tied to environmental behavior, consumer identity is tied to purchasing behavior. When more time is taken up in consumer activities, the consumer identity flourishes, and less time is available for cultivating our ecological identity.

But the greatest motivator for studying consumption and consumerism may in the end be self-preservation. All signs point to increasing difficulty in sustaining ecological life-support systems and thus the human populations dependent on them. Pollution, depletion, and resource damage continue to worsen, taking an enormous toll on ecosystems and human health. As developing countries increase their rates of consumption, the rate of environmental impact increases even faster. Multiply this by the growing world population and an aspiring global consumer class and the result is only more alarming. While predictions indicate population levels may eventually stabilize, rates of consumption seem only to be growing.

Before proceeding much further, let me clarify some of these terms and provide a little historical context for this current wave of consumerism. Neva Goodwin, director of the Tufts Global Development and Environmental Institute, defines the consumer society as characterized by its use of leisure time for spending money and for its belief that owning things is

3

the primary means to happiness, the assumed primary goal in life. In a consumption-oriented society, your identity is tied more to what you consume than to what you produce. "Consumerism" as a belief system accepts consumption "as the way to self-development, self-realization, and self-fulfillment."[5] At its 1997 international meeting in Japan, the Buddhist Think Sangha defined consumerism further as

> the dominant culture of a modernizing invasive industrialism which stimulates—yet can never satisfy—the urge for a strong sense of self to overlay the angst and sense of lack in the human condition. As a result, goods, services, and experiences are consumed beyond any reasonable need. This undermines the ecosystem, the quality of life, and particularly traditional cultures and communities and the possibility of spiritual liberation.[6]

British cultural theorists Yiannis Gabriel and Tim Lang identify five understandings of "consumerism," which reveal its complexity in sociocultural discourse. It can be seen as (1) a moral doctrine for developed countries—the vehicle to freedom and power as well as happiness; (2) a social ideology for establishing class distinctions; (3) an economic ideology for global development (in contrast to the austerity of communism); (4) a political ideology, with the modern state protecting transnational corporations; and (5) a social movement promoting the rights of consumers.[7]

Consumption per se is not inherently problematic. Everyone must consume to survive. But when it becomes an end in itself or the primary measure of economic success, then it overruns other social goals of well-being. Looking back to some of the origins of today's consumerism, historian Peter Stearns describes the consumer society of mid-nineteenth-century Europe, where the commercial economy was developing rapidly.[8] Trade with global colonies sparked interest in cotton from India and porcelain from China. Small shops and markets took up the practice of advertising to promote a range of personal products from perfume to parasols. With increased prosperity from expanded trade, especially the slave trade, more goods were sold for profit. The rationalist philosophy of the time reinforced secular values, undercutting the importance of traditional religious values of restraint and frugality.

In the early years of the United States, consumerism was slow to take off because of the financial struggle for independence and the strong Puritan values. But once the country stabilized and manufacturing expanded, an explosion of consumer goods entered the marketplace. The first department stores with their wide array of products and changing fashions were all the rage. Agencies dedicated specifically to advertising developed persuasive techniques to help producers compete effectively. With the invention of radio, and later television, advertisers spread their gospel far and wide.

The consumer society we know today took shape in the 1920s with the emergence of brand names and packaged, processed foods for a growing urban culture. Economists deemed mass consumption beyond basic needs as key to U.S. economic and political success. Supporting the economy was (and still is) touted as a patriotic duty. Though consumption slowed temporarily during the Great Depression and World War II, after the war the boom was on. Inspired by the stunning success of wartime production, government leaders expanded their vision of the United States as a major world economic leader. President Dwight Eisenhower's chief economic advisor proclaimed that the ultimate purpose of the American economy was "to produce more consumer goods."[9]

Since the 1950s, a significant factor driving consumption has been the steady commercialization of the household economy. In earlier times, people managed their own cooking, gardening, food storage, laundry, and clothes making. As women shifted into the labor market, these functions shifted into the money economy. Business soared in fast food, household appliances, and ready-made clothing. With the advent of efficient shipping and globalized trade, consumerism spread beyond the borders of the industrialized countries. Coca-Cola products are now found in more than 170 countries; McDonald's opens two thousand new restaurants each day somewhere in the world.[10] As the values and structures of this wave of consumerism have spread around the globe, they have been met with both fascination and resistance. People in Japan took rapid adoption of Western goods as a sign of modernization, releasing them from two hundred years of isolation. People in the Middle East, in contrast, targeted consumerism as a threat to Islamic moral and social principles.

What makes the current wave of consumerism distinct from previous eras is that it encompasses the entire world community and gravely threatens the future health of the planet. The ecological consequences of manufacturing, waste, and global trade now affect every region and country. Environmental or social impacts in one region multiply in cascading complexity as products travel around the world to expanding markets. The pace of economic globalization over the last decade has accelerated so rapidly it is impossible even to keep track of all the changes. It seems that affluenza has penetrated every reach of the globe.

SCOPE OF IMPACT

What exactly does this global consumption look like on the ground? Let's take an example that illustrates the far-reaching impacts of North American consumption—our beloved coffee. Say the average person drinks two cups a day. A year's worth of coffee is about eighteen pounds of beans per year, which requires twelve coffee trees along with eleven pounds of fertilizer and pesticides. In the processing, forty pounds of coffee pulp are released into rivers, consuming life-supporting oxygen as they decompose. The beans travel to the United States and are roasted using natural gas. After being packed in multilayer bags, they are shipped by trucks (getting six miles to the gallon) to a regional warehouse. Coffee is the second-leading export crop in the world after oil and is the second-largest source of foreign income for developing nations. In the cool highlands of Costa Rica, Brazil, and Colombia, thousands of acres of biologically rich tropical forest have been cleared to support the North American boom in espresso shops.[11]

What about the other items on our breakfast table? Orange juice from Brazil, grapes from Chile, apples from New Zealand, cocoa from Malaysia, bananas from Costa Rica—all of these appear at the supermarket with production and shipping costs virtually invisible. An average bite of American food travels more than twelve hundred miles from field to fork. Food processing, packaging, distribution, and storage in the United States use 17 percent of all energy consumption, and food packaging makes up 20 percent of municipal solid waste. More than 6.5 million tons of food travel around the earth each year, with global markets competing for consumers' dollars. This unfortunately leads producers to cut costs, raising the hazards of food-borne disease.[12] The global consumer class eats the lion's share of the world's meat and consumes in one form or another 40 percent of the world's grain.

Indicators show that the consumer class is responsible for most of the environmental impact on the planet. Industrial nations use 62 percent of the world's oil, with the United States' oil use alone increasing over the last ten years by 2.7 million barrels a day. Though Americans comprise less than 5 percent of the earth's people, they produce 25 percent of greenhouse gas emissions. The global consumer class is responsible for 90 percent of the chlorofluorocarbons destroying the ozone layer and 96 percent of the world's radioactive waste.[13] Per capita fossil fuel use is conspicuously highest for people in the United States. The total number of cars in the world has gone from 50 million in 1950 to 500 million in 1990 and is projected to double again by 2015.[14]

Today the picture is changing dramatically as more and more of the world joins the consumer class. Of the estimated 1.7 billion members of the consumer class, nearly half are now in the developing world. China, for example, added eleven thousand more cars to its streets every day in 2003. In India the film and electronics industries are growing rapidly, supplying economic support for a consumer lifestyle. Together China and India's consumer class is 20 percent of the world total, larger than the entire consumer class of western Europe. If the average Chinese consumer increased his or her energy budget to American levels, China would need 90 million barrels of oil each day—11 million more than were even produced each day in 2001 for all the world's consumers.[15]

As the global consumer class grows, so does consumer waste. Americans remain the waste champions, producing 51 percent more waste per person than any other industrialized nation. Certain product waste streams are growing at an astonishing rate, especially electronic waste. By 2005 the global collection of used cell phones may top 500 million, most destined for landfills. Obsolete computers are an even greater challenge, with more than half a billion sold in 2002. Electronic waste is the source of 70 percent of the heavy metals found in U.S. landfills. Many computers are recycled to China as part of the toxics trade flow, with workers picking through parts by hand for anything of value.[16]

Environmental impacts alone are reason enough to challenge the explosion of global consumerism. But social, psychological, and human health are also strongly affected by consumer values and priorities. Mass-marketing techniques perfected in the United States are now employed on every continent, impacting local values and eroding cultural self-esteem. Helena Norberg-Hodge has documented the rapid erosion of local values in Ladakh and Bhutan.[17] Contact with goods from outside the culture has dramatically increased the desire to buy them. In a very short time, local people have come to see their internal standards of value as secondary to the high status represented by American goods. Industrial-scale, chemically dependent cash-cropping systems have replaced locally adapted agricultural practices in order to supply consumer goods. For Norberg-Hodge, economic globalization is establishing a social monoculture, destroying cultural as well as ecological diversity in its wake.

Psychological effects may be harder to measure, but David Loy and others suggest that the drive to consume has displaced the psychic space once filled by religion, family, and community. More time spent on personal lifestyle pleasures tends to mean less time spent in civic engagement and public life. Kalle Lasn, author of *Culture Jam*, speaks of "microjolts of commercial pollution" that flood our brains—about three thousand marketing messages per day. "Every day, an estimated 12 billion display ads, 3 million radio commercials, and more than 200,000 TV commercials are dumped into North Americans' collective unconscious."[18] Around the world, dollars spent on advertising reached $446 billion in 2002. Advertisers will now go everywhere and anywhere to sell their products, even printing logos on hot dogs and eggs! With competition so fierce for the consumer dollar, people are barraged by sales pitches on subways, at cash registers, in airports, and on ski lifts. Even if they forget the ad, they entrain the message: There is a product to solve life's every problem.

Advertising deliberately promotes a climate of self-centeredness revolving around material desires, setting up stereotypes that foster greed, status envy, hyperstimulation, and at root, a sense of psychological dissatisfaction and inadequacy. Children are particularly vulnerable to commercial brainwashing, easily replacing their authentic needs and wants with what they've been told to want. It is not uncommon for people to turn to shopping to alleviate their suffering. If this becomes a deeply entrenched habit, they become "shopaholics," caught in a cycle of desire and dissatisfaction.[19]

Author Bill McKibben once did the experiment of watching every minute of television that was aired on a single day by the largest cable system at the time.[20] He concluded that the central theme, repeated on ad after ad, was this: "You are the most important thing on earth." Can this really be the primary orientation of our times? In place of caring for others, look out for yourself. Instead of communing with God or nature, surf the shopping channel. McKibben calls this "I-dolatry," the extreme self-referencing fostered by the profiteers of consumerism.

Understandably, psychic numbing and depression are not uncommon among those afflicted with affluenza. Physical as well as mental diseases of consumption are on the rise. Being a member of an affluent society is correlated with high rates of heart disease, cancer, and diabetes. More than a billion people worldwide are now overweight or obese. Though consumerism offers many attractive opportunities for pleasure and comfort, its hidden shadow is now becoming alarmingly visible.

ROLE FOR RELIGION

What is the role for religion in responding to this state of affairs? How should religious leaders and institutions engage the moral dimensions of consumerism? For some denominations, the environmental crisis has served as a wake-up call, inspiring study groups and greening projects. Others raise issues of global inequity, the condition of the poor, the driving presence of greed in the world economy. Religions have historically played an important role in raising fundamental questions about the quality and meaning of life. Over the last decade there has been increasing scholarly attention as well as activism addressing environmental issues from a religious perspective.[21] The Center for a New American Dream, among others, has developed specific projects addressing the moral concerns related to consumerism.

Gary Gardner, Worldwatch Institute researcher, points to five significant assets religions can contribute to the global dialogue on environment (and consumerism).[22] For one, religions wield considerable moral authority, both in their own pulpits and in some political arenas. They have, as a body, a very large membership base and extensive material resources (both financial and real estate) that can be engaged to raise awareness. They are also a strong influence in shaping worldviews and would be supportive in questioning consumerist ideology from more deeply rooted values. Perhaps their greatest asset is the religious capacity for building community and social capital. Some of the most intractable aspects of consumerism will be dislodged only through creating better infrastructures for well-being. Religiously based communities hold great potential for leading the way.

Consumer resistance movements have almost always been morally driven.[23] Gandhi promoted the values of frugality and local production, urging his followers to boycott British goods. The Japanese consumer co-op movement resisted the government's plan to import U.S. rice, defending the values of self-sufficiency. When Ralph Nader took on the automobile industry, he challenged the collusion and secrecy behind commercial interests. Recent resistance movements have taken up ethical issues related to environmental protection and fair trade. First World consumers have found ways to join in solidarity with Third World producers, offering moral alternatives to sweatshop clothing and unfair trade pressures. Activist campaigns questioning bioengineered crops have catalyzed a storm of global doubt, slowing consumer acceptance of genetically engineered products. By engaging the moral issues involved in these concerns, religious institutions could expand citizen participation considerably, advancing both knowledge and moral integrity.

Given these possibilities, is there a particular role for Buddhism to play? To date, Buddhist initiatives in this conversation have been modest. Several books have popularized Buddhist values of simplicity and restraint, most notably E. F. Schumacher's *Small Is Beautiful* and Gary Snyder's *The Practice of the Wild*. Some Western Buddhist teachers have taken up particular themes relating to consumption—Philip Kapleau on vegetarianism and Robert Aitken on reducing wants and needs. Thich Nhat Hanh has expanded the fifth precept (no abuse of delusion-producing substances) to include junk television, advertising, magazines, and candy.[24] Among scholars, Rita Gross has explored Buddhist positions regarding population, consumption, and the environment.[25] Leading Thai intellectual Phra Payutto has written on Buddhist economics; activist Sulak Sivaraksa has advocated Buddhist principles of compassion and skillful means in economic development.[26] Philosopher David Loy has addressed poverty, greed, and the driving psychology of "lack" as it plays out in consumerism.[27]

As I have worked with authors on the chapters in this book, it has become more and more clear that Buddhism offers many useful and compelling paths for unlearning consumerism. Buddhist philosophy begins with the deep grasp of suffering as the fundamental ground of existence. This opens the way for examining the wide scope of suffering related to consumerism—for people certainly, but also for plants and animals, mountains and rivers. Suffering or fear of suffering (economically or politically) can also be seen as driving the actions and policies of nation-states. The suffering takes countless forms at many levels, from individual to structural systems. Because consumerism is a completely human phenomenon, every aspect of it reflects human fallibility and suffering.

Looking to the causes of suffering, the Buddhist approach focuses on desire or craving: "Desires are endless, I vow to put an end to them." This line in a Zen chant indicates the comprehensive scope of desire—for things, states of mind, preferences, and above all, the desire for relief from suffering. This is the condition of life, a driving force of our basic animal existence. We may think that consumerism is to blame for making our lives miserable, but actually our lives are already filled with suffering. Consumerism only magnifies this condition by multiplying desire.

Perhaps the most useful of the Buddhist teachings is the insight into the emptiness of the ego self. This view holds the key to releasing attachment to the constant self-inflating messages of consumerism. From a Buddhist perspective, what we perceive as the individual self is actually a fleeting aggregation of form and energy, shaped by countless causes and conditions. Believing in an autonomous independent self is a serious delusion in this view. Buddhist practice helps in breaking through the multiple reinforcing beliefs and activities that reify the false self. Many time-proven techniques have been developed to work with the persistent habits of mind that protect this self. Koans, meditation, visualizations, monastic training all provide opportunities for unraveling these false views. With hooks at every turn, consumerism presents a remarkably rich field for practice.

Seeing this teaching of emptiness from the other side, we find another useful Buddhist perspective—the law of interdependence. If all existence is shaped by causes and conditions, we can study the nature of those conditions and see how they interrelate. The Buddhist view shifts emphasis from objects or beings to the relationships that form them. A relational worldview is not unique to Buddhism, but coupled with emptiness, it becomes a powerful tool for dismantling the structures of consumerism. The many examples in this book show how this relational understanding can support ethical restraint and fruitful inquiry. It can also point the way to creating alternatives to consumerism, making new links of codependence that support well-being over material wealth.

It would be misleading to imply that Buddhism has all the answers. It certainly doesn't. Many have criticized Buddhism for being weak on structural analysis of social systems (such as consumerism) and equally weak on activist strategies for social change. Buddhism does not carry the great charge for social justice, for example, that the Abrahamic traditions hold. It is an open question whether Buddhism can be a force for social change regarding consumerism. It may be that the greatest Buddhist contribution to this arena will be at the individual level, helping people evaluate lifestyle and consumer choices. But there are some fledgling examples in Japan and Thailand that show what is possible when Buddhist leadership and teaching are engaged.

This book arose out of my own concern that accelerating levels of consumption have gone way beyond any intelligent limits of sustainability. No one is steering the planetary ship; instead all parties seem bent on pursuing their own short-term individual goals. How to work with such a planet-sized koan? I knew I could not penetrate the puzzle on my own enough to make a difference. But I thought Buddhism might offer some handholds, some time-tested teachings to temper the raging appetites around the globe.

The work in this book builds on several earlier collections of readings on Buddhism and ecology.[28] The most recent of these, *Dharma Rain*, laid out a broad range of published texts, commentaries, and personal explorations that frame an introduction to Buddhist sources of environmentalism. I wanted to follow up on this with some fresh thinking, what might be called "constructive theology" in Christian terms. What new light could experienced Buddhist thinkers bring to the rascally problems of consumerism? I looked for Buddhist teachers, scholars, and practitioners who shared some of my concern for the environment and who were interested in bringing their bright minds to this arena of environmental thought. I asked them each to follow their own strongest leads, drawing on the teachings they knew best. It was important to me that this book reflect Theravada, Zen, Tibetan, and Pure Land views to show how each tradition might work with consumerism.

I felt a Buddhist nonjudgmental perspective could be very helpful in looking deeply at the complex conundrum of consumerism. Evangelical anticonsumerism messages tend to be simplistic and often don't advance the conversation much at all. I really wanted to know in the biggest sense: What is going on here? How deeply can we look, accepting fully that we are all in the soup together? As I worked with the authors, we taught each other in the editing process, refining insights and clarifying the specific elements of Buddhist thought that offer skillful means for understanding. Though many topics have been addressed here, we sense we have just scratched the surface of this Big Conversation.

The book is organized into three sections, with five or six essays in each section. The first section, "Getting Hooked: Desire and Attachment," contains pieces that describe in Buddhist terms what is actually going on in the process of consumption. The authors look at greed, delusion, and attachment, showing how the common phenomenon of "being hooked" illuminates ego clinging. The second section, "Practicing with Desire: Using Buddhist Tools," contains essays that explain Buddhist methods for working with desire or craving and the urge to consume. This includes the Four Noble Truths, the Three Refuges, the Twelve Links of Codependent Origination, causal analysis, the Middle Way, and Dogen's being-time sutra. The third section, "Buddhist Ethics of Consumption," focuses on particular Buddhist principles or virtues that might be useful in developing Buddhist guidelines for consumer choices. These essays draw on classic texts and current initiatives to lift up Buddhist values such as simplicity, frugality, generosity, and nonharming.

My hope for the book is that it provides many springboards for conversation—for Buddhists and non-Buddhists alike. For activists working in the field, I hope these essays will support your own quest for moral direction in the work. For students of Buddhism, I hope this writing will add to your understanding of Buddhism in the everyday world. For all those interested in the speeding train of consumerism, I hope this book adds to your capacity for preventing a disastrous train wreck!

The authors of these pieces have been generous and gracious through every step of the process with me. I deeply appreciate their willingness to work with my editing suggestions with an open mind. They each took great care in crafting their essays, speaking strongly from personal practice experience and knowledge of Buddhist teachings. They have given their best good-faith effort in preparing these essays; all errors that remain are fully my own.

PART ONE

Getting Hooked

Desire and Attachment

Desire, Delusion, and DVDs

Joseph Goldstein

SOME TIME AGO, His Holiness the Dalai Lama was giving a series of teachings in Los Angeles. Every day on his way from the hotel to where he was speaking, he was driven down a particular street filled with people selling all the latest high-tech gadgets. At first he just looked with interest at the different things in the windows as he passed by. By the end of the week, he found himself wanting things even though he didn't know what they were! Desire is *very* strong. It is hardwired into our biology as part of what helps us survive. If even the Dalai Lama sees wanting arise in the mind, we know this is not trivial conditioning.

In the early years of my practice, as I sat in Bodh Gaya with my teacher, Anagarika Munindra, he would often speak of the difficulty of escaping the gravitational field of the world of sense pleasures. Our lives seem to revolve around desire for ever-new experiences, even as we see how fleeting they are. All the things we gather in our lives will inevitably be dispersed. Either we lose interest in them (as so often happens), or they break, or they remain in the corner of some closet until we move or die. Yet the tendency toward accumulation is very strong. Our homes somehow keep filling with stuff.

Covetousness, the wanting mind, the feeling that we never have enough, is seen in Buddhism as unskillful action of the mind. In the framework of the Buddhist cosmology and the different realms of existence, this covetous mind state is most extreme in the hungry-ghost realm. Hungry ghosts are often depicted as having huge stomachs and pinhole mouths, showing how they are incapable of ever feeling satisfied. In our own culture, we might call it "catalog consciousness," obsessively rifling through the pages to see what else we might want. This is "wanting to want," a disease our culture keeps nourishing.

Why do we invest so much energy in acquisition? There may be many psychological underpinnings of this behavior, seeing it as compensatory action, even at times compulsion for some deeper lack. But we can also understand the force behind this habit of accumulation in a simpler way, namely, the profound influence our consumer society has on our minds. It continually reinforces desires and wanting, often co-opting spiritual values to do so. One of the examples I use a lot in talking about desire is a magazine advertisement for a fancy SUV. There on the glossy page is a view of a beautiful couple in front of their expensive car, surrounded by hundreds of objects, all supposedly contributing to their happiness. The caption on the ad reads, "To be one with everything, you need one of everything."

The wonderful paradox of the spiritual path is that transitory phenomena as objects of our desire leave us feeling unfulfilled, while as objects of mindfulness they can become vehicles of awakening. When we try to possess and hold on to things or experiences that are fleeting in nature, we are left feeling finally unsatisfied. Yet when we look with mindful attention at the constantly changing nature of these same things or experiences, we are no longer quite so driven by the thirst of desire. By mindfulness, I mean the quality of paying full attention to the moment, opening to the truth of change and impermanence. We all know that things change, but how many of us live and act from that place of understanding? The more deeply we can see the impermanent nature of reality, the less seduced we are by impermanent phenomena such as consumer goods.

Mindfulness training keeps us focused in a very precise way on the law of dependent origination. Through paying close attention, we can follow the links of how we get caught in desire—sensing, contact, feelings, desire, grasping, and so on. To be released from this chain of dependent origination, we can work to break the connection between feelings and desire. Each link depends on the others; if any of the conditions cease to exist, the entire cycle of desire is disrupted. We can observe the conditioning of contact, noting the feeling of pleasantness, and then stay mindful of that feeling.

One of the things I discovered in my own practice, which speaks to my relation to consumerism, was how desire works on very subtle levels. For example, when I'm on retreat and I find myself desiring a cup of tea, I might be inclined to get up and gratify that desire. This is because I am focusing strongly on the object of my wanting, the cup of tea. But if I shift my focus from the object to the anticipated feeling of satisfaction, I can be aware that it is the pleasant feelings associated with the tea that are really what I am after. It is then much easier to remember that these feelings are fleeting. Remembering this impermanence, I am less hooked by the object of desire. If we focus on the object, which appears to be more real, it is harder to resist the desire; we are more fooled by the apparent substantiality of the object and less able to see its impermanence. When we focus on the feelings, we have a greater chance of remembering the impermanent nature of feeling, thus breaking the link that generates the wanting. Still, the habit pattern of wanting is very strong.

Some might say that the primary emotional motivator for consumerism is greed. But this greed is itself born from delusion. Delusion is characterized by confusion, bewilderment, by not seeing things as they are. We call this delusion of mind "ignorance." A central focus of Buddhist teaching is the suffering that comes from delusion or ignorance, the delusion of holding a fundamentally wrong view. Greed is fed by one particularly strong aspect of delusion, namely, the delusion of a separate, independently existing self. The big question for the Buddha was how to awaken from this ignorance.

We usually think of self-centeredness as a personality problem, something our friends might suggest we go to therapy for. But *self-centered* has a more fundamental meaning. Self-centeredness occurs when we create or hold a sense of self at the center of our lives, a reference point for all we think and sense and feel. The self-center is the idea or felt sense of someone behind all experience to whom it is happening. Most of us live in the powerful field of this self-center, circling around our hopes and fears, our plans and worries, our work and relationships, and our multitude of possessions.

There are many different descriptions of awakening, but all Buddhist traditions converge in one understanding of what liberates the mind. The Buddha expressed it clearly and unequivocally: "Nothing whatsoever is to be clung to as 'I' or 'mine.' Whoever has heard this truth has heard all the Teachings, whoever practices this truth has practiced all the Teachings, whoever has realized this truth has realized all the Teachings."[1] This is the essential unifying experience of freedom—the heart of liberation: nothing whatsoever is to be clung to as "I" or "mine." Our unfolding experience keeps changing—sometimes it is pleasant, sometimes unpleasant—but the practice of freedom is always the same, namely liberation through nonclinging.

The Buddha pointed out the major arenas of attachment, in both our meditation practice and our daily lives. We can investigate these attachments in our minds, learn how to let them go, and thus practice the mind of freedom. The attachment of pleasant feelings reveals a lot about the power of addiction, fascination, and enchantment. Thus we have my wanting that cup of tea on retreat, or wanting the pleasant feelings it might generate. On a deeper level, we can cling to pleasant experiences in meditation, feelings of great rapture, calm, happiness, and peace.

We can also become quite attached to our opinions and views about things, attached to being right. Clinging to views is subtler than attachments to sense pleasures, which, though they run deep, are usually not difficult to notice. But the views and opinions we hold are often difficult to see, even though they determine how we perceive the world. Attachment or clinging to views, even if they are worthy or just, can create problems and actually be counterproductive. People involved in critiquing consumerism, for example, can be quite attached to their perspectives, attacking others for their actions and differing points of view. This is not good for one's own mental health and is not necessarily the most effective strategy for social change. Nobody wants to hear a diatribe. The energy of that is very draining. In the name of letting go of consumer objects, the critics are actually holding on to views. I think a careful distinction could be drawn here between attachment and commitment. We can be totally committed to social or political change and still keep our minds and hearts open and inclusive.

The deepest attachment that conditions our lives and understanding is the clinging to the concept of self. Whenever we identify with any particular aspect of our experience, we create a felt sense of self. There are many examples of this. We see this clearly in the relationship we have to our bodies and all that we buy to keep them beautiful, healthy, youthful. This body, which we hold and cherish, seems to define our root answer to the question "Who am I?" It is reflected in our fear of death and resistance to aging. We also create a sense of self when we identify with thoughts or when we identify with the stories we make up about our experience. Thoughts are tremendously seductive. When they go unnoticed, they have compelling power; they become the dictators of the mind. Thoughts of the new car we want or the bigger house we must have can carry great weight in determining our actions.

LIBERATION THROUGH NONCLINGING

Although renunciation is a central aspect of the Buddha's teachings, many of us in the West have a difficult time with this idea. Renunciation is not a particularly appreciated cultural value. And even if we are somewhat aware of its value, it may not be all that inspiring. In Saint Augustine's famous prayer, he says "Dear Lord, make me chaste, but not yet." But another way of talking about renunciation is through understanding it as "nonaddiction." Whereas "renunciation" feels like a burden or sense of deprivation, "nonaddiction" implies freedom, which is something all of us want. Using familiar language and awareness about addiction, we can investigate addictions to food, television, to consuming itself. This language helps to identify the problem and suggests the possibility of freedom.

From a Buddhist perspective (not necessarily an economic one), the basic renunciation is internal. In the Buddha's time there were many wealthy people living the good life of that era, who were able through practice to achieve some understanding of the nature of desire. Unless one chooses the monastic path, I don't think it is essential to give up a comfortable lifestyle in order to practice renunciation. The inner work is in letting go, in the renunciation of the wandering mind, of afflictive emotions, of the idea of self. The Buddha taught people in a wide range of lifestyles, from kings to paupers. In one teaching he said that it is better to live in a palace and be free of desire than to be in a cave consumed by the wanting mind. Often the issue was excess, not the consuming itself. At one point the Buddha counseled a king who was a glutton. The Buddha spoke with him about the importance of letting go of that addiction for his own health and well-being. When addiction results in excess, renunciation offers a route to freedom.

Meditative retreat situations provide some support for reducing consumer urges. People come on retreats for many reasons, one being to de-stress from work, relationships, or personal problems. Consumerism is not usually at the top of their list of concerns. Those who come to Buddhist centers tend to be already preselected for values congruent with reduced consumerism. But even if it is not why they came on retreat, people often find huge relief in being in a situation that doesn't feed the wanting. On retreat they are able to temporarily experience the ease and simplicity of monastic life. That was one of the great things about living in India all those years; we were just living so simply. We all had very little money, and we kept our wants to basic needs. But even in this narrow field, the consuming mind could still wonder—"Oh, where can I get a nice shawl?" Generally people seem to appreciate being in a place where there is not much opportunity to consume.

Silence is another strong support for weakening greed. With relatively little eye contact and no talking, people feel less need to present themselves to other people. The whole self-image machine goes into slow motion. At the Insight Meditation Society (IMS) center there is nothing to buy, no bookstore, no vending machines—there are very few distractions. Yogis are encouraged to stay on the grounds and avoid whatever few consumerist temptations there are in a small New England town. Still, some do wander off in search of a hamburger, or whatever it is they think they need.

Our center, like a number of others, is in a rural setting, so people often do walking meditation out in nature, calmed by the trees and the land. This also helps tame the acquiring mind. When you're out in nature, you are just present with what is there; you feel less need for something to consume. On the three-month fall retreats, being outside is an especially strong support for renunciation. As the leaves turn and the season settles in toward winter, it is a very inner-directed time of year.

Buddhist centers can also be very useful in helping people clarify their motivations. For me, this is an essential aspect of practice and understanding. A Tibetan phrase expresses it well: "Everything rests on the tip of motivation." There is a significant difference, both in how we feel and in the effect on others, between actions motivated by greed and those motivated by generosity—even when the outward action appears to be the same. The consequences of each motivation will be very different, both in the moment and in the long run. Given the importance of motivation in affecting the results of our actions, it becomes essential that we actually know what our motivations are. This is not easy. If we stay unaware, we simply play out all the habits of our conditioning, including the way we have been conditioned as consumers.

People who come on retreat can study their motivations deliberately and then use this capacity in the world to clarify their reasons for action. Motivation can be very subtle and thus can benefit from awareness training. It takes a lot of practice to look closely at our intentions. Most of us tend to think that basically our motivations are pure, but it is much more complex than that. More often they are mixed, conflicting, ambiguous. This applies to most acts of buying, but really it applies to everything. Media and marketers promoting consumerist messages can play on these mixed motivations and highlight particular internal messages, in effect giving them more air-time. This then makes it harder to recognize and connect with other motivations that may be driven into the background beneath those loudspeakers. I feel that meditation retreats are essential just to give people a chance to study their motivation and develop some clarity that can help them when they return to a more complicated world.

Commitment to Buddhist practice does not necessarily require a radical change in lifestyle. But it may suggest a change in our time allocation that reflects a shift of priorities. People are often amazed that almost one hundred people have been coming each year to the three-month retreats at IMS. They wonder, how do they get the time to do that? When something becomes a very high priority, people figure it out and find the time, even if it takes several years of planning. In general though, after meditation retreats, even highly committed Buddhists continue to live in the way they're accustomed to. It is very unusual to see students simplify their lives drastically, give away all their belongings and savings, and become monks or nuns, although I have seen this happen. Even short of such a level of letting go, everyone can cultivate renunciation in the form of practicing greater generosity.

The practice of generosity can serve as a corrective to addictive consumerism. Generosity enacts the quality of nongreed; it is a willingness to give, to share, to let go. It may be the giving of time, energy, resources, love, and even in rare cases, one's own life for the benefit and welfare of others. Generosity weakens the tendency of attachment and grasping and is intimately connected with the feeling of lovingkindness. People who experience the power and joy of generosity will also experience its effect on consuming. The cultivation of generosity offers a very strong antidote to the wanting mind and would be a powerful corrective if taken up in a widespread way across our culture.

REDUCING HARM

So we can ask the question: Within our culture, what constitutes excess? Are we consuming much more than we actually need—even if we are not leading a renunciate lifestyle? We can also ask, what is excess in the context of our culture within the global economy? These are two different questions, for what may appear to be commonplace or moderate in most homes in America would be seen as excess in the context of the global economy. We can use these questions either as bludgeons of self-judgment or as thoughtful inquiry into our lives and the choices we make, including our choice of what to consume. Recently I purchased a DVD player. But since I already had a perfectly good VCR, was buying the DVD excessive? Does it represent greed? It may be completely ordinary in many American households, but do I need it? These are questions that are, at the least, worth asking.

In order to survive, we have to consume, but by what guidelines do we choose what and how much? The first and most fundamental principle to apply is nonharming. Often this becomes a matter of education. People don't usually know what harm is caused by the products they use or which brand is most harmful. I have heard of a project in the making that could be helpful in this regard. Someone is developing a reference tool, somewhat like a palm pilot in design, that could call up product information from a computerized network as you shop. You could plug in "Cheerios" and it would tell you the social and environmental impacts of producing this cereal. This would give you some basis for your decision; otherwise you just don't know. It would be the equivalent of the guidebooks published by Co-op America and others that evaluate products for relative degree of harm and social responsibility. This could significantly raise the level of awareness for a shopper concerned about nonharming.

Sometimes we know something is harmful, but we don't know it deeply enough. There is a great need for education here, similar to the educational process in this country about smoking. For years people knew smoking was unhealthy, but it took years and years of repeating the message to generate society-wide levels of understanding. It required a certain critical mass with a consistency of behavior across society to start changing things. People may know what is good to do, but until understanding reaches some critical mass, social behavior probably won't change.

Let's look at these criteria in relation to what we literally consume, that is, our food. Debates about this have been alive as far back as the time of the Buddha. One monk in the early sangha (the Buddhist community of followers) urged the Buddha to make a rule saying all monks should be vegetarian. Instead, based on his own experience, the Buddha found the middle way between extremes of self-indulgence and unnecessary austerity. He recognized that within certain guidelines, it was important for the monks to accept any food offering as they went on their alms rounds. They were not to ask that an animal be killed for their food or accept meat if an animal had been killed especially for them. But if a family was sharing what they had cooked for themselves, then it was all right for the monks to receive it.

How do we apply this in our culture today, where food is neatly packaged in the market and there is not much connection with its source? Some people who recognize the harm in raising and slaughtering beef refrain from eating meat. Others for health reasons may need to eat meat. Some people, such as those in many native cultures, embrace the larger cycles of birth and death in nature and act from that understanding. There is no one right answer to this question of what to eat. Our task is to investigate different options, not holding the taking of life lightly, and with whatever we consume to maintain a heart of compassion.

We can extend the questions from consumer products to the consciousness produced by consuming. Even if something does not appear to harm the environment or those who make the product, does it still harm the purchaser or consumer in some way? Once a visiting teacher asked me to check out all the most gruesome videos I could find for him. Although I found the request rather strange, he said the videos provided a way for him to consciously put himself in disturbing situations to see if he could stay free within them. Rightly done, this could be a very strong practice in developing equanimity. Of course, it would also be very easy to rationalize more unwholesome motivation. In more ordinary modes of shopping or consuming, we can watch what is happening in our own minds. If we can bring mindfulness to this arena, then it allows us to make wise choices.

Should Buddhist teachers do more in addressing consumerism as an important current issue? There is a wide range of engagement with this topic among Buddhist teachers. Some address the issues of consumerism and its impact on society very directly; others talk more about understanding the nature and power of desire in the mind. As with all areas of social concern, the more information we have, the wiser our deliberations will be. So a great challenge is finding ways to make this information more available.

One point, though, that I would like to emphasize is the understanding that there is not a hierarchy of compassionate action in the world. Somebody meditating in a cave for years working for enlightenment is as much an activist as somebody out there fighting overconsumption and waste. This is not always obvious to people. If you think of the Buddha's past lives and then take a snapshot of just one life as a monk meditating in the forest, one might well ask, how was he helping the world? But if we see that one life in the context of his whole journey of awakening and all the compassionate action that followed from that awakening, then we get a fuller picture. The key is motivation; it is not the action itself, because there is a wide range of compassionate action possible, some of which will look like compassion and some of which will not. What is important is the motivation behind what someone is doing and how free his or her mind is in doing it.

Mindfulness is the foundation of understanding. It contributes to wise attention and helps us distinguish what is skillful action from what is unskillful. Without mindfulness, we don't know what our minds are doing or what the effects of our actions will be. As we bring awareness to our lives in the world, we discover on deeper and deeper levels the nature of desire and wanting, the implications of consumer consciousness, and the suffering of attachment. Yet it is right here in every moment of wanting that we find the possibilities of greater freedom.

2

How We Get Hooked, How We Get Unhooked

Pema Chödrön

This essay was delivered originally as a teaching on the process of attachment. In it, Pema Chödrön addresses how habits and addictions are cumulative forms of attachment protecting us from the insecurity of living in a changing world. Although she is not addressing consumerism directly, her comments offer useful Buddhist teachings on the fundamental processes at work around desire and craving. She explains how refraining from being hooked can open up the possibility for wisdom to arise, allowing more spaciousness in dealing with ourselves and others. With practice, this wisdom becomes a stronger force than attachment, helping us practice goodness and equanimity, Buddhist virtues that counteract the values of consumerism.

YOU ARE TRYING to make a point with a co-worker or your partner. At one moment her face is open and she is listening, and at the next, her eyes cloud over or her jaw tenses. What is it that you're seeing? Someone criticizes you. They criticize your work or your appearance or your child. At moments like that, what is it you feel? It has a familiar taste in your mouth, it has a familiar smell. Once you begin to notice it, you feel as if this experience has been happening forever. The Tibetan word for this is *shenpa*. It is usually translated "attachment," but a more descriptive translation might be "hooked." When *shenpa* hooks us, we are likely to get stuck. We could call *shenpa* "that sticky feeling." It is an everyday experience. Even a spot on your new sweater can take you there. At the subtlest level, we feel a tightening, a tensing, a sense of closing down. Then we feel a sense of withdrawing, of not wanting to be where we are. That is the hooked quality. That tight feeling has the power to hook us into self-denigration, blame, anger, jealousy, and other emotions that lead to words and actions that end up poisoning us.

Do you remember the fairy tale in which toads hop out of the princess's mouth whenever she starts to say mean words? That is how being hooked can feel. Yet we don't stop—we can't stop—because we are in the habit of associating whatever we are doing with relief from our own discomfort. This is the *shenpa* syndrome. The word *attachment* doesn't quite translate what is happening. It is a quality of experience that's not easy to describe but that everyone knows well. *Shenpa* is usually involuntary, and it gets right to the root of why we suffer.

Someone looks at us in a certain way, or we hear a certain song, we smell a certain smell, we walk into a certain room, and *boom*. The feeling may have nothing to do with the present, and nevertheless, there it is. When we were practicing recognizing *shenpa* at Gampo Abbey, we discovered that some of us could feel it even when a particular person simply sat down next to us at the dining table.

Shenpa thrives on the underlying insecurity of living in a world that is always changing. We experience this insecurity as a background of slight unease or restlessness. We all want some kind of relief from that unease, so we turn to what we enjoy—food, alcohol, drugs, sex, work, or shopping. In moderation what we enjoy might be very delightful. We can appreciate its taste and its presence in our life. But when we empower it with the idea that it will bring us comfort, that it will remove our unease, we get hooked.

We could also call *shenpa* "the urge"—the urge to smoke that cigarette, to overeat, to have another drink, to indulge our addiction, whatever it is. Sometimes *shenpa* is so strong that we are willing to die getting this short-term symptomatic relief. The momentum behind the urge or craving is so strong that we never pull out of the habitual pattern of turning to poison for comfort. It does not necessarily have to involve a substance or a particular thing; it can be saying thoughtless words or approaching everything with a comparing mind. That is a major hook. Something triggers an old pattern we would rather not feel, and we tighten up and hook into comparing or criticizing. This gives us a puffed-up satisfaction and a feeling of control that provides short-term relief from uneasiness.

Those of us with strong addictions know that working with habitual patterns begins with the willingness to fully acknowledge our urge, and then the willingness *not* to act on it. This business of not acting out is called refraining. Traditionally it is known as renunciation. What we renounce or refrain from is not food, things, sex, or relationships per se. We renounce and refrain from the *shenpa*. When we talk about refraining from *shenpa*, we do not mean trying to cast it out; we mean trying to see the *shenpa* clearly and experiencing it. If we can see *shenpa* just as we are starting to close down, when we feel the tightening, then the possibility exists to catch the urge to do the habitual thing and to choose not to do it.

Without meditation practice, this is almost impossible. Generally we don't catch the tightening until we have indulged the urge to scratch our itch in some habitual way. And unless we equate refraining with loving-kindness and friendliness toward ourselves, refraining feels like putting on a straitjacket. We struggle against it. The Tibetan word for renunciation is *shenlok*, which means turning *shenpa* upside down, shaking it up. When we feel the tightening, somehow we have to know how to open up the space without getting hooked into our habitual pattern.

In practicing with *shenpa*, first we try to recognize it. The best place to do this is on the meditation cushion. Sitting practice teaches us how to open and relax to whatever arises, without picking and choosing. It teaches us to experience the urge and the uneasiness fully and to interrupt the momentum that usually follows. We do this by not following after the thoughts and by learning to come back to the present moment. We practice staying with the uneasiness, the tightening, the itch of *shenpa*. We train in sitting still with our desires, with our conditioned hooks. This is how we learn to stop the chain reaction of habitual patterns that otherwise rule our lives. This is how we weaken the patterns that keep us hooked into discomfort that we mistake as comfort. We label the spin-off "thinking" and return to the present moment. Yet even in meditation, we can experience *shenpa*.

Let's say, for example, that in one meditation session you felt settled and open. Thoughts came and went, but they didn't hook you. They were like clouds in the sky that dissolved when you acknowledged them. You were able to return to the present moment without a sense of struggle. Afterward you are hooked on that very pleasant experience: "I did it right, I got it right. That's how it should always be, that's the model." Getting caught like that builds arrogance, and conversely it builds poverty, because your next session is nothing like that. In fact, your "bad" session is even worse now because you are hooked on the "good" one. You sat there obsessing about something at home or at work. You worried and you fretted; you got caught up in fear or anger. At the end of the session you feel discouraged—it was "bad," and there is only yourself to blame.

Is there something inherently wrong or right with either meditation experience? Only the *shenpa*. The *shenpa* we feel toward "good" meditation hooks us into how it's "supposed" to be, and that sets us up for *shenpa* toward how it's not "supposed" to be. Yet the meditation is just what it is. We, however, get caught in our idea of meditation: that's the *shenpa*, that root stickiness. This is ego clinging or self-absorption. When we are hooked on the idea of good experience, self-absorption gets stronger; when we are hooked on the idea of bad experience, self-absorption gets stronger. This is why we, as practitioners, are taught not to judge ourselves, not to get caught in good or bad.

What we really need to do is address things just as they are. Learning to recognize *shenpa* teaches us the meaning of not being attached to this world. Not being attached has nothing to do with this world. It has to do with *shenpa*—being hooked by what we associate with comfort. All we are trying to do is not to feel our uneasiness. But when we do this, we never get to the root of practice. The root is experiencing the itch as well as the urge to scratch, and then not acting it out.

If we are willing to practice this way over time, prajna begins to kick in. Prajna is clear seeing, our innate intelligence, our wisdom. With prajna we begin to see the whole chain reaction clearly. As we practice, this wisdom becomes a stronger force than *shenpa*. That in itself has the power to stop the chain reaction. Prajna is not ego involved. It is the wisdom found in basic goodness, openness, and equanimity—all of which cut through self-absorption. With prajna we can see what will open up space for less attachment. Ego-bound habituation is just the opposite—a compulsion to fill up space in our own particular style. Some of us close down space by hammering our point through; others do it by trying to smooth the waters.

As students of Buddhism we are taught that whatever arises is fresh, the essence of realization. That is the basic view. But how do we see whatever arises as the essence of realization when the fact of the matter is, we have work to do? The key is to look into *shenpa*. The work we have to do is about coming to know that we are tensing or hooked or "all worked up." That is the essence of realization. The earlier we catch it, the easier *shenpa* is to work with, but even catching it when we are already all worked up is good. Sometimes we have to go through the whole cycle even though we see what we are doing. The urge is so strong, the hook so sharp, the habitual pattern so sticky, that there are times when we can't do anything about it. There is something we can do after the fact, however. We can go sit on the meditation cushion and rerun the story. Maybe we start with remembering the all-worked-up feeling and get in touch with that. We can look clearly at the *shenpa* in retrospect; this is very helpful. It is also helpful to see *shenpa* arising in little ways, where the hook is not so sharp.

Buddhists are speaking about *shenpa* when they say, "Don't get caught in the content: observe the underlying quality—the clinging, the desire, the attachment." Sitting meditation teaches us how to see that tangent before we go off on it. To engage this training on the cushion, where it is relatively easy and pleasant to do, is a way to prepare ourselves to stay calm and clear when we get all worked up. Then we train in seeing *shenpa* wherever we are. Say something to another person and maybe you will feel that tensing arise. Rather than get caught in a story line about how right or wrong you are, you can take it as an opportunity to be present with the hooked quality. You can use it as an opportunity to stay with the tightness without acting upon it. Let that training be your base.

You can also practice recognizing *shenpa* out in nature. Practice sitting still and catching the moment when you close down. Or practice in a crowd, watching one person at a time. When you are silent, you get hooked by mental dialogue. You talk to yourself about badness or goodness: me-bad or they-bad, this-right or that-wrong. Just to see this is a practice. You will be intrigued by how you will involuntarily shut down and get hooked, one way or another. Just keep labeling these thoughts and coming back to the immediacy of the feeling. That is the way to break the chain reaction.

Once we are aware of *shenpa*, we begin to notice it in other people. We see them shutting down. We see that they have been hooked and that nothing is going to get through to them. At that moment we are experiencing prajna, the basic intelligence that comes through when we are not caught up in escaping our unease. With prajna we can see what is happening with others; we can see when they have been hooked. Then we can give the situation some space. One way to do that is by opening up the space on the spot through meditation. Be quiet and place your mind on your breath. Hold your mind in place with great openness and curiosity toward the other person. Asking a question is another way of creating space around that sticky feeling. So is postponing your discussion to another time.

At Gampo Abbey we are very fortunate that everybody is excited about working with *shenpa*. So many words I've tried have become ammunition that people use against themselves. But we feel some kind of gladness about working with *shenpa*, perhaps because the word is unfamiliar. We can acknowledge what is happening with clear seeing, without aiming it at ourselves. Since no one particularly likes to have *shenpa* pointed out, people at the Abbey make deals like this: "When you see me getting hooked, just pull your ear lobe, and if I see you getting hooked, I'll do the same. Or if you see it in yourself, and I'm not picking up on it, at least give some little sign that maybe this isn't the time to continue this discussion." This is how we help each other cultivate prajna, clear seeing.

We could think of this whole process in terms of four Rs: *recognizing* the *shenpa, refraining* from scratching, *relaxing* into the underlying urge to scratch, and then *resolving* to continue to interrupt our habitual patterns like this for the rest of our lives. What do you do when you don't do the habitual thing? You are left with your urge. That is how you become more in touch with the craving and the wanting to move away. You learn to relax with it. Then you resolve to keep practicing this way.

Working with *shenpa* softens us up. Once we see how we get hooked and how we get swept along by the momentum, there is no way to be arrogant. The trick is to keep seeing. You don't want to let the softening and humility turn into self-denigration. That is just another hook. Because we have been strengthening the whole habituated situation for a long, long time, we can't expect to undo it overnight. It is not a one-shot deal. It takes lovingkindness to recognize; it takes practice to refrain; it takes willingness to relax; it takes determination to keep training this way. It helps to remember that we may experience two billion kinds of itches and seven quadrillion types of scratching with various degrees of intensity, but there is really only one root *shenpa*: ego clinging. The branch *shenpa*s are all our different styles of scratching that itch.

I recently saw a cartoon of three fish swimming around a hook. One fish is saying to the others, "The secret is nonattachment." That is a cartoon about *shenpa*: the secret is—don't bite that hook. If we can catch ourselves at that place where the urge to bite is strong, we can at least get a bigger perspective on what is happening. As we practice this way, we gain confidence in our own wisdom, and it begins to guide us toward the fundamental aspect of our being—spaciousness, warmth, and spontaneity.

3

The Inner Pursuit
of Happiness

Ruben L. F. Habito

AS I WORK ON MY COMPUTER, my two sons sit lazily in front of the
television watching their morning cartoons. Every now and then I hear
them blurting out, "I want that!" These outbursts signal times between cartoon segments when ads for new toys or new brands of snacks are flashed
before their eyes. This scenario in my own household deep in the heart of
Texas literally brings home the state of American society, aptly characterized as a "Consumer's Republic" by author Lisabeth Cohen.[1] Sometimes
my sons are lucky enough to get hold of one of those coveted items as a
birthday or Christmas present, or they save up weeks of allowance to buy it
themselves. Yet usually within a few days these gadgets are laid aside or rel-
egated to the storage box with piles of other toys acquired in the past. Reflecting on this all-too-often repeated pattern, I wonder: Did they *really*
want that? Already their interest has shifted to another gizmo that has
caught their attention in the ads.

Reflecting on what I learn observing my two children, it seems that acquiring a specific object of one's desire brings but short-lived satisfaction.

But more significantly, acquisition itself does not quench desire but only heightens desire for other objects not yet in one's possession and thus leads to increased dissatisfaction. In her book on consumption trends in American society, Juliet Schor reports that "the story of the eighties and nineties is that millions of Americans ended the period having more but feeling poorer."[2] Although people tended to have more consumer goods than a decade or two earlier, they had less of a sense of overall satisfaction with their lives. More people felt they were further than ever from their ideal of "the good life," which is linked with owning an array of consumer goods deemed "necessary." Schor's recent book builds upon her earlier, bestselling book, *The Overworked American*, which characterizes the lifestyle of many Americans as a "cycle of work and spend,"[3] leaving people in a chronic state of dissatisfaction and frustration.

It was just such a sense of dissatisfaction that led a young man named Gautama, who lived in northern India around the fifth or sixth century BCE, to set everything else aside and seek a way out. His search took him in different directions until he came to sit under a tree in contemplation. At this point he arrived at what has been described as the "place of peace" (*santam padam*), born out of "the extinction of all craving" (*nibbana*), an experience that transformed him into an awakened one or Buddha. His experience, and the message that drew its source from that experience and his subsequent way of life, came to inspire millions of human beings throughout the centuries to this day.

My main task in this essay is to listen with an attentive ear to what the Buddha taught, to reflect on its implications for living in a globalized culture of consumption, and to look for hints that may break us out of this cycle. I begin with an affirmation that the pursuit of happiness is the corollary to the overcoming of dissatisfaction. This pursuit is an underlying dynamism that motivates human beings in our life projects, in our thoughts, words, and deeds. Taking a panoramic view of human history and contemporary global culture, we can identify several areas wherein human beings have sought and continue to seek this elusive happiness. In short, human history has been propelled in great part by the pursuit of three basic desires: the desire to possess, the desire to know, and the desire for thrill and sustained pleasure. Each of these plays a significant role in today's runaway consumeristic culture. And each is easily observable in our own everyday experiences.

THE ACQUISITIVE MODE AND THE
CYCLE OF DISSATISFACTION

The Desire to Have More

Our pursuit of happiness generally leads us in the direction of wanting to have more of the good things of life, thinking that this is what would make us happy. This is a very natural human urge. The very commonness of it makes us vulnerable to manipulation. We are bombarded with images, slogans, and all sorts of signals by the media and by educational, economic, political, and other institutions, leading us to believe that unless we have this or that particular item, we are nothing. And so we strive with all our efforts to acquire those things that we consider conditions for our attainment of happiness. It could be a fashionable house in the right part of town, the dream vacation package, the ideal romantic partner. It could be some kind of designer clothing, or the right brand of shoes, the perfect wine to offer friends. Each thing seems to be the necessary prerequisite for a particular state of happiness.

Social and cultural commentators concur that it is this desire to *have more* that keeps the economy going and the world running. Author Lisabeth Cohen describes how in the 1950s, following the Second World War, a powerful consensus of government, business, and labor emerged. Their combined message was that "buying everything in sight" was the best way to serve the national interest and the best way to fulfill one's duty as a citizen.

Cohen examines the mass consumption–driven economy-cum-sociopolitical-cultural system of postwar America from various angles. Such a system was meant to "provide jobs, purchasing power, and investment dollars, while also allowing Americans to live better than ever before, to participate in political decision-making on an equal footing with their similarly prospering neighbors, and to exercise their cherished freedoms by making independent choices in markets and politics."[4] Trends in the following decades, however, indicate that what materialized was the exact opposite of these ideals of social egalitarianism, democratic participation, and political freedom. For example, between 1979 and 1997, the richest fifth's average income jumped from nine to fifteen times the income of the poorest fifth. The consumption-driven system also has led to the growing fragmentation and heightened inequality in American society, and these inequalities in turn have brought about disenfranchisement in educational, cultural, and political realms of social life.

In his assessment of contemporary consumer culture, Thomas Hine describes the psychological and sociological mechanisms involved in shopping, noting the pathological tendencies in those who might be called "shopping addicts." An act of shopping can be a manifestation of power, responsibility, discovery, self-expression, and other positive values. But at the same time, it can be a symptom of deeply rooted insecurity and an escape from responsibility or replacement for meaningful action. He suggests how "our insecurities leave us open to psychological manipulation, which in turn keeps the engine running."[5]

The human drive to want more and more things comes from a deeply felt sense of *lack*. Buddhist philosopher David Loy has called this lack a basic character of our human existence in this phenomenal world.[6] Our activities in this world are motivated largely by the need to fill in this inherent lack we feel at the heart of our being. And yet, the more we seek to fill this lack by following our craving to have more and more—in short, living in the acquisitive mode—the less we are truly satisfied, and thus continue in a state of unfulfillment and frustration.

An underlying assumption of the dominant mode of life in today's consumer society is that "you are what you have." Furthermore, if you have it, flaunt it. It is in having this or that particular item, whether it be a Gucci handbag or a nifty Vespa that we find our identity and our worth in life. This mode of life drives us in the direction of wanting more and more, believing that having more is the key to happiness.[7] However, sooner or later we realize that the more we have, the more we still want. And thus we realize that we can never *really* be satisfied with what we already have. In short, this desire to have more keeps us in a constant state of dissatisfaction. Even in the process of acquiring things we desire, we see that there is always more that we still do not possess. Those who succeed in acquiring most or even all of their prerequisites for happiness may still get the gnawing feeling expressed in the Peggy Lee song: "Is that all there is?"

The Desire to Know More

A second area of craving is the desire to know more, accelerated by the information technology now widely available to the general public. In our computerized culture, the almost universal accessibility of the Internet (given a certain level of economic status) and its varieties of services has opened new avenues of human pursuit. The World Wide Web has also radically transformed our consciousness and opened new horizons of knowledge never before imagined. It is not an exaggeration to say that we are in the midst of a knowledge revolution in human history. The fulcrum of this lies in "information technologies (microelectronics, informatics, and telecommunications) around which a constellation of major scientific discoveries and applications (in biotechnology, new materials, lasers, renewable energy, etc.) is transforming the material basis of our world."[8]

The revolution in information technology that undergirds our twenty-first-century global society is propelled by the natural human desire to know, and to know *more and more*. This desire to know is an inherent aspect of our being human, as Aristotle pointed out long ago. The underlying presupposition is that knowledge is power—the more we know, the more powerful we can be.

The scientific method as a fundamental procedure in our quest for knowledge has ushered in tremendous discoveries about the way things work and has brought about momentous transformations in human civilization. For better or for worse, it has given us enormous power over our natural environment. It has given us the confidence that with adequate knowledge, we humans can control the natural world. Hence we tend to assume that any problem we face can be resolved by further research resulting in further knowledge that will then put us in control. Scientific advances since 1900 have pushed the frontiers of our knowledge further and further out into the expanding universe and further and further into the intricate workings of the subatomic world. With the cracking of the genetic code and the mapping of human DNA, we have attained a radically new level of understanding of the human organism.

There is indeed a certain satisfaction in the acquisition of new knowledge. We all have tasted the feeling of competence in mastering new domains such as a foreign language or a musical instrument. However, as with the desire to *have* more, the desire to *know* more is constantly being met by the realization that there is always more still left that is unknown. This only sparks the desire to know even more, drawing human beings in directions where no one has gone before.

If we dispassionately survey our contemporary world, we cannot help but notice the stark contrast between our ideal of universal happiness—the expected outcome of more knowledge and mastery over nature—and the actual realities of our global situation. We cannot help but see an ever-increasing gap between the haves and have-nots, with hundreds of millions living and dying in subhuman conditions. We can't help but see the heightened tension among different sectors of our human community, leading to armed conflicts around the world. We can't help but see the increasingly critical situation of ecological destruction, from ozone depletion to the extinction of thousands of species. All this indicates that we have not been able to harness our knowledge to provide the wisdom we need to live well and be genuinely happy as a global community. The desire to know that drives our mental pursuits presupposes, as well as accentuates, the dichotomy between knower and known. I see the world and other people as "out there," separate from me, and therefore fundamentally cut off from my field of concern as I seek my own happiness.

Never before in the history of the world have we human beings had access to so much knowledge and information. But looking at the history of the last hundred years, the gap between what we know and how to use that knowledge for greater happiness has never been greater. Indicator after indicator affirms that we have not been able to put our knowledge at the service of our communal human well-being. This is a gap that is crying out for redress.

The Desire for Thrill and Pleasure

A third feature in the engine that keeps our contemporary global consumer culture running is the relentless pursuit of thrill and pleasure. The entertainment industry is ever ready to offer the latest kinds of thrills. Reality TV seeks to capture the mass audience with yet another adventure challenge, allowing the ordinary Joe or Jane to become an overnight celebrity. The film industry keeps on churning out new blockbuster films that compete for weekly box-office ratings. Ever newer varieties of video and computer games keep children fixated on their little machines that give them the thrill of competition. The sports industry likewise continues to capture the attention of fans who find their highs in the excitement of competitive spectator games.

And yet, we realize, the more we seek new sources of thrill, the less we feel truly satisfied. We may find momentary enjoyment in these thrills, but it is followed by an inner emptiness that can only be filled with a new source of pleasure. This is literally documented in cases of drug and alcohol consumption. Again, we come to the realization that our search for thrill keeps us in a perpetually dissatisfied condition.

The pursuit of thrill in our contemporary society is fanned by titillating images and attractive offers presented to us on television and through the Web. The fact that these images and offerings are able to sway multitudes, generating huge profits for entrepreneurs and providers, indicates that people apparently feel a need for such thrills. This indicates the inner lack many of us feel, which clamors to be filled precisely by these thrills offered for mass consumption.

But as anyone knows who has sought out some kind of high—whether it be the final play-off of the World Series or the euphoria from homegrown marijuana—these thrills do not last. Eventually the altered state wears off and we are left low instead of high. This then leads us to crave the next high. Hence the chronic state of dissatisfaction is only heightened, as we look to some external stimulus we think will offer that thrill or pleasure, whether it be alcohol, tobacco, drugs, the cinema, television, food, coffee, chocolates, sex, or shopping.

The desire to *have more*, the desire to *know more*, and the desire for *more thrill* and pleasure are basic components of what can be described as an *acquisitive mode of being*. As I have tried to demonstrate, such a mode of being attains not happiness but only a chronic state of dissatisfaction and a heightened sense of frustration. Can we envision a different mode of life, one that leads not to dissatisfaction and frustration but to genuine happiness and contentment? Exploring this question, I turn to a tradition that has addressed this very question for more than twenty-five centuries.

TOWARD A CONTEMPLATIVE MODE: THE INVERSION OF THREE DESIRES

In his process of seeking to overcome dissatisfaction (*dukkha*) and attain true inner peace, the Buddha came to realize that neither the relentless pursuit of desire nor the opposite extreme, self-deprivation through rigorous asceticism and mortification, could lead him to happiness. He arrived at what has been called the Middle Way between these two extremes. This middle way was reflected in his inner stance as he settled down under a tree in contemplation, taking a straight look at things as they are.[9]

It was this contemplative attitude that became the condition for the momentous awakening experience that opened him to the true path of peace (*santam padam*) and that came to define his contribution to humanity as a buddha (awakened one). This experience was a pivotal moment that illumined the Buddha's understanding of reality and transformed his entire life. From this moment on, he no longer was a seeker of truth but was now one who had awakened to the liberating truth (*dharma*). The Buddha's contemplative attitude was foundational to his transformative experience. And in return, his experience of awakening grounded him in the contemplative mode of being throughout his entire life.

How can we describe the features of this contemplative mode that opened the Buddha to his awakening experience? Taking our cue from the three kinds of desire that generate dissatisfaction, we can understand the contemplative mode as an inversion of these three desires.

Awareness of Being

As we begin to see through the inherent contradictions in the acquisitive mode of life, we may come to a point where we are stopped in our tracks, unable to go on with our unsatisfactory habits of buying and consuming. In this pause, there can be an opening. We may hear an inner call, inviting us to change direction. Literally stopping and beholding what is going on— in other words, assuming a contemplative mode—can be the key to an entirely different perspective on ourselves and the world.

Instead of pursuing the craving to have more, the contemplative mode involves an inner attitude of simply beholding "what there is, just as it is." When asked by his followers how they too could arrive at the peace of mind that characterized the Buddha's life, the Buddha is said to have replied, "*Ehi passiko.*" "Come and see." This is the invitation to enter a contemplative mode of being.

The instructions are straightforward: simply to behold what is there before us. Following basic guidelines of meditation, or simply sitting and watching our breath with the inner eye of our mind, we may get glimpses of a realm that can only be characterized as "not this, not that." This is a realm not like the one we are accustomed to in our ordinary life with its wants and needs that clamor constantly for our attention. Instead, this is a realm that can fill our hearts with a sense of fullness, a sense of rest, a sense of being truly at home. In this realm we are able to taste a full *awareness of being.*

Let me illustrate how this contemplative mode can arise by comparing two modes of walking. We take it to be common sense that we walk because we want to go from point A to point B. We walk, for example, to get to the other side of the street, or from the parking lot to the grocery store. In this mode of walking, the act of moving our legs is simply a means to get us where we intend to go. We are generally conscious of the time at our disposal to get there, and we tend to hurry so we can get there faster. The value of the walking is then entirely dependent on whether it takes us where we want to go in the allotted time frame. It is a means to an end and nothing else.

There is, however, a mode of walking where the point is simply to experience the pure act of "just walking." In this mode of walking we open ourselves to a realm that goes beyond "walking in order to go somewhere" to experience "walking for the sake of walking itself." Here the act of moving our legs is an event that we are able to experience and relish as such. We may taste the wonder of being able to do this act at all, that is, moving our legs so we maintain our balance, finding our whole body swaying with the rhythm, experiencing the simple and glorious fact of . . . being able to walk.

I should note that this second mode need not mean that we do not actually get from one place to another. True, we may choose to walk in a way that takes us around in a circle within a given space, as in a meditation hall. But we may also choose to walk from the parking lot to the grocery store.

Though the setting may be the same, the inner attitude that we bear makes a world of difference. The first mode can be compared with what I have described as the acquisitive mode of life; the second mode reflects a contemplative mode of being. In this mode the walking is totally independent of the linear time spent in engaging in it and can in fact lead one to an experience of the timeless.

Contemplative experience can open one's mind and heart to a kind of satisfaction not to be gained by the acquisitive or time-and-space-consuming mode of movement. It has nothing to do with gaining or not gaining, arriving or not arriving. The contemplative mode offers an inner satisfaction that is not dependent on external conditions and is thus an experience in the realm of the unconditional. Such an experience can lead to a tremendous sense of inner peace and release, freeing one from the shackles of desire for consumer goods. As we walk in the contemplative mode, our sense of inner lack is overturned to usher in an awareness of the fullness of being.

Nondual Knowing

As we take this stance of beholding, simply "seeing things as they are," we may come to that most revolutionary of discoveries in the inner journey of the spirit. Put inadequately into words, this is the discovery that what makes "me" what I am most truly is intimately connected to what makes the world what it is. In short, it is an experiential realization of what the Buddha saw in his moment of awakening. He articulated this insight as "the doctrine of interdependent co-arising" (*pratitya-samutpada*), elaborated upon by Buddhist thinkers through the ages.

Coming to this discovery is to realize, intimately, experientially, that what happens to each and every sentient being in this world happens to my very own self. It means experiencing the pain of each and every being as my own pain and, conversely, each one's joy as mine. It is to undergo a momentous transformation in the way I see the world and myself. The experiential realization of intimate connectedness is *nondual knowing*, a sharp contrast to the knowledge-acquiring mind. It is this experience of nonduality that can unleash the powers of wisdom to flow out into acts of compassion.

From the contemplative view, as I look at the world, I realize that I am seeing my own self. The world is no other than what I am. And conversely, what I am is no other than what the world is. To know the world is thus not different from knowing myself. As thirteenth-century Japanese Zen master Dogen writes, "I came to realize clearly that mind is no other than mountains and rivers, the great earth, the sun, the moon, the stars."[10] Beholding the mountains and rivers and the wonders of the natural world, I see these as manifestations of mind, the same as my own mind, my own self. From this nondual way of knowing, the leveling of mountains and the cutting of trees, the pollution of rivers, the ongoing loss of species, are not events "out there" but are things happening right at the heart of my being. This causes me deep pain.

The realization that "we *are* the world" can bridge the gap between our scientific knowledge and the wisdom we need to direct this knowledge to our well-being as we live together in this Earth community. Grounded in the experiential realization that the world is not separate from ourselves, and therefore that the world's well-being is our own well-being, we can harness our knowledge and technological acumen to uproot the sources of individual and social suffering.

Up to this point in human history, we have pursued our desire to know in a way that has given us mastery over the laws of physics, chemistry, biology, and even over our own bodies. The dualistic mode of knowing, while giving us power over nature, has also led to great disparity between the haves and the have-nots of the world. We have used this mode of knowing, for example, to master the techniques and economics of factory farming, raising cattle, pigs, and chickens in large quantities for mass consumption. Engaging the nondual mode of knowing, we empathize with the cattle, pigs, and chickens being mass-produced in this way and *know* that something is not quite right. This mode of knowing can lead us to question how such a system can treat countless living beings in this way and to question our own eating habits dependent on this system. It can also empower us to take action toward transforming the situation and reducing the suffering.

Nondual knowing is prominent in the cultivation of the contemplative mode. In the well-known *Metta Sutta*, a scriptural text from early Buddhism, it is described as a stance of being engaged with the world "as a mother toward her only child."[11] This wisdom manifests itself as compassion, grounded in a way of being that offers oneself and one's whole life toward the healing of the wounds of the world. Albert Einstein, a major figure in the human quest for knowledge in the twentieth century, made this connection between knowledge and wisdom:

> A human being is part of the whole called by us the universe, a part limited in time and space. Humans experience themselves, their thoughts, and feelings as something separated from the rest, a kind of optical delusion of their consciousness. This delusion is a kind of prison for us, restricting us to our personal desires and to affection for a few persons nearest to us. Our task must be to free ourselves from this prison by widening our circle of love and compassion to embrace all living creatures and the whole of nature in its beauty.[12]

Unconditioned Joy

Cultivating the contemplative mode requires setting aside the pursuit of certain kinds of "thrills" that would obstruct this cultivation. This "setting aside" need not be a heroic act of self-denial and asceticism but can be a simple response to an inner voice, a call of the heart to a deeper kind of joy. It is turning toward an inner satisfaction more satisfying than any pleasure dependent on external conditions or stimuli.

For example, we may be in the habit of leaving the television on to keep us company in a lonely house, or of turning on the radio while driving to occupy our bored minds. But we may come to a moment when we see this dependence on directionless external stimuli for diversion as truly distasteful, depriving us of a deeper pleasure. This deeper pleasure is what we taste in moments of silence and simple attention to what is going on around us. Setting aside the pursuit of thrills through external stimuli is a response to that inner voice inviting us to a deeper kind of satisfaction.

Following this inner call, we may be led to search further by reading books on spiritual practice. Reading such books may begin to fill our hearts with yet a new longing—the longing to become a spiritual person, finding satisfaction in spiritual instead of material pleasures. But this itself can throw us into another cycle of dissatisfaction. We read book after book and find our minds filled with ideas that we are not able to incorporate into our way of living. We may also easily fall into what Chögyam Trungpa called "spiritual materialism," or perhaps, "spiritual consumerism." We may be misled into thinking that we are "worth something" because of the many spiritual books we have read, considering ourselves better than others caught in the pursuit of more tangible thrills.

But we may also come to see that all this pleasurable Buddhist reading is not really making any significant dent in the cycle of dissatisfaction that led us to the reading in the first place. We realize that we have done enough reading and that it is now time to take another significant step. Having looked at the menu from various angles, it is now time to set the menu aside, order our food, and then begin to eat. It is this insight that leads us to embark on some form of contemplative practice that can yield more sustained satisfaction.

Finding a community of contemplative practice, with a reliable teacher who can serve as a spiritual guide, can take us to new levels of experiencing joy in our lives. As we engage seriously in contemplative practice, we hear an inner voice inviting us toward a satisfaction that is deeper than anything external stimuli can offer. As we take up spiritual practice of the contemplative mode, we begin to relish a new kind of fruit in our life. A most apt way of describing this fruit is *unconditioned joy*. This can be felt in various degrees of intensity, from the mild sense of inner tranquillity after meditation practice to an intense ecstatic experience whose effect and implications can be felt throughout the rest of one's life.

This experience of unconditioned joy can begin to enter one's life even in the midst of the normal struggles of day-to-day existence. It is not based on a change in external factors in one's life; it is not dependent on some condition we impose or suppose. At best one can perhaps acknowledge it as a gift, a gift of the universe to one who is disposed to receive. This unconditioned joy can be triggered by something as simple as the sight of a tree or the smell of a flower. One can perhaps say that it is a deeply felt affirmation of the fact that "it is good to be." And this affirmation is one that stands in spite of the ups and downs of life, in spite of the actual condition we are in or the state of the world. We can also describe it as experiencing a dimension that is unconditional and universally available to anyone, anywhere, regardless of social or economic status, age, gender, physical condition, ethnic origin, and so on.

Alan Clements, who lived in Burma as a monk for a number of years and now teaches in California, describes it this way:

> The practice of meditation became a wonderful new way of life. I was amazed to see how awareness put eyes and ears where there had been none. It enhanced perception and revealed greater nuance and dimension. Sounds were accentuated. Colors became brighter. Tastes, more subtle and sweeter. Smells more fragrant. At times it felt like every cell in my body was undulating with orgasmic bliss. Watching the fog lift in the early morning was a dance in itself—the play of photons, like tiny prisms refracting thousands of infinitesimal rainbows on the eye. The smell of the gardenia bush just outside my window became a symphony of textured scents. I fell in love with the simplicity of just being.[13]

Even a small taste of this unconditioned joy can free us from the driving desire to keep seeking thrills in manifold ways. We will be able to see through those impulses that urge us to buy this or that or seek the thrill of diversionary recreation to fill an inner lack. In fact, we may even come to realize that those cheap thrills are almost distasteful compared with the inner joy experienced in "simply being."

THE INNER PURSUIT OF HAPPINESS

I began this essay with an affirmation of the pursuit of happiness as an underlying dynamism that motivates human thought, word, and deed. Most of the time we humans are trapped in the delusive idea of a self that is separate from the world, leading us to pursue an elusive ideal of happiness. Caught in a cycle of dissatisfaction, we stay locked in the acquisitive mode, hooked on the desire to have more, to know more, and to experience more pleasures and thrills.

Seeing through this cycle of dissatisfaction can become a turning point in our lives as it was in the life of Gautama Buddha. It can enable us to hear an inner voice, calling us to a different definition of happiness. This is an inward way that can take us from the dissatisfaction of not having and bring us to an awareness of the fullness of being. It can connect our pursuit of knowledge of the objective world with the knowledge of our own true selves, opening our lives to the cultivation of wisdom and compassion. It can also redirect our pursuit of thrills and pleasures to the inward journey that will open to us the exquisite taste of "the simplicity of just being," an experience of unconditioned joy.

These experiences are not available in the shopping mall, but they are available with every step we take. We have the choice to transform these three driving desires in each act that relates to consuming. Strange as it might seem, we can actually take the basic drives behind consumerism and turn them around to pursue the Buddha's path. This is not only possible, it is crucially necessary to reduce the rising suffering in the world caused by our mindless consumer habits. As we replace the acquisitive mode with the contemplative mode, we will be in a "win-win situation," overcoming our own suffering and dissatisfaction and at the same time helping to reduce the cause of others' suffering.

4

Young Buddhists in Shopping Shangri-la

Sumi Loundon

I NEVER UNDERSTOOD the importance of Martha Stewart's products until I bought my first house. In a quest for the perfect curtains to grace my new box window, I visited many stores in the mall. When I finally found my dream curtains, my heart fell. Window treatments, I discovered, are expensive—forty dollars for one curtain! Then my mother told me about Kmart. I was overjoyed to find a wide array of tasteful treatments at much lower prices. Feeling satisfyingly domestic, I hung the new yellow curtains in my kitchen and went to bed. My thoughts were awhirl with planning my next shopping trip in search of area rugs, lamps, and bookshelves. Then I stopped myself. Previous nights had been marked by an easy floating off, remembering friends and thinking about something I'd read—meaningful thoughts. Now my mind was seized with a kind of acquisitiveness I had never experienced before. What had happened to the values of frugality I absorbed from my counterculture childhood?

I was raised by staunchly anticonsumer parents in the 1970s. We lived in a small Zen community in rural New Hampshire that grew its own food, pressed its own tofu, and used hand-me-down toys and clothes for its many kids. Our large house had the sparest of furnishings, many of them from donation or handmade from old lumber. Imagine being a child in those circumstances! Such a place gave me reverence for any object that could be mine. Nothing was disposable. Everything should be shared. One took only what was truly needed. It wasn't until I was seven that I ever stepped into a department store. Because most things were brought by one or two staff to the community, no one needed to go out to buy things. Most items were in bulk, without brand names, such as sacks of flour and beans and huge boxes of powdered milk.

Though we were laypeople with families, my counterculture parents and their friends cultivated a monastic-like asceticism to attain the highest realization. In contrast to my peers who were raised in single-family homes with a certain consumer diet, I had been brought up with material starvation and Buddhist rhetoric that still undergird my sensibilities. That rhetoric, birthed in the religious experimentation of the sixties, taught: "Buddhism teaches nonattachment. Worldly things create attachment. Therefore, we should not have things." My father was so antimaterialist that when I cooed over a little mirrored music box, he saw my expression of desire as grounds for throwing the box out. He would sometimes sing Madonna's "Material Girl" as a way of getting me to deny that I was materialistic.

Twenty years later and still a Buddhist, my attitude toward consumerism might be surprising for someone raised in a self-sufficient community with generic goods and meditators' mind before materialists' matter. The fact that I bought a house, have a retirement plan and dental insurance, and own a new loveseat is a sharp contrast to my parents, who at my age consciously rejected these things in pursuit of awakening.

Today I have a complex relationship to consumerism. On the one hand, I feel almost nauseated walking through Kmart. With thirty brands of shampoo in different colors and smells, consumer culture feels excessive to the point of decadence. On the other hand, the severity of the anticonsumerism I endured as a kid bordered on deprivation. This internal conflict around consumerism is heightened when I shop in a Buddhist boutique. Today's kapok-filled zafus are prettier than the newspaper-bound-with-masking-tape one my parents made for me, but is a hand-stitched, Egyptian cotton, organic-dyed, silk-edged, monastery-made, pricey cushion with color-coordinated zabuton necessary to my meditation success?

For a number of years, especially as I went through an elite college with many privileged kids who grew up near malls, I thought that I might be the only young person who felt ambivalent about consumerism. In graduate school, when I began searching for and interviewing hundreds of young Buddhists in America, I found that I was not alone. Like mine, my peers' relationship to consumerism is complex. To explore this complexity, this chapter draws upon my own experience and anecdotal evidence. While this writing is not based on a comprehensive survey, I hope to provide an impression of my generation's attitudes toward consumerism as well as some initial reflections on what they may mean.

YOUNG BUDDHIST ATTITUDES

Unlike the childhood of my parents, my generation has had greater exposure to two opposite dimensions around consumerism, both bequests of the baby boomers. On the one hand, we have been raised with recycling (at home, in schools), with some ideas about environmentalism (one can buy Sierra Club greeting cards at any store, read about global warming), with access to theories about consumerism (reading Marx in high school), and with exposure to sophisticated understandings of psychology (such as Daniel Goleman's). On the other hand, we have been the most heavily marketed-to generation of consumers. Once retailers discovered that brand affinity begins as early as age three, they aimed their advertisements to children specifically to inculcate consumer values and label loyalty. Given that my generation has been lobbied from both sides, it is not surprising to find young Buddhists who are disgusted, delighted, or at ease with consumerism, or some combination of these conflicting attitudes.

Within this contemporary context, baby-boomer Buddhists have provided frameworks for placing consumerism in a dharma path. Reading articles by baby-boomer Buddhists such as Ken Kraft and Allan Hunt-Badiner as well as books such as *Dharma Rain*, young Buddhists absorb a range of lessons. Significantly, baby-boomer Buddhists themselves have changed their relationship toward consumerism, just as my parents rejoined the comfortable class in the eighties after asceticism in the seventies. As a result, today's young Buddhists select from more than forty years of models. Some are still inspired by early writings such as Jack Kerouac's *The Dharma Bums*, which puts forward one type of relationship to possessions, while others might pick up a later writing. Yet, even while my generation takes its cues from baby-boomer ideals, many are creating their own philosophies.

Although I found there are as many views on consumerism as there are young Buddhists, it appears that young Buddhists fall roughly into three camps: nonconsumers, at-ease consumers, and conscious consumers. The first group consists of young people who have taken up a monastic path, either emulating it as a layperson or receiving traditional ordination. Counterintuitively, although these young Buddhists, who are as Buddhist as they come in the West, live materially simplified lives, I would not consider them to be *anti*consumerists. Many are not likely to picket Kmart or go to an antiglobalization rally or read *Adbusters* or *Utne Reader*, nor are they likely to buy farmers' market produce over agribusiness goods. One person told me that his monk friends actually get excited about a trip to the mall to purchase the latest computer software! Therefore, because of the nonawareness of consumerism as an issue in their dharma path, I would characterize most of the young, ascetic-leaning Buddhists today as *non*consumerist rather than as anticonsumerist.

One example comes to mind: I remember a freshman at my college who came from a middle-class background. His dorm room had as much stuff as other students'—skis, posters, stereo, clothes, knickknacks. He began attending a morning meditation group on campus. He became so interested in the practice that he shipped himself off to Japan, meditated like crazy in the Rinzai lineage for two years, and came back as a monk. After I had graduated, I visited him at the dorm his senior year. His room was completely bare except for a laptop and two thin blankets spread on the hardwood floor. He wore a neatly arranged gray monk's robe that he had sewn himself. However, the motivation behind his asceticism had more to do with the value of a simple life in cultivating enlightenment than with being *against* American consumer values.

My college friend's adopted ascetic life reflects a trend among many young people who get turned on to the dharma. Introduced to Buddhism through a college course or meditation class, reading a beginner's book on Buddhism, attending a public talk, they waste no time in going right for the ultimate goal of awakening. This includes shedding all material excess from earlier years, even what might normally be considered material necessities. The simplicity of an ascetic life, they say, allows them to focus on the important goal of full awakening. Some say that simplicity gives them the freedom to dedicate themselves to helping others instead of concerning themselves with a house, nuclear family, and wealth-generating profession. One young nun wrote that having a shaved head relieved her from having to think about buying shampoo or choosing a hairstyle. Still others come back from Buddhist-studies programs in Asia and, having seen that others do with much less and are actually happier people, decide to simplify their own lives.

The second camp might be termed anti-anticonsumers or at-ease consumers. This tiny group of young Buddhists is aware that Westernized Buddhism has a lot to say about rejecting consumerism but chooses to remain a part of consumer culture nevertheless. There is a sense of guilty pleasure in rejecting anticonsumerism reflected in what James Silberstein writes:

My girlfriend and I recently had a discussion about consumerism, a word which comes off pejoratively as sounding greedy and animalistic, lacking in reason or awareness. After we discussed our disgust with the idea of being a consumer, we both admitted to being full-fledged, card-holding members of the cult of consumerism.[1]

I can identify with this feeling. Sometimes it seems as if the rhetoric on anticonsumerism is delivered so vehemently that one seesaws between agreeing and saying, "Whatever. Let's enjoy ourselves." It may be that this anti-anticonsumerism sentiment follows a larger trend: after a decade of consciousness around fat-free foods, the American public seems to be enjoying a fad in comfort foods such as deep-fried Twinkies and deep-fried cheesecake, items even more fatty than those in the pre-anti-fatty-food era.

In conversations with young Buddhists, I wasn't surprised to find those for whom consumerism wasn't a big deal (nonconsumers) or those for whom anticonsumerism had become a turnoff (at-ease consumers). I *am* surprised that I have yet to meet young Buddhists who are actual anticonsumerists! Investigating this a little further, I found that there are two types of young Buddhists who begin at different ends—as anticonsumers and as unaware consumers—but arrive at the same place: conscious consumerism.

Some conscious consumers have preexisting anticonsumer opinions into which Buddhism later plays a role. Hilary Miller, fifteen, writes,

> Personally, I have felt anti-consumerism sentiments, and was, even before I discovered Buddhism, planning to get rid of many of my things and live more simply. Still, it was difficult to do so because I was so attached, inexplicably, to most of the things I owned. Buddhism helped me free myself from the tyranny of these objects, and I honestly don't miss them. Getting rid of them was actually liberating.[2]

Among anticonsumers who become Buddhist, an unexpected thing happens: radical anticonsumer views soften. A twenty-one-year-old who describes himself as an Eco-Anarchist-Buddhist writes,

> I was always really "anti-consumerism," but I think that Buddhism has helped to replace consumerism with something more positive. At one point reading Marx and *Adbusters* magazine drove my anti-consumerism. Now, I have just learned to be happy without trying to constantly grab everything I see and buy it. When I can see clearly, I find that I don't need these things.[3]

Likewise, Corey Flanders, a Nyingma practitioner in his thirties, writes,

> Before I became a Buddhist, over seven years ago, I remember reviling consumerism as if it were necessarily an evil or negative expression or symptom of greed. Now I'd say that Buddhism has shaped my attitude in that I am much more accepting of consumerism. I think it's pretty much a natural impulse for human beings to search for and acquire that which they believe will make them happy. There is something pure and true about consumerism, as it is a barometer of that impulse and therefore a powerful metaphor which may serve to help one's understanding of human life and drives. This understanding, for me, is a cornerstone of compassion. I mean *I want* the SUV and *I want* the beautiful clothes and *I want . . . whatever*, and I can recognize the patterns of consumerism in myself and, consequently, in others.[4]

Dan Fisher, a graduate student at Naropa University, makes a similar point in reflecting that Buddhism has changed his attitude toward consumerism in that he doesn't see the practice of each as mutually exclusive: who he is as a Buddhist is who he is as a consumer and vice versa.[5] Thus, anticonsumerism is seen as too extreme for a system that advocates a middle path, so anticonsumers who become Buddhist adopt a more positive stance toward consumerism.

Other conscious consumers have benefited from dharma teachings that move them from mindless consumerism toward consumer awareness. Young Buddhists say that teachings on desire and nonattachment are influential. In addition, the Buddhist doctrine of interdependence leads young Buddhists to consider how consumption affects not just the mind but the environment. Seunghee Ham, a Korean high school student, writes that when she came to an adult understanding of Buddhism, she consciously changed her behavior:

> When I grasped the idea of interdependence, it became clear to me that my own life depended on so many elements that I could merely be the combination of all those around me. This realization has kindled my passion to preserve the environment, the biggest sacrifice of consumerism. I now lecture my brother to take short showers, rummage through the trash bag for anything recyclable, and most important, spend less.[6]

This contemporary type of consumer awareness is milder than that of the Buddhists of my parents' generation, who, as young adults, sharply critiqued consumer culture by radically changing their habits, through handmade goods, farming, recycled clothing, generic and bulk foods, self-sufficiency. Perhaps the moderated views of these young Buddhists are the result of the baby boomers' influence, since most of the anticonsumer baby boomers have themselves relaxed the anticonsumerism of their early twenties. For example, I am surely less anticonsumer today because my parents have returned to a middle-class lifestyle (now my mom has dental insurance, a reclining loveseat, and horror of horrors, a new, not-cheap, car!).

This is not to say that Buddhism today doesn't give rise to radical anticonsumer positions. It does. But it appears that at some point in the development of their views, young Buddhists come to a middle ground. Jeff Wilson, Web editor for *Tricycle*, captures this growth:

> At first, the convert Zen[7] I imbibed came with a strong rhetoric of simplicity and nonattachment, which led me to criticize people caught up in the samsara of endless consumption. If true peace and happiness came only from within, related to the mind and not one's possessions, then consumerism seemed like a very literal form of disease and madness. Later, as I began to notice that a lot of the teachers of convert Zen themselves had fancy cars and expensive altar ornaments, I began to think about whether it was possible to live a life of nonattachment to both consumerism and anticonsumerism, especially since at the end of the day we all must operate within the real world.[8]

Though here I simply describe the current attitudes of young Buddhists, I predict that conscious consumerism will fuel the dominant ideology as my generation matures. Where can we go with conscious consumerism? Is it simply an easy way out, allowing us to be comfortable consumers and sanctimonious Buddhists at the same time? Or does it help us approach consumerism realistically, preventing us from falling into the self-centeredness of the antiworldly dharma bums or the severity of anticonsumerism among young baby boomers? Is this a middle path simply because the two ends of the debate have been drawn up by American decadence and radical anticonsumerists? Or might we be pioneering a truly balanced approach that wisely accommodates individual psychological, spiritual, and economic needs with larger communities' environmental and social justice needs?

CONSUMING BUDDHISM

The conscious consumerism I find among my Buddhist peers is heightened when it comes to the material dimension of Buddhism itself. At an idealistic level, young people see Buddhism as a philosophy, science, psychology, and practice, not a religion associated with an abundance of products that one can buy. Given that Buddhism teaches nonattachment, where is the place for a teak altar set or an expensive Buddha statue? For this reason, some students disparage "boutique" Buddhism and the way Buddhism has become popularized through chic Zen clothing, Samsara perfume, a rock band named Nirvana. I myself went through a phase of disgust as I watched the principles from my Zen commune—intimate, immediate, practiced— become mainstreamed, stereotyped, and seemingly watered down by desk-set rock gardens, Yoda's lines in "Star Wars," and *Dharma & Greg*. I felt I could understand why Catholics objected to the crucifix necklace fashion that gripped teens in the late eighties. I didn't want the heart of my religion ripped out by consumer culture. I'm not the only one who feels this way. Again, from Hilary Miller:

> Has anyone else noticed the new trend? Malas (Buddhist prayer beads) have been turned into some kind of cheap new jewelry. I see them daily at my school, often on the wrists of people who strike me as very un-Buddhist (although I know we all have Buddha nature, some people hide it really well). Sometimes I have an almost irrepressible urge to go up to one of these people and politely inform them that they are wearing a copy of a religious tool. What really annoys me, though, is not the people that wear them (they are merely ignorant, not malicious), but the people who first manufactured these bracelets. Obviously they knew that their product had Buddhist origins or they would not have named them "karma beads." Why does our society have to commercialize everything in this way? . . . What right do people have to sell religious items like costume jewelry? I try not to be bothered by it, I really do, and I succeed for the most part. But I just don't understand why the people who manufacture these things don't understand that what they are doing is insulting.[9]

At one time I shared Hilary's dismay, yet as I have gotten to know the different paths by which young people are drawn to Buddhism, my view has changed. For many young people, the first contact with Buddhism is precisely through consumer avenues. Monster book chains have a wide selection of books written in accessible language, from personal (Dinty Moore's *The Accidental Buddhist*) to scholarly (Don Lopez's *The Story of Buddhism*), from practice (Bhante Gunaratana's *Mindfulness in Plain English*) to popular (His Holiness the Dalai Lama's *The Art of Happiness*, which made a quiet appearance on an episode of *Friends*). I would estimate that more than half of all young people first learn about Buddhism through a book, and often that book was checked out from the local public library. The Beastie Boys, a rock band that has done some Buddhistic songs and whose lead singer, Adam Yauch, is a dedicated Buddhist, may have done much to draw young people to Buddhism. Young people find the Buddha figure, with that peaceful enigmatic smile and gentle but attentive pose, to be more attractive than the crucified Jesus from church. These statues invite young people to ask why the Buddha looks like that. Films such as *Kundun, Seven Years in Tibet, Bulletproof Monk,* and *Little Buddha* have also been a powerful popular Buddhist introduction for young people. These movies offer some basic doctrines around rebirth, karma, inner peace, and freedom that young people are curious about in their search for meaning.

"Hard-core" Buddhists, who do intensive meditation retreats or have a more philosophical style of Buddhism, tend to dismiss the value of consumer-Buddhist stuff—books, statues, music, movies—in initiating someone into the path. Yet, important seeds are planted from that initial consumer contact, and these should not be dismissed. For some young people, the seed may lie dormant for several years. When a crisis arises—death in the family, a major breakup, a car accident—that seed can germinate in the person's process of finding meaning and purpose. Although I personally did not come to Buddhism through a material source, many highly committed young Buddhists began their journey with the things that consumer Buddhism sells. It has taken me some time to see the value of this.

Despite the wide-ranging discourse in Buddhist magazines, living-room meditation groups, and casual conversation on how Buddhism is being cheapened by Buddhist materialism, young people seem to take a conscious consumer approach with Buddhist goods, as they do with consumer goods in general. Connie Pham writes, "The dharma is not something you can buy or sell; it's free for the taking. So despite threats of 'spiritual materialism,' ultimately the dharma, like everything else that sustains life, is free."[10] Corey Flanders considers, "Is Buddhism becoming too consumeristic? No. How can a way of practice become consumeristic? Consumerism/Western materialism may be pulling Buddhism into its structure, using it to make money, but that is natural. That is its function. It will try to co-opt whatever it can for its purpose."[11] Jeff Wilson reflects,

"In the West, we hear lots of dire warnings about Buddhism becoming consumeristic. It seems like they are being called for out of a romantic notion of what 'pure Buddhism' should be, which always strikes me as an impossible ideal. If people wish to consume Buddhist goods, so long as they don't do so in support of illegal practices (such as stolen Asian artworks), that's okay."[12] If young Buddhists continue to develop a philosophy around conscious consumerism, then we will also need to think about how Buddhist products are regarded within that.

YOUNG BUDDHIST ATTITUDES IN ASIA

The Buddhist students at University Sains Malaya in Penang have two large shared houses just near the campus. The living rooms have been converted into meditation spaces with Buddha altars, while some of the dedicated students live upstairs. The cohousing bulletin board has the same lists one finds in Western communities: chore assignments, community meetings, telephone messages. Yet, inquire as to the students' majors and one finds that these dedicated young Buddhists concentrate on economics, computer programming, communications, and science. These majors lead to successful middle-class professions. The students in Penang wear white shirts and slacks and have conservative haircuts. Young Asians in places like Penang, many from lesser circumstances than Western youth, aspire to be middle class, own a home, have professional standing, and acquire enough things to live comfortably.

In contrast to the Penang students, Buddhist students in Western universities choose majors in religion, anthropology, arts, and history. These majors lead pretty much nowhere practical (I write this as a fine arts major myself). The students of Buddhist groups in the West usually wear decidedly nonmainstream clothes—sometimes even the Asian clothes that Asians themselves no longer wear—and redefine the limits of hair. Many of the Western youth have the opposite goal from their Asian peers: having grown up in conventional American society, they reject it and seek alternatives.

While Buddhist youth in both Asia and the West are highly committed to their faith traditions, their dispositions around consumerism and material goods are strikingly different. The wide gap between these two cultures suggests that being Buddhist does not perforce give rise to a view on consumerism. For the young Asians in developing countries whom I met, the compatibility of being Buddhist and striving for success and material stability is not a burning question. Likewise, I have not found consumerism to be a big concern among first-generation Asians in America who are also seeking to establish a basic, middle-class life here. It turns out that young Asians from wealthy families have dispositions more aligned with young, affluent Westerners.

I find this contrast fascinating. Why, among certain Buddhists, is the question of consumerism so big? Why do young Western Buddhists, second-generation Asian Americans, and well-off Asians highlight certain dharma teachings—on desire, nonattachment, interdependence—and relate that to consumerist culture? We might take two things away from this correlation.

First, I suggest that those from good circumstances are nearly overwhelmed by American consumerism. Thus, Buddhism's nonattachment may be the diet for consumer gluttony. A high school Buddhist wrote, "I wonder if there is a growing movement of youth who are tired of materialism and propaganda aimed at us and the culture the corporate businesses are trying to sell?"[13] For people like this, perhaps Buddhist teachings offer tremendous psychological relief and are a remedy for societies that have become excessively affluent.

Second, the sociological issue of class appears to be a motivating force in how Buddhism and consumerism have become intertwined. For example, not all traditions of Buddhism, as they have evolved in America, speak to consumerism. Soka Gakkai not only tolerates material success but also includes ways to achieve material success through chanting practices. Could this encouragement be why Soka Gakkai International–USA has had much greater success reaching lower socioeconomic classes—thereby including a greater diversity of ethnic groups—than have Zen, Theravada, or Vajrayana lineages? Given that an ethics of conscious consumerism is dominant among middle- and upper-class young Buddhists, perhaps we should not assume this ethics automatically applies to everyone. Or, in developing this ethic further, we may need to consider the psychological effects of economic class as a motivating force.

While traveling in Malaysia, I was struck by the fact that Malaysians want material goods just as much as Americans. If they have the means to get them, they will! Greed seems to be human, not specifically American.

The same thing applies to Buddhist goods. There are just as many Buddhist items for sale in Asia as there are in America, if not more. If anything, one finds even tackier stuff. We are upset about malas hawked as power beads? Check out Buddha cell phone straps, Buddha car talismans, Buddha mouse pads, monk dolls, monk stationery, and so on that can be found in any temple or mall boutique. We in the United States might deal with our ambivalence around Buddhist goods by reflecting on the place of these goods for Buddhists in Asia.

REFLECTION

Doing a little fieldwork for this essay, I recently returned to Kmart. On my way, I stopped by Home Depot to check into buying a new water heater for my house. I must say that buying a water heater does not create the intense craving mind of consumerism. It's practical, it's necessary. I did not feel fussy about the fact that water heaters came in only one color (white), for example. I did not feel defined by my water heater. It was a clean, clear, and stress-free shopping experience.

I then went to Kmart partly because I had some real needs—we're tired of using a cup as a ladle—and partly just to wander the aisles and see if anything leaped out at me as being a necessity. I came to the socks section, hoping to buy something basic but stylish. I was proud of myself for not checking Lands' End online first. No, I thought, no one really sees socks, so I will buy what is functional and long lasting so as not to waste resources. But after searching the entire wall of socks, I could not find anything I liked. I felt myself growing fussy and annoyed. Can't this store stock itself right? I began looking at the other customers who were walking around in a daze at all the stuff. I heard a man ask his wife if there were any Martha Stewart versions of their desired object. I sighed, leaned on my cart, and headed for the checkout counter, where one could buy, just in case I forgot, American flag stickers. "Oh, yeah," I thought, "this is what consumerism is about: creating an identity through what we buy, being dissatisfied even with abundance, and being a good, all-consuming American."

There is no question that I am grateful for some of the anticonsumerism views I was raised with on the Zen commune. At the same time, I won't be raising my own children in such deprived circumstances. Fortunately for my generation, we have many more avenues in which to realistically infuse Buddhist principles into a conscious consumerism. We have decent socially responsible investing funds. There are established social activism groups who make a real difference. We have access to abundant alternative food vendors who are socially and environmentally conscious. In colleges, there are plenty of courses on environmentalism, Buddhism, media awareness, and social responsibility as well as student organizations devoted to activism. More so than for our parents when they were young, we can take jobs in nonmainstream professions and get paid for our work. Young Buddhists can take advantage of these opportunities, bestowed by the babyboomer Buddhists. At the same time, we should become more conscious of our dominant consumerism views and perhaps critique and develop them into a theory.

In the meantime, I can't wait for Martha Stewart to develop her own line of meditation cushions.

5

Marketing the Dharma

Thubten Chödrön

WHEN WE TURN to spirituality, we may think that we're leaving behind
the corruption of the world for higher purposes. But our old ways of thinking do not disappear; they follow us, coloring the way we approach spiritual practice. Since we have all been raised to be good consumers—getting
the most while paying the least—we carry our consumer mentality as teachers and students of religion right into our spiritual practice.

Although much of what is said below pertains to newer spiritual students, it also applies to those of us who have practiced the Dharma for years
and are now seen as teachers. We, too, must reflect on how consumerist
conditioning has influenced us. Until we reach the culmination of the path,
we remain imperfect sentient beings and Dharma students.

How consumer mentality influences spiritual practice has been a topic
of ongoing interest to me for a variety of reasons. My first Dharma teacher,
Ven. Zopa Rinpoche, talked continually about "attachment to the happiness of only this life." He stressed motivation as key to the difference between an action that was Dharma and one that wasn't. Did we act with the
thought seeking the happiness of only this life? Or did we act with a motivation that looked beyond our own temporary pleasure? An action seeking

only our own gain in this lifetime resembles the actions of animals, he said. Animals help their friends and harm their enemies. Animals want to be comfortable and to be "top dog." If, stripped of rationalizations and justifications, our actions are motivated by such thoughts, then we aren't making full use of our precious human life and the rare opportunity it affords us to practice the Dharma.

These were not easy words for me to hear. Previously I'd thought of myself as a good person, even a compassionate, spiritual one. But when I began to meditate and was honest about my motivations, I was alternately shocked and horrified. But I have been grateful to Zopa Rinpoche ever since, because right at the beginning he imprinted in my mind the importance of being aware of motivations and of consciously cultivating beneficial ones. This is not to say that I have been able to do it. Far more often than not, my mind is overpowered by thoughts of "my happiness now . . . or at least my happiness as soon as possible."

Consumer mentality, in which most of us in the West have been well schooled, is clearly rooted in attachment to the happiness of only this life. As a Dharma student and a so-called "teacher," over the years I have noticed my own tendencies in this area. In writing this piece, therefore, I speak as both a student and a teacher. Although most of the essay is written with the inclusive "we," this "we" is amorphous. It may or may not include you, the reader, or me, the writer, in all its usages. (For example, I don't have children, so the "we" meaning parents doesn't refer to me.) However, I didn't want to say "they," as if I were excluding you and me or pointing the finger at others. So, as you read "we," if the cushion fits, sit on it.

THE SPIRITUAL SEEKER AS CONSUMER

The Consumer Mind

How does consumerism manifest on the part of the student? One element of consumerism is seeking the best product. Thus many of us shop around for the best group, the most realized teacher, the highest practice. We go from this place to that, seeking the best spiritual product to "buy." We want the highest teachings and neglect foundational practices. Viewing ourselves as fully qualified disciples, we don't see much need for basic practices such as ethical discipline and restraint of the senses. Instead, we jump into the most advanced track.

As consumers, we want to be entertained. We'll attend a center as long as the teacher is entertaining—and a teacher must be entertaining these days to attract students. We like to hear interesting stories, told in an amusing way, and we want new and fascinating teachings. When we hear the same teachings over and over again, we get bored and set out to find something new and different.

Our practice environment should be interesting as well, so we seek out exotica. Practicing in the Tibetan tradition, I can say that Tibetan Buddhism certainly obliges this. While in Tibet many of these practices and accoutrements are simply part of the culture, in the West they have become exotic lures. High thrones for the teachers, brocade seat covers, and robes, long horns, short horns, bells, drums, processions, deep chanting, and, oh yes, hats! Yellow ones, red ones, black ones. With all the paraphernalia, how could one ever get bored practicing Tibetan Buddhism? Yet after a while we become jaded and are left with just our own minds, our own suffering. Having little endurance or commitment to practice or to teachers, we move on, seeking something more interesting. We neglect to see that repetition may be just what we need or that exploring the reason for our boredom could bring fresh insights. We also fail to notice that our teachers still do foundational practices and attend elementary teachings given by their spiritual mentors.

Consumer mentality insists on instant gratification of our desires. In spiritual life, we say we want a close relationship with a spiritual mentor, but when that mentor's spiritual guidance challenges our desires or pushes our ego's buttons too much, we stop going. At the beginning of our practice, we profess to be earnest spiritual seekers, aiming for enlightenment. But after the practice has remedied our immediate problem—upset from a divorce, grieving the loss of a loved one, and so forth—and we are happier, our attention shifts once again to seeking happiness from possessions, romance, technology, or career, and spiritual interest fades.

Today's consumer expects things to be easily available and obtainable without much effort. In past ages, spiritual aspirants underwent difficulty to meet teachers. Tibetans traversed the Himalayas to meet wise mentors in India; Chinese crossed the Takla Makan Desert and Karakoram Mountains to attend monasteries and bring back scriptures from India. But nowadays we think, "Why should we have to travel to attend teachings? The teacher should come to us! We have such busy lives we don't have time to go across the country, let alone to another continent." Forgetting that the seeker's very effort and struggle opens him or her to the teachings, we'd prefer that spiritual practice not disturb the flow of our life.

Receiving lengthy teachings or doing complex spiritual practices takes time that modern consumers don't have. Our time is taken up with families, jobs, hobbies, and sports; spiritual practice should not impinge on those pleasures and responsibilities. So we ask our teachers to "modernize" the teachings and practices—to shorten and simplify them—so that they will fit conveniently into our lives. As consumers functioning in a world of supply and demand, we take our business elsewhere if our wishes aren't satisfied.

The Dilemma of Dana

Asian Buddhists traditionally make offerings, or *dana,* to the monastic community to accumulate merit or positive potential that will bring a good rebirth. Looking at them, some Westerners say, "They're doing spiritual business. They are giving to get something for themselves." Thinking that Westerners are superior to Asians trapped in old traditions, we don't give to the monastic community. Instead we hold to the American work ethic and think monastics should go out and get a job.

When we do give dana (or donations), what is our attitude? At the end of a retreat, someone gives a "dana talk," explaining to everyone that dana is generosity freely given. "Think of all we've received from our teachers during this retreat. They have families, cars, mortgages, credit card bills, and for them to continue to teach us, they need our financial support." Hasn't dana then become another way of paying for a consumer service we've received?

We don't give to support earnest practitioners who don't teach. Instead, we give to teachers when we've received their services. We go through lots of mental gymnastics figuring out how much to give: "Let's see, if someone were to charge for this retreat, how much would be a reasonable price? That's what I'll give." We totally miss the point of dana, which is to take delight in giving and to give from our hearts.

According to the consumer mentality, we pay as we go. But dana is a long-term commitment that is part of our practice. We give because we want to be free from the hindrance of miserliness; we offer dana because we appreciate the teachings and practitioners. When we give dana properly, we don't offer less for a two-day retreat than for a four-day retreat. Instead we give because we want to support practitioners who live simply and devote their time to spiritual study and practice. We give to make the teachings available to new people.

Consumerism breeds self-centeredness. Spiritual practice often becomes centered on "me," my needs, my wishes, what is convenient for me, what works for me. When we go to a religious place or event, we think, "What can I get from this? How will it benefit *me*?" A dharma center, temple, or monastery becomes a place where we go to receive, not to give. If an activity doesn't meet our needs, we don't have the time or money to support it.

I regularly visit an Asian temple in Houston where they hold summer camps for kids. Working in the kitchen, cooking food for a hundred people, are parents, students, grandparents, single adults, and couples without kids. Many people who don't have children are willing to spend four or five days cooking or running children's programs. Why? Because they enjoy being part of a community. They care about children and the future of society. They want to give their time and energy to support something worthwhile for others. Giving is part of their spiritual practice, and they relish it. They enjoy giving, in contrast to consumers who enjoy receiving.

Why do Westerners have trouble creating community? After all, most of us feel a deep longing for community, but still we keep our distance and maintain our autonomy. My guess is that this has to do with the *c* word, the word we are very frightened of. No, it's not *cancer*, although that undoubtedly is frightening. The *c* word we mistrust is *commitment*. If we commit, our shopping around ceases. We have responsibility not just to others but to ourselves. We commit to a daily practice; we commit to attending regular dharma classes in order to nourish our hearts; we commit to attending yearly retreats. We commit time to plan activities at the dharma center, monastery, or temple. We commit energy to plan the Sunday school program instead of just dropping our kids off in the hope that someone else will teach them the dharma. We commit goodwill to serving our teachers and fellow practitioners. This cuts into our time to be with family, to watch TV, go to the gym, talk on the phone, do e-mail, browse catalogs, frequent the mall, and go on vacation. In short, it requires that we divert time that ordinarily goes toward worldly pleasure into time leading to dharma happiness.

Somehow we mistakenly think that commitment means being trapped. In fact, when we make wise, well-thought-out commitments, they free us. They enable us to enter deeply into our practice and shed our defenses before our teachers and fellow practitioners. We develop trust in others and ourselves and learn to be fearlessly open. And most of all, we stick with a teacher and a practice long enough so that the dharma can actually transform our minds. As one student said, "We keep showing up, whether we're happy or unhappy, whether we understand the teaching or not. We keep coming, instead of getting discouraged or distracted." Only with commitment can we actually taste the dharma.

The Enchantment of Status

In a consumer society, people derive status from using certain products. Similarly, being close to a famous Dharma teacher uplifts a student's spiritual status. Having that teacher stay in our home, ride in our car, bless our religious objects, sign a photo, and so forth gives us something to display to others. These days one of the best ways to become close to a teacher is by being a big donor, thus obliging teachers to see you in order to show their appreciation. We wouldn't want to give anonymously and miss a possible reward.

We also gain status by possessing valuable spiritual items. We buy beautiful statues and exquisite paintings of religious figures, which we display on elaborate altars in our homes. On the altars, too, are photos of ourselves with various spiritual masters. When dharma friends visit, we make sure they admire our collection of artifacts, but when relatives visit, we discreetly cover them to avoid their inquiries. We have the latest spiritual books (preferably autographed by a famous author), a comfy meditation cushion (or two), and the requisite prayer beads (made of crystal or stone, not plastic, and blessed by a holy being).

In addition, we collect spiritual events. We proudly rattle off a list of retreats we have attended or initiations we have taken and advise new students about which events and teachers are mediocre and which they must not miss. As experienced connoisseurs, we critique retreat centers for newcomers. We boast of attending large teachings by famous teachers and mention that as a teacher was making his way through the crowd, he stopped to greet us, or while he was sitting on the Dharma throne, he smiled directly at us. Meanwhile, we pat ourselves on the back for being such sincere practitioners.

Similar to the status-seeking attitude is one that idolizes great figures. In consumer society we worship movie stars, sports stars, and political leaders, thinking that everything they do is wonderful. As teenagers we wanted to emulate them; now, as semicynical adults, we idolize them for awhile and buy the things they advertise. But later, when we see their human failings, we blame them and become discouraged.

The same happens with our Dharma teachers. For a while we are in love with our guru: He's so wonderful; his compassion makes the room shine. She's so humorous and warm. He's an incarnation of a very high yogi. She's clairvoyant. We sit around and drink tea and talk about our teachers, telling stories about cute incidents, reciting tales of their great qualities. Sometimes there is subtle competition over who has the highest teacher or who can tell the greatest stories. We revel in newcomers' wide-eyed fascination as they listen to us; we're jealous of those who have better stories.

When our teachers do things we don't agree with, or worse yet, when their behavior appears all too human, we feel betrayed. We are disappointed or indignant, just as when we discover politicians' scams, movie stars' mental illnesses, and sports stars' greed. But we don't realize that our previous attitude was a setup for our present feelings.

What is it in us that makes us seek someone who is perfect? And what does "perfect" mean, anyhow? Does it mean that the person does what we want when we want him to do it? Does it mean she agrees with all our opinions and ideas and lavishes praise on us? I believe this tendency toward idolization relates to the consumer mentality that seeks "the best, or your money back." We have a steady diet of advertisements that condition us to become enthralled with grand expectations of happiness when we buy *this* product, vote for *this* candidate, see *this* film, or attend *this* game. We bring our unrealistic wishes for perfection and satisfaction into our spiritual practice, projecting them on teachers and meditation practices.

SPIRITUAL MENTORS AND CONSUMERISM

Marketing the Dharma

Consumer mentality influences teachers as well. In a consumer culture, advertising boasts about the excellent qualities of a product. Following this pattern, notices of Dharma events don't just announce an event but actively sell a product, that is, the teacher or the teaching. Most ads display an enticing photo of a spiritual master who is either smiling radiantly or looking wisely into the distance. He or she, the ads declare, is a highly realized, well-respected, fully accomplished master. The topic being taught is a secret teaching that in the past was given only to a select number of qualified disciples. It is the supreme teaching by which previous masters have attained enlightenment. You can receive this for a mere $99.95 plus dana for the teacher. Register early to reserve a seat or you'll be left out. What happened to the age-old custom of humble masters who kept their qualities hidden?

With sincere motivation, informing people who could benefit from a spiritual teaching or retreat is valid and necessary. Can this be done without hype in a culture that thrives on hype? This is a dilemma for many of us because we came to the Dharma partly because of a dislike for the hype and hard sell of consumer society. We want to let people know about Dharma events so they can benefit from the teachings, but we prefer simple announcements. However, these get lost amid the many attractive ads and fascinating flyers. For teachers to draw people to Dharma events, they need to have a title or two, and they must appear "high" or important. His Holiness the Dalai Lama has remarked that people who are unknown in Asia come to the West and suddenly become lamas and rinpoches with a string of titles before their name and a retinue of devotees behind them.

Personally, I find this issue difficult. *Venerable* or *bhikshuni* indicates I'm a monastic (at least in my tradition, though *Venerable* is used differently by others). That's fair enough, because I've been ordained since 1977. However, I have nowhere near the qualities of my teachers and therefore do not want people to address me as "lama," a title that in my tradition is reserved for well-respected teachers. On the other hand, some people who are much newer in the dharma are called "lama"—sometimes because their tradition uses the word differently, sometimes for other reasons. So people ask me, "How come you're not a lama?" When I explain why I don't use that title, they think I'm odd, because in a Western consumer culture, we are taught to display our qualities and make ourselves look good.

To market a product, it must be appealing to potential buyers. The Buddhist teaching of skillful means—teaching according to the disposition and interests of the students—is necessary to guide people on the path. But when do skillful means degenerate into pleasing students so that teachers will have more students? Do we omit particular ideas or teachings or explain them away because potential students don't like them and will stop coming? How much do teachers water down the scriptures in the name of skillful means, when our motivation is actually attracting and maintaining a large following?

There is much danger in this, because it is easy to teach something that looks like Dharma but is a mixture of Dharma and our own ideas and preferences. Sometimes we aren't even aware we do it, because we receive great praise from numerous students, who say, "Your teachings are wonderful!" And since more people are coming to our talks and more people are buying our books and tapes, we think what we're doing must be good.

Success Is in Numbers

In a consumer economy, success is measured by numbers. Thus many spiritual teachers hope attendance at teachings will be high, dana will continually increase, their books will sell well, and invitations to speak on television and radio programs will be plentiful. To what extent do teachers decide where to teach based on the amount of dana they will receive? Is it just coincidence that many teachers go to wealthy communities? How many teachers go to developing countries or to lower-income areas in our own country where dana is meager?

Financial resources are necessary to spread the teachings. How can teachers procure support consistent with right livelihood? Do we drop hints, flatter, or subtly coerce people so that they offer money to us or to our organization? Do we give donors extra perks that are denied to other devotees who may be more sincere but not as well off?

For monastic teachers, the issue of personal livelihood is much simpler. We don't need a lot because our precepts set parameters on our lifestyle. We don't have many or diverse clothes, we don't wear jewelry or cosmetics, we don't own a house or a car, nor do we have children to support. For lay teachers with families and a middle-class lifestyle, this is trickier.

But both lay and monastic teachers have organizations that support Dharma study and practice and sometimes social welfare projects as well. As someone trying to start an abbey in North America, I struggle with this. As an individual monastic, I didn't need much. I was careful not to view people in terms of who had money and who didn't. But to begin a monastery, more is needed. Many people have suggested fundraising ideas that I have vetoed because they involve pressuring, schmoozing, or giving perks to those who give. I would like people to donate to the abbey because they value the Buddha's teachings, appreciate monastics, and want to see the Dharma flourish in the West. I want them to give because they take delight in giving and feel good about contributing to worthwhile projects. How can I share my enthusiasm for the abbey in a respectful way that accords with my own principles?

THE DISADVANTAGES OF SPIRITUAL CONSUMERISM

Consumer mentality in spiritual students and teachers brings disadvantages to both ourselves and others. In terms of ourselves, it draws us away from actualizing our deepest spiritual aspirations. As mentioned earlier, the distinction between dharma and nondharma actions is made primarily in terms of motivation. Motivations seeking only the happiness of this life are considered worldly because they focus on our own immediate happiness. Motivations aspiring for good future rebirth, liberation, and enlightenment are spiritual because they seek longer-term goals that benefit self *and* others.

When describing a mind seeking the happiness of only this life, the Buddha outlined eight worldly concerns. These eight fall into four pairs: (1) delight in receiving money and material possessions; displeasure or upset at not receiving or being separated from them, (2) delight in praise, approval, and ego-pleasing words; displeasure at criticism and disapproval, (3) delight in having a good reputation and image; displeasure when they are tainted, and (4) delight when contacting pleasurable sense objects—sights, sounds, smells, tastes, and tactile objects; displeasure when encountering unpleasant sense objects. When I examine my mental states, most of them consist of these eight. Personally speaking, I find having a pure spiritual motivation is actually quite difficult. I hope that others who suffer similarly from worldly motivations aren't afraid to admit it to themselves and others. Only through being honest with ourselves can we purify our minds and hearts.

Consumer mentality in spiritual seekers is clearly involved with the eight worldly concerns. While it is often masked by clever rationalizations, it still enslaves us to the happiness of only this life. When that mind is operating, true spiritual practice cannot occur. We may come to the Dharma with sincere aspirations and devotion, but when old self-centered habits creep into our motivations, we lose what we cherish the most. We may put a lot of time and energy into activities that look spiritual but aren't because the motivation is tainted with the eight worldly concerns. In this way our consumer mentality can sabotage our spiritual practice and noble aspirations.

Perhaps most distressing is the harmful impact spiritual consumerism can have on others. Dharma teachings have been passed down for centuries by practitioners who took great care to preserve their true meaning expressed accurately. The consumer mentality threatens this purity by enticing teachers to "adjust" the meaning of the teachings in order to draw bigger crowds or to have a better reputation. This deprives future generations of spiritual instructions that are true to their source. It can cause others to lose faith in the efficacy of practice because they see teachers speaking one thing but acting the opposite. That is, we talk about the disadvantages of samsara and generating the determination to be free from it, but we act in ways that show our craving for samsara's pleasures. Seeing this, students may think that the teachings don't really work, that the Dharma is a sham. This devastates their possibility for enlightenment. In addition, consumer mentality allures spiritual institutions into creating structures that harm the very people they promise to help. This occurs because the purpose of the institution shifts subtly from serving others to self-preservation.

REMEDIES

In the *Pathamalokadhamma Sutra*, the Buddha said:

> *Among humans, these things, namely,*
> *Gain, loss, status, disrepute, blame, praise, pleasure, and pain*
> *Naturally are impermanent, uncertain, and liable to change.*
> *The wise, ever mindful, understand these things*
> *And contemplate them as always shifting and changing.*
> *Thus, delightful things cannot oppress their minds,*
> *They have no reaction to disagreeable things,*
> *They have abandoned all liking and disliking (for worldly*
>   *concerns).*
> *Further, they know the path of nirvana, dust-free and without*
>   *sorrow,*
> *They have reached the other shore of existence and know this*
>   *correctly.*[1]

One of the foremost antidotes to the eight worldly concerns is the meditation on impermanence and death. By seeing pleasure from the eight worldly concerns as transient, we lose interest in them. By seeing the worldly concerns as uncertain, we are disinclined to exert so much energy into procuring and protecting them.

Struggling for worldly happiness is wearying. We may work very hard to attain the four pleasures and be free from the four displeasures, but we are not necessarily successful. Why? Because we can't control the external world and everything in it. Therefore, it is more valuable to transform our minds. By freeing the mind from attachment, hostility, and ignorance, we will be able to be internally content no matter how much wealth we have, no matter what people say about us, and no matter what we experience. Attaining stable peace—nirvana—is the purpose of Dharma practice.

Part of the remedy lies in asking ourselves, "What does it mean to be successful?" We have been conditioned that the eight worldly concerns constitute success, but do they? We know people who are successful by worldly standards—they have wealth, good relationships, status, and sense pleasures galore—but many of them are miserable. Are these people actually successful? Isn't a better measure of success our internal experience of peace and joy? If so, we need to focus on developing this through spiritual practice.

So whether our consumer mentality functions in the shopping mall or the meditation hall, I propose that we try to catch it when it arises and bring our minds back to what is truly important: compassion and wisdom. Let's revive appreciation for the traditional model of a practitioner—a renounced being who lives a life of simplicity and humility, sincerity and endeavor, kindness and compassion. Let's choose teachers with these qualities and cultivate these qualities in ourselves. Let's keep our spiritual institutions on track by having only as much organizational structure as needed to facilitate the teaching and practice of the Dharma.

Buddhists are attempting to introduce Dharma values and establish a substantial role for the Buddha's teachings in Western culture. The consumer mentality is a great obstacle to reorienting people toward spiritual values and aims that would benefit them. Our collective challenge is to practice and teach the Dharma in ways that not only benefit contemporary culture but also preserve the purity of the Buddha's teachings.

6

You Are What You Download

Diana Winston

LET'S IMAGINE THE BUDDHA ON FOOT, traversing dusty northern India a few hundred years before the birth of Christ. Wandering and spreading the word from village to village, stopping only during the rainy season, he is followed by a retinue of shaved-head men and women, all of whom see him as the Holy One, the Enlightened, the World Knower. Each word from his mouth is like nectar to the disciples, quenching their thirst for knowledge, leading them to the supreme happiness. The great sage carries a begging bowl, a razor, a second set of robes, and a worn-out but still functioning laptop with an extra set of batteries. Even the Buddha needed to check his e-mail.

This image may not work for you. Never mind the anachronism. In truth, it's hard to imagine the Buddha surfing the Web. He was an oral tradition kind of guy, for starters. If the Buddha were around these days, I bet he would have a lot to say about Internet technology and its effect on our minds. Does the Internet oppose his teachings of moderation, restraint, nonconfusion, and nongreed? What about the Buddhist precept against clouding or confusing the mind with intoxicants? Is the Internet an intoxicant, sending us further into the delusion of separateness, wanting, control, and self? To answer these questions, the Buddha would point us computer-age denizens directly to our own minds. It's all there, in this fathom-long body, so he said.

He might ask us: Does it matter what you fill your head with? From the Buddha's perspective, the answer is unquestionably yes. Everything affects us. The law of karma reminds us that each action—no matter how tiny—has an effect. And effects are cumulative: "With single drops of water, the water bucket fills." What kind of mental habitat do we want to create? What kind of self (to use Buddhist language) gets constructed each time we add another drop of water, possibly from a questionable source, into our mind? And might the accumulation of those drops drive us into activity we might not be too happy about later, such as Web shopping for antique dinnerware?

The popular belief, so I hear, is that we don't need to worry about what goes into our heads. We forget everything. Watching violence on television does not necessarily reproduce violent acts in the real world, the theory goes. After all, we have natural filters, we humans are infinitely adaptable, and smart to boot. We'll forget the unimportant or awful stuff and retain what really matters, like which cable station is which number on the channel changer.

My own experience as a meditator, spending hours and hours observing my mind, has shown me without a shadow of doubt that we *are* affected by what enters our minds, although we don't always see it right away. If we feed our minds with greed-inducing information, we are certain to get more greedy. The Internet, once hailed as a revolutionary, time-saving communication technology, has turned out for the most part to be a time-wasting, greed-inducing, glorified shopping channel. As with most things in America, consumerism reigns. And our poor minds pay the cost.

THE CLOUDED MIND

I'm a bit of a meditation junkie. I gravitate toward long periods of structured silent retreat, say, three months at a time. I practice vipassana, or insight meditation, where I observe the moment-to-moment experience in my mind and body: my breath, body sensations, thoughts, and emotions. On these retreats I meditate in silence for sometimes fourteen hours a day, every day, no break. I am not supposed to talk to anyone, read, write, watch TV, open a newspaper, or go online. The point is to clear the mind of the usual distractions of everyday life in order to see where my mind is clinging or creating a sense of "self," and then to find freedom through letting go. So on retreat I empty out my mind, and in all that residual mental space, everything I ever ingested floats to the surface. Yes, it is still in there, although it's hard to say where.

On long retreats I remember the tiniest supposedly insignificant experiences, like the time I fought with my friend Karen when we were four because she wanted to color the entire coloring book red and I protested for variety's sake; or my dad teaching me to listen to rain; or the wallpaper in my bedroom and the way the light shone in between the tree leaves and created moving shadow puppets on the wall; the smells and views of the little hill town in India where I lived for six months; and the time I first kissed someone, who shall remain nameless.

While meditating, my mind has yielded at all hours of the day, without relief, unending rounds of seventies commercials, television jingles, Broadway musicals, "The Brady Bunch" and other TV theme songs, monologues from acting class, bad rock and roll, previous discussions, good rock and roll, songs from summer camp . . . *the ants go marching one by one, hurrah, hurrah.* . . . They have not gone away. Worse, when I try to sit still to find peace and calm, they come back to haunt me. (I will say, however, that in all these years of meditating, quantitative algebra has yet to materialize.)

No, this mind has not forgotten. It is all in there, especially strong and violent stuff. An avid fan of Salman Rushdie, I once snatched up the first novel of his former wife, Marianne Wiggins, with anticipation, assuming great minds must think alike. Before long I found myself unable to put down an oeuvre on cannibalism. The plot chronicled a group of young girls who, shipwrecked on a desert island, resort to dining on each other. I have scarcely encountered in literature anything as horrific as the little girls gleefully roasting the forearms of the ship captain and devouring the ghastly morsels. I quickly put it out of my mind. Or so I thought. A few years later, in the midst of another long meditation retreat, graphic replays from Wiggins's book tortured me. For a week I walked the halls of the meditation center like a wraith, tormented by images I couldn't exorcise. Ultimately they played themselves out, thanks to vigilant mindfulness. I followed the experience with a heartfelt vow: From this day on I will never take anything into my poor mind that I don't want to see later.

Are meditators encouraged to hold to a basic level of ethics because you might not like what you see otherwise? If you are morally in good shape, maybe you don't spend hours on the cushion engaged in remorse, regret, and guilt. But what if you're not? *I shouldn't have told her that story, but it was just too good to keep to myself,* or *I should never have shoplifted the Bonne Bell lip gloss from CVS; the ants go marching two by two, hurrah, hurrah.* Ethics gives us a framework to abide by. As part of our personal ethics, we can lean toward simplicity, renunciation, and generosity rather than complication, gaining, and consuming. Thich Nhat Hanh's interpretation of the fifth precept invites us not to cloud our mind with *any* kind of intoxicant, including TV and the Internet, in addition to the usual drugs and alcohol listed in the Buddhist texts.[1] If we try to follow this precept, we may try to avoid online stimulants and the apparatus of shopping in order to maintain some peace of mind. We can create a life infinitely less cluttered with stuff—internally and externally.

But if we do find ourselves inexorably drawn to the Internet, what happens when we deliberately imbibe excessive, violent, stupid, pointless, titillating, and prodigious information in a direct link from our computer to our brain? As an Internet user, my already full mind is privy to vast new fields of information, stories, poems, bad jokes, sites, commentary, porn, pet projects, hoaxes, dating opportunities, music, chat rooms, sweepstakes offers, commercials, products, advertisements. *Do I need more stuff in there?* I have hundreds of books I haven't yet read. I have interesting friends whose brains I haven't picked, countries I've never visited, films still to see—and libraries, remember them?

Now I cannot help but think Internet thoughts. My everyday discussions refer to links and URLs and sites. Once I commented to a friend that our conversation had become a Web site. We headed in one direction and a tangent sent us off in another, which led to another, and so on. We were clicking conversational links. "Would you hit Back?" he asked me. "I'm lost."

What do we want in our minds? More junk? If so, log on. Do we really want to keep jamming in this useless, vaguely entertaining, often not even true, never-ending information? It will stay in there, I guarantee. And it will come out to haunt us. The question is, will it make us better people? Yes, yes, I know, we can learn very important things from the Internet. Alternative press has flourished, as has alternative political campaigning. I have access to new media studies, hip peace events in Bangladesh and Colombia, left-wing critiques of the war of the month. They used it in Chiapas. They organized with it in Seattle. I am not denying any of this. If you think I'm only complaining, you are missing my point.

But what kind of karma is being created from daily, less-inspired use of the World Wide Web? What sort of self is being constructed? Will the Internet make us ethical, kind, generous, or compassionate? Will it make our minds and lives more spacious and relaxed? Or will it inflame our greed, leading us to consume? With all that ingested junk, and access to much, much more, how does the Internet affect our basic ability to free our minds? Is it a tool for enslavement or for liberation?

DEPENDENT (OR NOT) ORIGINATION

On the day I realized that I could have anything I wanted over the Internet, I bought ten new books, a subscription to a simple-living magazine, and a pair of black leather boots, and sent myself the daily quotes of the Buddha. The Buddha sent me an e-mail about the law of karma. He said actions have results. If I plant a plum pit, I will get a plum tree. If I practice greed, I will be more greedy. If I practice generosity, I will be more generous. Buddhism 101.

The Buddhist teachings explain on a microscopic, almost neurological level how attachment works and the self gets created. We encounter, for example, a desirable object. At the moment of visual, aural, or touch contact with that object, a pleasant feeling arises in our minds or bodies. This pleasant feeling comes from a variety of places—past habit, training, media, standards of cool, socioeconomics, karma, and so on. With this contact, we associate the pleasant feeling with the object. The feeling itself is wonderful. In order to sustain the feeling, we think we need to *get* the object. We cling to the feeling and then to the object itself that we think has produced the feeling. We get attached, and voilà, the "self" is born.

Another way of saying this is, we feel something nice (pleasant feeling), we reach out for it (craving), grasp our hand tightly around it and don't let go (clinging), and then there is a birth of the self (becoming). It works in reverse too: an unpleasant feeling results in not wanting and ultimately pushing away (aversion). In Buddhist philosophy, this chain of events is called dependent origination—nothing is independently produced. This chain is happening continuously at such a rapid rate that we are seldom aware of this process. They say it is the driving force by which we live our lives. We are unconsciously responding to pleasant or unpleasant stimuli, but all we know is that we have to have the new DVD player.

Dependent origination teaches how we automatically grab for an object to stop the aching and sustain the pleasantness. In effect, we are trying to put an end to our suffering, which is certainly understandable. The chain can seem hopeless—we are controlled by an unconscious process, running toward pleasant experience and away from what is unpleasant. But this is where mindful awareness comes in, which is really the key. Mindfulness is the part of our mind that knows exactly what is happening when it is happening. It is present, aware, and connected to the moment. It has a liberating power in that it can help us to see clearly. Through the power of mindfulness, it is possible to short-circuit the cycle and prevent the automatic response. If at any moment we apply mindful awareness to the cycle of contact, pleasant feelings, wanting, and clinging, we need not move on to the next link of the chain.

We can notice *Wow, I want a pair of boots.* We can feel the feeling of desire in our bodies (aching in the chest or gut area, pounding heart) and notice the accompanying thoughts (*they're perfect, I can't live without them*). Then we can apply mindfulness to these sensations or thoughts. When we see them clearly for what they are—merely thoughts and sensations, not truths about ourselves—the mind may let go. We may relax some, soften the belly, notice: "Hey, it's just a thought." By seeing it clearly, the mind can let go and stop the forward thrust into attachment, purchase, and the boot-addicted self.

The revolutionary insight brought to us by the Buddha is that actually it is painful to want. Letting go of wanting stops the pain. Getting what we want only temporarily soothes the wound. Buddhist wisdom teaches us that a desire doesn't have to be fulfilled to make it go away. We can recognize and let go of the desire. We can break the chain. All we have to do is catch a single point on the cycle. *Oh look, there's pleasant contact with a desirable pair of boots! Oh, I feel body sensations of longing for them, hmm. Oh, I feel myself wanting!* If we can bring mindfulness here, we can break the chain. It is up to us; we are not slaves to an automatic process. We don't have to buy the boots. The desire for them may fade through the power of mindfully witnessing dependent origination.

Part of breaking the chain depends on our ability to have some space for reflection. But what happens when our reflection time is limited? What happens when we throw the speed of the Internet into this equation? Over the last decade, the space between a desire and the satisfaction of that desire has almost disappeared. Back in the Stone Age (before 1994, when the

Internet was just a toy for computer geeks and the military), if you wanted something, there was a process. You could think about it, visualize the item, research the product, save money, compare the item at several shops, ask your friends for advice. Yes, there were mail-order catalogs, and I suppose even the shopping channel existed back then, but there was some consideration in the process to get something you wanted. Not that this would necessarily deter you, but in those halcyon days, purchasing an object required work.

On the day of the planned purchase, perhaps you asked a friend to join you, drove to the shop, found parking, discovered the desired object was or wasn't there, or they didn't have your size, browsed other things, talked with a salesperson, stopped for a late lunch, and finally, when descending upon your desired object, perhaps reneged—"Well this may not be exactly what I want after all." Today you peruse the Internet and log on to a shopping Web site. You want something—anything, really. It's the CD you never realized you needed, but now you will die without it. There it is. Great. How much? No problem, it's on sale! You type in your credit card number (or your computer—in true Orwellian fashion—remembers it), hit a control key, and it is yours.

Pleasant feeling, wanting feeling, and instantaneous action—all in just a few seconds. There is no time for mindfulness to prevent the inevitable purchase. We have no time to get free. It is easy to act quickly when there are no obstacles. We don't have to go anywhere, talk to anyone, discuss, debate, consider, or compare. We merely have to press a button.

What happens when space and distance are removed in the buying process? What happens when every possible desire can (appear to) be fulfilled at the click of a mouse? When getting an object is taken for granted in the wanting? When millions of young minds are taught that they can have anything they want whenever they want it? What are they taking into their minds, nonstop, with no filters whatsoever? What happens when these children grow up? What will happen to those sweet Buddhist values of nongreed, compassion, and generosity? We may be in for some trouble. In the new millennium, thanks to the Internet, the process is so sped up that we have no built-in physical moment to break the cycle. Could the Internet and its rapacious commerce be contributing to the breakdown of the social fabric? It seems we have become slaves to an even quicker version of dependent origination. The profusion of objects is endless; we attain them at lightning speed. This is not good news, contrary to all the press.

GO REALITY

There must be an antidote to this proliferation. There must be a way out of the constructed self that has been birthed through a field of never-ending consumer desires nestled among prodigious and useless information. There has to be a way to circumvent the nasty effects and the not-so-desirable self that now has been born. It will require some work. I'm not discounting the difficulties of swimming upstream in a culture addicted to speed and greed, but we have to start somewhere.

We might try a few guidelines for support. We could limit the time we spend on the Web and do our best to stick to it. I like to ask myself, do I really need to read the thirty-fifth analysis of the Patriot Act, or could I live without it? Or we might decide that for every hour we spend online, we spend two hours in nature or with friends. A one-to-two ratio, while arbitrary, seems appropriate, or at least a place to start. Another practice would be to pay close attention to how our mind feels upon unplugging. For me the aftermath is increasingly unpleasant and the groggy spaced-out feeling is becoming less and less desirable. Sometimes after a protracted, riveting session on eBay, I log off only to find I can barely tie my shoes. Oh, right, I have a body. A neighbor stops by and it takes about fifteen minutes before I connect with the actual experience of talking. I am stumbling as if I'm drunk, and my eyes are itchy, as if I've been in a sandstorm. Ultimately I normalize, but the transition period is definitely not fun. I now ask myself on a regular basis, would I rather take a walk or surf the Web? (Don't get me wrong, sometimes the Web wins.)

There is a host of potential practices we could try. We can program our computer so a "mindfulness bell" rings randomly, and the monitor goes blank temporarily, helping us stop in that moment, breathe, and sense the body. We can put little awareness reminders stickered to our computer. We could answer e-mails only on alternate days. If we work in an office, we could invite friends to stop by to remind us to breathe while we are on the computer. In that dreadful endless space between Web pages being loaded, we could perceive it not as a tragedy but as a moment for coming back to ourselves.

As for the consumer end, we might agree with ourselves that we will make no impulse buys on the Internet—everything must be considered within a day. Or if we're really addicted, no Internet shopping, period. But

I'm skeptical of the cold-turkey approach. If we really want to get radical and work at it, developing mindfulness will go a long way toward subverting the greed-inducing effects of the Internet. Learn to meditate, attend retreats, practice, practice, practice seeing the mind getting caught in craving, and learn to let go. Observe dependent origination at work in your life as frequently as you can. Notice pleasant sensations. Notice wanting. Notice clinging, notice self. Ultimately, develop mindfulness that's sharp and subtle enough to catch the pleasant sensations *while* online. That's the advanced practice, of course.

One of my friends, a computer expert for a meditation center, decided to try a personal "computer retreat." For several weeks he meditated five to six hours daily, and when he wasn't sitting he went online, answered e-mail, and attended to his computer responsibilities.

"Were you able to be mindful?" I asked incredulously.

"Well, not to the details of typing and reading, not each finger," he replied. "Of course my mind got sucked in. But in that retreat space, I was able to have a general sense of awareness. I could feel the presence of my body and watch myself when I got sucked in, and I could come back to the bodily experience."

How extraordinary: it may be possible to find freedom while interfacing with the machine. I suppose we need strong framing devices to override the force of habit.

On the ethical level, we have to ask ourselves what kind of person we want to be. Greedy and addicted, or generous and free? It *is* possible to cultivate the second set of qualities. We actually have the capability to develop our character through practice. We can generate the self we want to be. Who we become depends on each little action we take, one choice or one mouse click at a time. Whenever I fall in love with something I just *have* to buy—a new sweater, a fancy toaster, or even a doorstop—I ask myself this question: Ten minutes ago, did you even know the item existed? Somehow this simple reminder helps me to let go of the wanting.

In the end it may come down to that Buddhist value of contentment. Being with things exactly as they are and being perfectly content. Not needing anything other than what you already possess within you to be happy. Contentment isn't valued in this high-speed and high-greed culture. If people were content with what they have and who they are, why would they go shopping? Learning to cultivate and acknowledge your own contentment is a revolutionary act in these times. Every time you feel content—in a conversation, a meal, a sunset—really sense the contentment. What do your body and mind feel like? For me contentment holds a subtle quality of well-being, a peace or quiet happiness. My body feels fully present, relaxed. I could be smiling, but I don't have to be. Everything is simply enough. Nothing more is needed to be happy. We can train our minds to settle for less. Just this.

To address the systemic impacts of cyberspace, I thought it might be useful to start an advertising campaign called "Go Reality." It would remind people through television spots, print media, and flashing Internet ads that ordinary life, exactly as it is, is actually *better* than the virtual world. Posters would display zoned-out kids staring glassy-eyed at computer screens contrasted with other kids romping cheerfully through the woods. Celebrity spots could broadcast: "When was the last time you spoke to your child?" or "Real sex is better" or "Try nature, it's the real thing."

The Go Reality campaign could invade the Internet and promote disruption. Those horrible hijacking ads—the ones for dating and for loans that pop onto your screen when you hit the Web—could be rivaled with hijacking ads of our own. Whenever you go on a shopping Web site, a message could pop up: "Do you really need that?" "Save for your kids' education." "C'mon, you're wasting your money." We could buy banner ads on all the major commerce sites shouting the criminality of excessive shopping. *Reality*, we could proudly display, *means being okay with things as they are!*

It's a great idea. And I promise to get to work on it right away. But I just heard about a new discount Web site, and, well, sitting back and shopping is a heck of a lot easier than changing the world.

PART TWO

Practicing with Desire

Using Buddhist Tools

7

Cultivating the Wisdom Gaze

Judith Simmer-Brown

WHEN TIBETAN BUDDHIST LAMAS fled the Communist Chinese tyranny in 1959, many came to the West to study, teach, and practice the dharma. The culture they encountered, however, presented special challenges to a genuinely spiritual life. In contemporary America, the dominant obstacle they observed was the predominance of materialism, a lifestyle of acquisition that promotes self-grasping. Tibetan teachers have commented about how difficult it is for American students to practice meditation in a materialistic environment. Observing the difference from his Tibetan home, Khenpo Karthar Rinpoche remarked:

> Because Tibet is an untouched and uncivilized country, people are quite happy with the simplicity of life. They do not long for the comforts and luxury of life. As long as there is food to eat and a roof for shelter, they are very happy. With that state of mind, when they go to retreat, their mind is simple and the decision is quite complete. They think, "Even if I die of an illness during this retreat, I will let myself die. Even if I die of starvation during this retreat, I will let myself die. Even if I die from the difficulties and hardship of the vigorous practice, I will be happy to die."[1]

Buddhist scholar José Cabezón has suggested that traditional and contemporary Tibetans are primarily concerned about how material wealth "deflect[s] one from pursuing the true, inner wealth of spiritual perfection."[2] Wealth is viewed as ephemeral, and therefore rather than accumulating it, it is more important to spend and enjoy it while it is available, or to give it away. He refers to the thirteenth-century Tibetan master Sakya Pandita, who reflected that those who have wealth that they neither use nor give away must be either sick or a deprived spirit. "Accumulating wealth without using it is like accumulating the wood for one's own cremation. Those who do so are like bees, who put so much effort into manufacturing their honey only to have it taken away from them."[3] Accumulating wealth accrues many obstacles, for then the wealth must be protected and one's greedy tendencies are exacerbated. When accumulation of wealth is an end in itself, it can divert one from the spiritual path and create negative circumstances for future awakening.

More than thirty years ago my teacher, Ven. Chögyam Trungpa Rinpoche, wrote one of the first popular dharma books in America, *Cutting Through Spiritual Materialism*.[4] While on retreat in a Padmasambhava cave in Bhutan, Trungpa Rinpoche composed a ritual text called the *Sadhana of Mahamudra* that addressed the way in which contemporary societies are dominated by material concerns. This text was received in a visionary state as a *terma*, a hidden-treasure text, attributed to Padmasambhava as a contemporary contribution to the "dark age" of materialism. In the book, Rinpoche identified what he considered primary obstacles to spiritual development in the West.

Trungpa Rinpoche described the acquisitive pursuit that binds humans to suffering as the hallmark of construction of personal identity, or ego. To promote this core activity, three allegorical lords of materialism[5] pursue three levels of acquisitiveness: the *lord of form* refers to physical acquisition, the *lord of speech* to conceptual acquisition, and the *lord of mind* to acquisition in the spiritual realm. According to these descriptions, materialism must be challenged or it will co-opt our physical lives, our communities, and our spiritual cores. "Physical materialism" refers to the compulsive pursuit of pleasure, comfort, and security as a balm for all of our problems and concerns. Culturally, it is expressed today in the form of consumerism. "Psychological materialism" seeks to control the world through theory, ideology, and intellect. We mentally create constructs that keep us from having to be threatened, to be wrong, or to be confused, thus putting ourselves in control. In American life, psychological materialism is expressed in science and technology, medicine and psychology. On the most subtle level, "spiritual materialism" carries acquisitiveness into the realm of our own minds, into our own contemplative practice or prayer, sometimes expressed as religious exclusivism or extremism.

In all of these areas, our conscious minds attempt to remain in control in order to maintain a centralized awareness from which to defend a fortified position of power. Through this process, our egos use even spirituality to shield us from fear and insecurity. Rinpoche suggested that spiritual practice is often used for personal gain and protection, an expression of acquisitiveness. What are the signs of such an appropriation of spiritual practice? The *Sadhana of Mahamudra* identifies how, in our preoccupation with issues of control and power, we become "afraid of external phenomena, which are [our] own projections."[6] What this means is that when we take ourselves to be real, independently existing beings, then we mistake the world around us to be independent and real. And when we do this, we invite paranoia, fear, and panic. We are afraid of not being able to control the situation, and as the text states, "sadness and depression are always with us." These teachings suggest that, through Tibetan eyes, even our spiritual traditions are vulnerable to the acquisitiveness that so dominates our cultural life.

This Tibetan analysis gives much greater depth to concerns about the pervading damage to humanity perpetrated by patterns of consumerism and economic globalization. As communist countries throughout the world collapse, the capitalist global economy is all but unchallenged in its growth. Again and again, when traditional societies become modernized, consumerism presents an irresistible path. Global economic interests are now running the entire world. Do any centers of power still exist that are relatively untouched by this globalized network? John Cobb has suggested that religious peoples and communities have the potential to bring the only remaining challenge to transnational corporations and consumerism.[7] Cobb and others from Judeo-Christian theological traditions have applied themselves to the issues of globalization and challenged Asian and Western Buddhists to join in analyzing the issues as well as engaging solutions.[8]

As an American Buddhist new to economic analysis, I have little to add concerning the complexities of the global economy or patterns of consumerism. But my Buddhist practice and training have taught me one thing clearly: No fundamental transformation can take place anywhere without the joining of inner change and outer change. The pedagogy of "engaged Buddhism" builds on the recognition of the interdependence of all things—the suffering of others is also one's own suffering, and the violence of others is also one's own violence. The basic nature of suffering is seen as continuous throughout the world. For engaged Buddhists, "social work entails inner work, and social change and inner change are inseparable."[9] Thus, opening a text of economic analysis is opening to the suffering of the world before our eyes. Listening to the devastating truths of transnational corporate exploitation is encountering a global network of suffering. In order to work with these appropriately, we transform our personal despair, cynicism, and powerlessness into effective action. International development activist Helena Norberg-Hodge wrote:

> As engaged Buddhists, we have a responsibility to examine current economic trends carefully, in light of Buddhist teachings. I am convinced that such an examination will engender in us a desire to actively oppose the trend toward a global economy, and to help promote ways of life consistent with more Buddhist economics.[10]

ANALYSIS AS PRACTICE

Central to any Buddhist analysis is close and mindful contemplation of causes and conditions. Buddhist teachings emphasize that there is no first cause or divine creator responsible for the patterns of suffering we discover in our experience—there is no divinely ordained evil or degradation. Instead, Buddhism suggests that all occurrences and events are a result of multiple causes arising under ever-changing conditions. Consumerism and globalization have arisen from a web of many causes and conditions, no one of which is primary. If one deeply observes causes and conditions and the effects to which they lead, then one can identify the most strategically effective ways to change the patterns of suffering in our world. Any form of suffering can be alleviated if one can properly witness the patterns from which it springs and remove specific causes. What is required is a penetrating analysis to identify those that most influence the results.

Tibetan Buddhist philosophers have developed a particularly systematic method of examining causes and conditions. This paper will draw from the magisterial work by the Nyingma meditation master Jamgon Mipham

(1846–1912), called *The Gate for Entering the Way of a Pandita*.[11] Ju Mipham Rinpoche (as he is often referred to) begins his analysis of phenomena by saying:

> Nothing included under inner or outer phenomena has arisen without a cause. They have also not originated from an independent cause, an uncaused or permanent creator. . . . The fact that phenomena are produced based on the interdependence of their respective causes and conditions coming together is called dependent origination.[12]

His text divides all causality into two categories, applied here to the phenomenon of globalization: (1) *external* causes and their effects, observable in phenomena outside one's own mind stream such as cycles of nature, or social and economic patterns such as consumer behaviors; and (2) *internal* causes and their effects, related to one's own cognitive and emotional patterns and actions such as acquisitive greed and the consumptive behaviors that arise from this greed.

Using the traditional framework of analysis, the first important step is to identify the problem of globalization correctly. What do we mean by *globalization*? The president of the Nabisco Corporation approvingly called it "a world of homogeneous consumption."[13] The goal of economic globalization seems to be an international market in which everyone, no matter what latitude or longitude, eats the same food, wears the same clothing, and derives pleasure from the same entertainment. Because of globalization, people from quite diverse cultural backgrounds throughout the world now consume the same McDonald's food, James Bond movies, Nike shoes, and Coca-Cola drinks. Globalization can also be defined as a network of power, centered in transnational corporations and international financial institutions, that controls the flow of capital in order to promote the financial interests of the power elite to the detriment of all others.

The effects of globalization are threefold. First, sovereign governments no longer exist solely for their citizenry or their own national interests. In order to protect financial interests, transnational corporations have "bought" the executive branches of governments through financing campaigns or bribes. To further ensure power, corporations have also taken control of the legislative branches of government through lobbyists, campaign contributions, and term extensions. Having secured governments, corporate interests set the conditions in which policy is determined and control the flow and content of information.[14]

Second, globalization has deepened the gulf between the very rich and the poor both within nations and globally. The unrestrained market favors the rich over the poor and deepens global inequity, increasing the debt of poorer nations under the banner of development. In spite of market rhetoric that suggests that international development will bring the poor into prosperity, the actual result is an increasing economic apartheid.[15]

A third effect is the destruction of cultural and ecological diversity throughout the world. The impact of globalization on developing countries and rural economies is devastating. The global monoculture is eradicating cultural diversity, replacing locally adapted forms of production with industrial systems divorced from natural cycles. Agriculture has become centrally managed and chemically dependent, creating ecological deserts in many climates. In Norberg-Hodge's assessment, "globalization creates efficiency for corporations, but it also creates artificial scarcity for consumers, thus heightening competitive pressures. . . . Globalization means the undermining of the livelihoods and cultural identities of the *majority* of the world's peoples."[16]

Such an analysis may at first cause horror, shock, despair, and denial, but this is because there is not sufficient understanding of the phenomenon in question. When such a response arises, it is a signal to go more deeply into observing the nature of the phenomenon. Ju Mipham's method begins with an analysis of the causes and effects, recognizing that all such phenomena are not "givens" but are created through multiple causes. This challenges the view that many with the neoliberal agenda hold: that globalization is an inescapable result of market-driven patterns, a "given" of natural law. For many, the ideology of the market, with its supporting ideologies regarding commodification, market success, and consumption, seem to be forces that have taken on their own reality, an inevitable development of the natural-law market principles. Margaret Thatcher, for example, summed it up with an acronym: TINA, "there is no alternative."

Consumerism is considered a subset of this doctrine of natural law. From this perspective, human behavior is the basis of the entire global economy, for humans have limitless wants and are willing to exchange and even sacrifice in order to fulfill their desires. Driven by basic needs and invented or "fancied" needs, humans are willing to live meaningless, subordinate lives in corporate settings in order to gain temporary gratification derived from satisfaction of those needs. Sometimes the doctrine of the market has been supported by theological justification that it was ordained by God, and that God "implanted self-interest in the human breast as the motive force of progress. By following self-interest we follow God's will. Going against self-interest only inhibits God's plan."[17] With market doctrine elevated to the level of divine revelation, those who challenge globalization become heretics.

When we more closely scrutinize the global economy, we see two things: first, this system has not arisen without cause, and second, there is no single, identifiable cause for this phenomenon. All economic theories point to a variety of factors that have given rise to globalization: it has arisen based on the interdependence of causes and conditions coming together, known as dependent origination (*pratitya-samutpada*; Tib., *tendrel*). That such a conditioned process made up of a variety of causal factors has an inevitable course not subject to alteration is not congruent with Buddhist logic. If things have arisen from a cause, they are not permanently abiding, transcendently ordained entities. No matter how daunting or damaging they may appear, their existence is reliant upon their causes and conditions and therefore temporary.

If one can properly penetrate these causes, understanding their inner and outer aspects, it is possible to eliminate the causes and to bring about cessation or transformation. All activism must engage in such an analysis in order to effectively identify strategies to overcome social, political, or economic ills. What is important from a Buddhist perspective, however, is to apply the analysis rigorously, thoroughly, to both inner and outer phenomena until one has identified the strategic causes, the elimination of which will truly bring about transformation. Intellectual analysis is important, but it is never enough. One must also contemplate and meditate in order to fully engage the phenomenon in question.

IDENTIFYING THE CAUSES

Outer Causes

When we look deeply, we discover that there are many causes that have given rise to globalization. These causes link together in a vast network of causes, each influencing the others. The doctrine of the market has created principles of supply and demand, measures of market success, and the commodification of land as abstractions from the human realities in the global setting.[18] Philosopher activist Noam Chomsky argues that globalization is not a result of the "natural evolution" of Smith's principles of the market; rather, it has developed from the explosion of industries that have grown grotesquely through state-supported capital. Industries such as telecommunications have developed in a successful fail-safe strategy of "cost and risk socialized, profit privatized."[19] Subsidies, which began as a public expenditure for a social good, have given unfair advantage to favored industries—savings and loans, the airlines, the Internet, and public power, including oil, electricity, and nuclear power—ensuring their continued growth and economic success. One hundred leading transnational corporations on the Fortune 500 list have benefited directly from state protection and taxpayer subsidy; twenty would not have survived without public bailouts.[20]

Additional causes can be found in the special protections afforded corporations. Many trace these to a Supreme Court decision in 1886 that granted to corporations "honorary" individual rights ordinarily endowed to a human person.[21] This set into motion the "entity" status of the corporation, which has safeguarded special protections for its rights to profit and power. Using this privilege, corporations have extended their control over democratic institutions, communications systems, and commodities to the extent that they would deny the resources upon which people depend for livelihood. David Korten has observed:

> Corporations now enjoy unlimited life; virtual freedom of movement anywhere on the globe; control of the mass media; the ability to amass legions of lawyers and public relations specialists in support of their cause; and freedom from liability for the misdeeds of wholly owned subsidiaries. They also enjoy the presumed right to amass property and financial resources without limit; engage in any legal activity; bring liability suits against private citizens or civic organizations that challenge them; make contributions to individual candidates, political parties, and political action committees and deduct those contributions from taxable income as business expenses. . . . Step-by-step, largely through judge-made law, corporations have become far more powerful than ever intended by the people and governments that created them.[22]

Put in Buddhist terms, the "entity" status of the globalized market, which appears to many to be an irreversible and unstoppable force, does not withstand deep observation and analysis. Globalization can be identified as a conditioned phenomenon, brought about through protectionism, subsidies, and transnational control. In short, it has come about through human institutions and decision making, propelled by self-interest and the reduction of value to monetary and commodity status. Because it is a conditioned phenomenon, it can be reversed by strategic change of the supporting conditions. David Korten advocates restoring human rights solely to human persons; others recommend the removal of public subsidies for corporate ventures. An engaged Buddhist approach would be to identify strategic causes that might encourage change, even cessation, of the damaging effects of globalization.

Inner Causes: Desire and Ignorance

Analysis of outer causes and conditions is complemented by the analysis of inner causes and conditions: How is it that I myself contribute to the pattern of consumerism and economic globalization? What causes can I discover in my participation, and what causes can be eliminated in order to bring the global pattern to cessation? In Ju Mipham's analysis, the inner causes are found in two stages: first, through understanding the twelvefold chain of dependent origination based on desire and ignorance, and second, through the profound understanding of emptiness of inherent existence, or *shunyata*.[23]

As we have seen, the global economy thrives through the propagation and practice of consumption, which is the daily contribution of each individual to the success of the global market. From a Buddhist view, consumerism exploits the dual foundations of desire and ignorance, which are the basis for the repetitive round of suffering called samsara. The twelve links (*nidanas*) of dependent origination identify an inner pattern of suffering built on the cultivation of desire.[24] Sequential links establish the pattern of isolation, solidification of personal identity, and the impetus to confirm that identity in relationship to things and others. The expression of that impetus arises as desire (*trishna*, or *srepa*), which Ju Mipham calls "eager craving." The text speaks of three kinds of pleasure seeking: "the eager craving of desiring not to be separated from a pleasant sensation, the fearful craving of desiring to cast away an unpleasant sensation, and a self-sufficient abiding in regards to indifferent sensations."[25] In consumptive pursuits, it is craving for pleasure (*kama-trishna*) that is the most obvious motivation, but when we understand the nature of craving on a more pervasive level, the other two kinds of craving, for existence (*bhava-trishna*) and for nonexistence (*vibhava-trishna*), are also apparent. Purchases are made to advance one's desire for pleasure but also to give meaning and expression to one's very existence—"I shop, therefore I am." Hidden within this craving is also the death wish, the desire to spend to satiation, to bankruptcy, to extinction. Within the very act of consumption is the destructive message that suggests the depth of suffering involved.

An essential insight derived from this teaching on desire is that consumption is inherently painful. Even within the pleasure and drivenness of the consumer's impulse is self-recognition of pain. The purchase event may have a moment of thrill, but the experience is haunted by its fleeting quality (*anitya, mi-takpa*), its intangibility (*anatman, dakmepa*), and its unsatisfactoriness (*duhkha, duk-ngelwa*). Because of its inherent unsatisfactoriness, the true impact of which is not absorbed, the consumer is driven to purchase again and again. From this view, compulsive consumption is truly an addiction that carries the seeds of its own destruction.

Outer and inner patterns of cause and effect are successfully linked by a number of core industries in the global economy that exploit addictive desire. Alcohol and cigarettes are obvious addictions, but we can add to them the sweet-tooth craving fed by Nestlé and Coke, cleanliness fetishes satisfied by Procter & Gamble, and entertainment addictions serviced by Universal Studios. The transnational corporations welcome and nurture new "invented" addictions. As Daly and Cobb observed, "If people's wants are not naturally insatiable we must make them so, in order to keep the system going."[26]

A second inner cause in this teaching is that desire arises from basic ignorance (*avidya*, or *marikpa*), the "delusion of perceiving incorrectly and in disharmony with the nature of things."[27] This means that underneath our desire, we refuse to actually witness the pattern of how desire always leads to suffering. We do not see the underlying unsatisfactoriness of consumption and how pursuing our desires leads to more and more desire rather than the satiation of desire. The threat of seeing this pattern drives us to greater, more intricate and demanding desires that further obscure our ability to see clearly.

According to Buddhist teachings, it is never enough to address desire alone. Desire will never cease on its own because it is so fundamental to the human condition. When the relationship between desire and ignorance is understood, then we see that the way to transform desire is to transform ignorance. The classic antidote to basic ignorance is the cultivation of insight (*prajna, sherap*), the clear seeing of the pattern of suffering and the arising of the pattern. When these are seen directly and experientially, there naturally grows the wish to abandon desire and to develop alternative motivations in one's life. Gradually the realization dawns that all the factors that have dependently arisen giving shape to consumerism are themselves dependent upon other factors, and those too are also dependent phenomena.

Patterns of interdependence in the global economy are so complex that it is difficult to experientially witness the consequences of desire and ignorance on a personal level. Structural suffering in the global economy seems to be perpetrated by a large, amorphous system. Alan Senauke, of the Buddhist Peace Fellowship, observed, "No one seems to be directly responsible, because it is moved ahead by governments, corporations, and is seemingly anonymous."[28] This anonymity makes the task of Buddhist analysis more difficult, for it is impossible to fully know and comprehend the extent of the causes involved in everyday acts of consumption. Yet, in personally examining these patterns, it is much easier to observe the underlying causes of desire and ignorance.

Inner Causes: Emptiness and Interdependence

If the analysis of inner causes remained focused only on ignorance and desire, one could become excessively austere and judgmental in identifying the remedies to globalization. One might become obsessively driven to stop spending, boycott corporations, and drop out of a system seen to be inherently problematic. However, in the Mahayana tradition of the bodhisattva, or "awakened being" dedicated to the liberation of all, fundamental understanding of causes involves a radical paradigm shift. This paradigm shift pivots around the teachings concerned with emptiness and dependent origination, the second level of inner analysis suggested by Ju Mipham.[29]

From a Mahayana Buddhist perspective, the global economy and our involvement in it through consumerism lack inherent existence and are said to be emptiness (*shunyata, tongpa nyi*). Through outer and inner analysis we understand that the multiple factors that support the global economy, especially consumerism, are extraordinarily fragile. On an outer level, the global economy depends on the factors of law, scale, governmental protection, market principles, and infrastructure. On an inner level, consumerism and our support of the global economy rest on habitual patterns of desire based on all-pervading ignorance. But being so dependent makes this phenomenon vulnerable to change, in fact vulnerable in its very existence. Seeing that phenomena are so fragile and dependent, one realizes that there is no independent entity or phenomenon that can be isolated and identified as consumerism or a global economy. Its "entity" nature is ultimately false, posing to be (as we can see upon further analysis) what it is not. Globalization does not have the status of an ultimate or absolute being, even if we conventionally give it that status. If consumerism were an independently existing phenomenon, it would not have a beginning and it could never be dismantled. In the conventional view, consumerism appears to have always existed and will exist no matter what other changes in our economy occur. Likewise, the global economy appears to be the only economy, in fact the only reality of our time, and it is apparently permanent and indestructible.

In Mahayana Buddhism, the ultimate view of reality is just this view of emptiness. No phenomena have inherent existence, including ourselves. It is not just market economics that have been given misplaced concreteness; it is any kind of market, any kind of economy, global anything. This insight, which may be a stretch in conventional thinking, has implications for anyone approaching consumerism. When globalization is seen to exist as an actual entity, it appears to be intimidating, solid, a definitely unsolvable set of problems. But we have found, on further examination, that it cannot possibly exist inherently. Therefore, a "problematic" approach is also unsuitable. If we view the world as basically problematic or flawed, we become powerless to change it. If we understand the emptiness, the lack of inherent existence of these "problematic" phenomena, we take a more balanced and more confident view. This view allows us to see that because phenomena and therefore suffering do not exist inherently, they can be brought to an end. Ignorance about the ultimate nature of the global economy is the primary obstacle concerning its change and ultimately its cessation.

Seeing this view is not just a matter of analysis, it is a matter of meditation and realization. Meditation practice exposes the chaos and suffering of the world over and over again, but it also exposes the unconditional backdrop against which this suffering is experienced. This backdrop is the confidence that no phenomenon is evil, flawed, or resistant to influence on an absolute level. As Ju Mipham Rinpoche wrote:

> Realizing this, you understand that all things are merely an un-failing manifestation of interdependence. . . . They are hollow and false, and are devoid of self-nature. The one who understands that this is so, is unaffected by [beliefs] such as conceptualizing a self in the past, present or future.[30]

From a Mahayana perspective, no problems of human life are intractable. To conclude that they are is to give them more power and reality than they deserve or could possibly have. For this reason, there is tremendous emphasis in Mahayana Buddhism on understanding the nature of the problem deeply, clearly, and unflinchingly. In this view, the global economy is an apparition, an interdependent appearance whose ultimate nature is emptiness.

TRANSFORMING GLOBALIZATION AND CONSUMERISM

How would Mahayana Buddhism address the inequities, the systemic violence, the exploitation that arise from consumer culture and from the global economy? How could it respond to the prophetic voice found in Christianity and in some Buddhist movements? While Mahayana Buddhism does not have a prophetic voice, it does have a clear vision about the problems of human existence. From the outset, the Buddha exhibited awareness of social issues such as war, caste, abuse of power, and unethical activity. The root of all such evils, from his perspective, was a mistaken view about the nature of reality. He remained unconfused concerning his central insight, that social issues cannot be changed without a concerted focus on understanding this root error. The Buddhist teachings on compassion begin with personal clear seeing, but they do not end there.

The reason the compassion teachings go further, must go further, is that in Buddhism one cannot experience durable, unconditioned compassion without a direct experience of the lack of inherent existence of all beings.

The enormity of serious issues like globalization and consumerism can be overwhelming, moving one to a sense of urgency. If the urgency, however, is an impulsive response to the unbearable qualities of suffering, the aversion that arises toward suffering could lead one to unskillful acts based on what is called "idiot compassion,"[31] the impulsive response with insufficient understanding. This impulsive compassion can quickly become ineffective and cause personal burnout, since continuing endlessly in this way for the benefit of others is exhausting and ill directed. Good intention is never enough; it risks the dangers of impulsiveness and romanticism. Effective compassionate actions must be based on wisdom.

Compassionate action regarding globalization and consumerism can be grounded in the realm of spiritual activism. Having identified as directly as possible the multiple causes of the global economy, one strategically chooses to undo those causes. Such choices about what one can contribute are very individual. One person might make a commitment to meditation practice, cultivating the view of the inherently empty and interdependent nature of globalization and consumerism. Another may focus on changing legal protections or public subsidies for corporate interests. Someone else may focus on small-scale community building within the local region or environment. Whatever the choice, these efforts must be developed patiently, with a clear sense of the magnitude of the project. And from a Buddhist perspective, these efforts must be based in recognizing that every single act of clear seeing or compassionate action reverses in some small way one's ignorance concerning the basic nature of reality. At the same time, all of these actions change in some small way the entire phenomenon of globalization. Activism based on impatience with results, excess urgency, or romantic clinging to alternative outcomes will be limited in outcomes.

In circles of engaged Buddhists, discussions of constructive steps have focused on issues of scale and sustainability. The vastness of the problems of globalization have made it almost impossible to witness the broad-scale patterns of cause and effect. Smaller communities allow members to bear witness, to take ownership and responsibility for the life of the community, and to adjust to change more quickly than large communities—in short, smaller communities are generally more sustainable communities. *Turning Wheel*, the journal of the Buddhist Peace Fellowship, proposes a number of strategies for reduction of scale, localization, and decentralization. Many engaged Buddhists feel that there is a growing need for the development of political skills among American Buddhists, so that coalitions might more effectively support collaboration with other religious traditions on these common concerns. There is clearly a need for comprehensive spiritually based analyses of contemporary economic, social, ecological, and political systems.[32] Attention to the pressing issues of consumerism and globalization may generate a kind of Buddhist "liberation theology" that would combine the best of contemporary social and economic theory and practice with the full lens of Buddhist teachings.

In addition to spiritually based activism, compassionate action can be applied to the inner work of contemporary American life. Compassionate action can address the negative emotions that arise when one contemplates the phenomenon of consumerism in the context of the global economy. When contemplation is only partial, it despairs of any solution, further re-inforcing the basic ignorance that cannot see two things: the patterns of de-sire that perpetuate consumerism, and the belief in the inherent existence of the phenomena of consumerism and the global economy. Ju Mipham Rinpoche describes this as the cultivation of the "wisdom gaze" of depend-ent origination.[33] This gaze has the ability to deeply, accurately understand the basic nature of the issue; to clearly see the empty and interdependent qualities of globalization, based on many empty and interdependent causes; and to identify what can be strategically changed so that transformation may take place. Such a gaze empowers us to engage in the patient, compas-sionate work of relieving the suffering of the world.

No River Bigger than *Tanha*

Pracha Hutanuwatr and Jane Rasbash

"THE WORD *development* in Pali is *vaddhana*, which means messiness or making messiness; it can be messy with good things or messy with problems, sufferings, or chaos. In the modern world, development means the world is flooded with material things neglecting the spiritual aspects."[1] These are the words of Buddhadasa Bhikkhu, a renowned Buddhist monk and thinker of Siam.[2] Following on this, Sulak Sivaraksa, a lay Buddhist thinker and activist, claims that consumerism is a new demonic religion. This chapter focuses on the effects of consumerism in Siam and alternative visions and initiatives based on the work of Ven. Buddhadasa Bhikkhu and Ajahn Sulak Sivaraksa, founding fathers of the engaged Buddhist movement in Siam. The structure of this essay is based on the teachings of the Four Noble Truths. This means identifying problems, looking at causes, envisioning solutions, and outlining a path from the present reality to the desirable situation.

THE PERILS OF CONSUMERISM

Four countries in Southeast Asia—Laos, Cambodia, Burma, and Siam—face the conflict between Buddhist and capitalist values. Each is of Theravadan

Buddhist background and at different stages of Western-style development. To explore the First Noble Truth, identifying the problems, we will look at how consumerism affects traditional Buddhist societies in Southeast Asia. At one extreme is Siam, wholeheartedly following the Americanization process over the last fifty years. At the other extreme is Burma, trying to close the country to Western domination in every way.

In Yangon, the capital of Burma, if we visit Shwedagon, the most important pagoda of the country, we see Burmese of all ethnic backgrounds—monks, nuns, and laypeople—paying homage to the Buddha. Some pray and meditate; others perform devotions. The pagoda is crowded all day, every day of the year, from as early as 5:00 A.M. until 9:00 P.M. In Bangkok, the capital of Siam, if we visit the Emerald Buddha Temple, we see it is crowded all day, nearly every day of the year, but with foreign tourists. Only a few Thai are there paying homage to the Buddha. Instead, Thai people crowd the big shopping malls in Bangkok, such as Jusco, Lotus, Tesco, and Robinson, every day from opening until closing time. For most Thai these shopping malls are the new temples and consumerism is their religion, even though if asked they will say they are Buddhist.

What does it mean for the Thai to have consumerism as their religion? It means they define who they are by what they buy: wearing the right brand of dress, owning the right brand of watch, driving the right brand of car, eating at Japanese or Western restaurants, and for the neo–middle class, speaking English to each other. This devotion to consumerism is putting many Thais into debt, especially through the use of credit cards. Credit card companies encourage people to take on debt and then charge them interest that sucks away at their income. If you drive a Toyota pickup and dress like a rural farmer, the traffic police will stop you at checkpoints and and ask for money. But the next day, if you drive a Mercedes Benz and dress in a Western suit, the same policeman will bow his head to touch the tires of your car.

With few exceptions, the monks of Siam are naively welcoming this new religion, blending it with Buddhism as an unavoidable friend. The Thai Buddhist sangha that is supposed to generate Buddhist values of simplicity, generosity, and compassion is now almost completely under the spell of consumerism. Many monks compete with each other to possess consumer goods such as mobile phones, BMWs, and portable computers; others are obsessed with raising money from their newly rich parishioners to build ever-bigger Buddha statues and superfluous religious halls.

Whatever your social status in Siam, you have to climb to the top. If you are from a farming family, you must not be content with being a farmer. You have to buy education to escape from being a farmer to become someone else. If you are a monk, you have to climb up the sangha hierarchy or make yourself famous and have many followers. The whole ethos of Thai consumer society, especially the media and the education systems, inflicts a sense of inferiority. No matter who you are, you are never good enough. From a Buddhist perspective, this is a basic form of alienation. This existential sense of not being good enough (*vibhava-tanha*) has been stimulated by Western-dominated media and advertising to such an extent that young people in Siam reject who they are. Helena Norberg-Hodge explains this phenomenon of cultural alienation very clearly and powerfully in her book *Ancient Futures*.[3] Such alienation stems from the illusion of self competing and comparing with others to define who you are (*mana*). The consumer monoculture feeds on this human weakness. To have consumerism as a religion means that the aim of individual life and of society is to gain unlimited wealth, power, recognition, and sensual pleasure. The Buddha warned his followers not to cling to these four worldly temptations.[4] Yet the present social structures supporting consumerism encourage people to run after them madly.

In contrast to Siam, Burma has been greatly damaged by an authoritarian military junta and, luckily or unluckily, closed to the outside world for more than half a century. This means that except for the few corrupt top military families and some leaks through the Chinese and Thai borders, consumer monoculture has touched the lives of ordinary people very little. The Buddhist values of simplicity, generosity, compassion, and detachment from worldly success are still intact for most Burmese. Meditation practice is widespread, not only among the monks but also throughout the lay community. The Burmese are proud to wear colorful *lunghi* rather than the Western trousers and skirts that have been adopted in Bangkok and many other parts of Southeast Asia. Yangon street markets are full of producers selling indigenous vegetables, largely home-farmed and grown without chemicals.

Of course, with any small opening to the outside world, the big multinational corporations rush in and pollute the beautiful cities with advertising for Marlboro, 555 Levi's, Tiger beer, Phillips, and Sony, thus spoiling the verdant natural scenery. We do not know whether future democratic leadership in Burma will be aware enough of the dangers of consumerism to stop this trend. It is also a big question whether Americanization in Siam and the Philippines will rush into Burma once the country is opened. At least at this moment, Yangon, with its intricate old buildings and greenery, is much more beautiful than Bangkok, one of the most polluted cities in the world. Once renowned as the Venice of the East, a mystical city of canals and golden spires, Bangkok today is full of unfinished construction sites, ugly new buildings, superhighways, and shopping malls that are tearing the heart out of local communities.

In Siam, development over the past fifty years has overemphasized economic growth without adequate consideration for environmental sustainability, social justice, cultural diversity, and spiritual well-being. This economic growth has been possible only by gradually challenging the traditional Buddhist worldview and replacing it with consumerism. During the Vietnam War, when Americans wanted to prevent Siam from becoming communist, they sent "experts" to be advisors to the various Thai government departments. They urged the Thai government to request the Buddhist sangha to stop giving teachings on contentment (*santosa* or *santutthi*). If people were content and happy, they wouldn't want American-style development. To follow the new economic path of consumerism, they would need to feel that their way of life was inferior, underdeveloped, not good enough. Unfortunately almost the entire Buddhist sangha was tamed to follow this heretical suggestion except for Buddhadasa Bhikkhu, who saw the dangers of consumerism more than fifty years ago.

The government, business circles, and multinational corporations have used the education and mass media systems and gradually become very successful in uprooting basic Buddhist values from Thai society. Many thousands of self-reliant villages were persuaded to join the cash crop economy, and most are now in debt due to lack of control over the price and costs of their production. After decades of development, more and more farmers have lost their land to absentee landlords or to middlemen who trade their products. Debt-ridden villagers are migrating en masse to the big industrial areas to work in factories and the building trades. As rural communities disappear, people are robbed of their sustainable livelihoods as well as the social security of traditional ways of life. Children of even the better-off farmers are now leaving the countryside for big cities, where they will face further alienation and loss of community. In an abortive attempt to fill this void, the estranged turn to the instant gratification of consumerism, including abusive use of drugs and sex.

A few rural people and poor urban dwellers manage to join the middle class and live a material life with modern conveniences such as private cars, televisions, mobile phones, DVD players, modern houses, and so on. As competition is the name of the game, urban consumers are never satisfied with what they have. Soon the new car will be obsolete, the new computer must be upgraded. Many business executives live a stressful life, going to bed with a handful of drugs to help them sleep. Then they are up before five in the morning, feeding the children on their way to school, arriving in a fancy car that gives the children status.

From a Buddhist perspective, this cannot be a healthy way of life, as one is always driven by greed (*lobha*), anxiety and aggression (*dosa*), and the delusions of individualism and competition (*moha*). Moreover, this way of life is a life without community. In Buddhism a person cannot grow without a supportive community. A higher quality of life based on generosity (*dana*), compassion (*karuna*), and respect for others (*samanttata*) cannot be developed in an individualistic society. Without the maturity of these healthy qualities (*kusalamula*), however successful you are in terms of wealth, power, and recognition, you still experience a deep sense of lack, loneliness, and isolation.

CRAVING AND CONSUMERISM

We turn now to the Second Noble Truth to look for causes of the problem. According to Buddhist analysis, craving is the root cause of all suffering. The very core of consumerism is the amplification of craving, or *tanha*. Traditionally *tanha* is classified with three aspects: craving for sensual pleasure, craving for existence, and craving for nonexistence. In other words, *tanha* manifests in the three unwholesome roots (*akusala-mula*): greed (*lobha*), hatred (*dosa*), and delusion (*moha*). Seen in the context of consumerism, *lobha* is the need to acquire the four worldly states of unlimited wealth, power, recognition, and sensual pleasure. *Dosa* is the anxiety to acquire these, the fear of losing them, the anger, sadness, and depression (which can turn into aggressive violence) when they are lost or not attainable. *Moha* is the individualism and competition to attain these four states, the pride when one has them, and defining who you are according to what you have. These modern states of delusion also include endemic low self-esteem and feelings of not being good enough when you don't attain these four states, as well as jealousy when others get them and you don't.

In Siam we can see clearly that *tanha* does not manifest only on the individual level, as seen in accepted social values. It also manifests as structural violence in the form of the free-market economy, the control of media by transnational corporations, and state mechanisms that favor the rich against the poor. Another form of structural violence is the industrialization process that overuses natural resources for excessive human consumption without compassion to other beings.

To elaborate on *lobha*, consumerism and capitalism can be explained as modern forms of greed. Capitalism depends on market growth and cannot work without people consuming more and more. Everyone is completely dependent on the "free" yet very unjust market, as is illustrated by the ever-increasing gap between the haves and the have-nots. All over Southeast Asia, seeds of greed are stimulated as people are persuaded to move away from subsistence agriculture to cash crops or paid work. With little control over prices, wages, or work conditions, they struggle to provide for basic needs and fall into a deep unconscious insecurity that is fertile ground for the existential sense of lack at the root of consumer culture. Along the Thai coast, fisherfolk have been living for generations on their daily fishing catches with their small boats and simple tools. In recent years a few modern large-scale trawlers from big companies in Bangkok catch all the fish with superefficient equipment, driving thousands of rural fisherfolk into destitution. This is a clear example of how the greed of big companies supported by the structural violence of the free market can destroy the livelihood of many people.

To elaborate on *dosa* (hatred), this is related to the lust for power that is so alluring as the sense of lack becomes more apparent. In the struggle for survival and later for the coveted goods, there is a fine line between acquisition, competition, and hatred. On a societal level *dosa* leads to unjust structures that not only support capitalism but also condone war and human rights abuses. Transnational corporations in Siam appear to have little interest in or accountability to the true needs of the people, seeing them only as consumers of their products. A Suzuki Motor Corporation factory near Bangkok, for example, took advantage of the economic crash in 1997 to lay off eight thousand workers with the pretext of preserving the factory. In reality they wanted to replace the old machines with new technology that used much less labor. During the labor-relations dispute, the government sided with the Japanese company, as they were afraid that the Japanese would withdraw their investment in Siam.

To elaborate on *moha* (delusion), sophisticated marketing techniques fuel greed and confused views by promoting satisfaction through ever-increasing accumulation. Basic needs expand and luxuries become necessities. In Siam and Burma plastic bags have replaced banana leaves to contain food, jeans and modern clothes are preferred to sarongs, then people buy motorcycles and refrigerators, and on it goes. Sadly, it seems that despite this accumulation of material things, the void inside is never filled. Manipulation of this perceived sense of lack is what the capitalist system relies on. Perhaps one of the great delusions is that this is seen as progress. The entire modern education system and mass media in Siam underpin the promotion of *moha*. It makes young people look down on traditional Buddhist values of generosity, compassion, and respect for nature and turn instead to individualism, competition, and a mindset that strives to conquer nature. Television and other vapid media are replacing the traditional role of the elders. In even the most remote Thai villages, people no longer chat with each other in the evening but instead sit in front of a TV screen watching Bangkok soap operas and violent movies from Hollywood.

Of course *tanha* has existed in all societies at all times since history has been recorded. However, in nonconsumeristic societies past and present, people have learned to curb this *tanha* so that harm to individuals, community, and nature is kept to a minimum. It is only in today's consumer monoculture that *tanha* has been eulogized as a desirable value. In contrast to the consumerist worldview, Buddhist teachings advocate reducing and eliminating *tanha* as the path to happiness. This conflict in views is represented by the following equation:

$$\text{Happiness} = \frac{\text{satisfying } tanha}{tanha}$$

Happiness can be increased either by satisfying *tanha* more often or by reducing *tanha* itself. While consumerism chooses the former and Buddhism the latter, the Buddhist argument is that the more you try to satisfy *tanha*, the more it will increase. As the Buddha said, "There is no river bigger than *tanha*." This implies that *tanha* is something ultimately insatiable. A society where *tanha* is encouraged is Mara's playground, with few winners and many losers. In this process the winners are not real winners, for on the road to acquisition they create oppression and inflict great suffering on many people. The processes of colonization, industrialization, development, and globalization are *tanha* operating in the macroscale of structural violence.

If we look at the nation-state of Siam, we can see that the social structure is an internal colonization system, where Bangkok imperialism dominates, subjugates, and exploits the whole country culturally, politically, and economically. This is definitely not a nonviolent social structure promoting and encouraging Buddhist values. Instead the social structures of violence (*vihimsa*) promote *tanha* in the form of greed, hate, and delusion.

Thai activist Sulak Sivaraksa challenges this capitalist trend as unethical:

> People believe science and technology will solve everything. The rich will get richer and even the poor will eventually get richer, but I don't believe in this trend. This trend is what I call the Eurocentric trend, which has become predominant because it has the best record in human rights, freedom, individualism, convenience, technology, etc. In this trend right now, Japan is even superseding Europe and North America.
>
> I feel that this trend is fundamentally wrong. Of course it creates something good, but it is fundamentally wrong, because it is unethical. The rich become rich at the expense of the poor and exploit natural resources. Look at the USA. They have 6% of the world's population using over 40% of the world's resources. Japan is also moving in this direction, which means that the gap between rich and poor will increase there too. . . . On top of this the rich are not happy. Fundamentally, this model is ethically and spiritually wrong because people are devoid of peace within. This is why I challenge this model.[5]

As *tanha* becomes globalized, the scale of suffering has amplified immensely around the world through the spread of consumerism. It is clear from the Buddhist point of view that *tanha* in the minds of the people works in tandem with *tanha* in the violent social structures to reinforce unprecedented suffering in the present society.

VISION FOR ALTERNATIVES

Turning now to the Third Noble Truth, from a Buddhist point of view, the way of peace and happiness (*santisukkha*) is to reduce unwholesome aspects of life and society (*akusala*) and encourage growth of the wholesome qualities. In other words, the greed, violence, individualism, and competition that presently dominate society must be curbed, and generosity, compassion, cooperation, and interconnection must be promoted. These wholesome values must be encouraged at both individual and structural levels.

During the left-right political debate of the seventies, Buddhadasa Bhikkhu voiced the strong criticism that the present mode of development was the path to madness and messiness. He proposed that the sangha model be used as an ideal for social reconstruction. He coined the term *Dhammic Socialism* as an alternative to the present system. He not only presented a theoretical framework but also experimented with creating and living in an alternative community for monks and nuns, which became the famous Suan Mokkh (Garden of Liberation). In contrast to Marxism, Dhammic Socialism sees human beings as part of the natural system, not as the dominating agent. Hence, human beings should live a materially very simple life and devote their energy to cultivating the Buddha potential within.[6]

Buddhadasa's Dhammic Socialism would produce a society that provides an environment for individual growth so that one can be fully human. Buddhadasa spoke about "simple living, higher thinking" as a more attractive ideal than gaining wealth and power. To live this good life he offered detailed methods of self-training and meditation, developing ways to look at the world with a free mind.[7] Buddhadasa felt that a life with limited but enough material well-being was more conducive to fully developing human potential than a life of too much material concern.

Buddhadasa also felt it was important for human beings to live a life close to nature. People should be friends with nature and not try to conquer nature. His favorite saying was that the Buddha was born, got enlightened, lived and taught and died in nature. For him a good society is not one full of artificial artifacts that separate us from the natural environment, as in Bangkok. Rather, the ideal habitat for Buddhist culture is the rural and semiforest life such as at Suan Mokkh. In his own life close to nature, Buddhadasa observed his natural surroundings and came to the conclusion that nature works in a cooperative way. To prove this to visitors, he always pointed to a big tree in front of his hut, where many small trees and plants grew together with the tree, along with a number of wild animals such as birds, squirrels, and lizards. He suggested that human society should be organized in this cooperative spirit. Nature operates under specific laws; the most important of these is the law of interdependence. So, he would say, as human beings we have to understand this and behave accordingly if we want to have a good life and good society.[8] For Buddhadasa, the cultivation of a free mind, cooperative spirit, and living close to nature are practices in harmony with the laws of nature.

Sulak Sivaraksa, in contrast, developed his alternative vision from a different background. While Buddhadasa trained mostly through studying and practicing in the forest, Sulak trained in the United Kingdom in the 1950s, where he became well acquainted with Western ways of argument. His vision of an alternative to consumerism is quite similar in essence, even though his work is based in Bangkok, the center of Thai consumerism itself. He also proposed the Buddhist sangha as a prototype for the emerging countercivilization. For him the sangha in its pure state is an ideal society based on nonviolent ethics where cooperation and egalitarian democracy have remained intact for millennia.[9] Sulak feels that Buddhism must take the issues of poverty and exploitation by the rich very seriously. In his ideal Buddhist society, under righteous and effective decentralized administration, there would not be any poverty. Everyone would enjoy economic self-sufficiency except the monks and nuns, who would intentionally be sustained by the surplus material resources of the lay community. This would then enable the laypeople to be guided by the monks' lifestyle and spiritual progress.

Sulak feels, as did Buddhadasa, that if Buddhists want to play a meaningful role in reinforcing peace, sustainability, and justice in the world, they must question the present consumer monoculture and the violent structures that support it. Though there are no blueprints for a consumerism-free society, Sulak sees the original Buddhist sangha with liberty, equality, and fraternity as the paradigm for lay society to follow. Sulak feels that in the past the Thais followed these ideals, but they have now gone wrong. So, in a way, they need to go back, but that is easier said than done. It is essential, however, to make a very clear stand to confront consumerism and capitalism. In this he feels that Buddhists must work with Christians, Muslims, and others to create a more just and peaceful society.

Sulak's vision for sustainable alternatives is rooted neither in the capitalist story of personal emancipation nor in the communist ethos of collectivism. He is well aware of the potential dangers of misuse of power in both.

> At one time people thought the Marxist approach would be the answer. Unfortunately Marxism failed, because instead of using the socialist approach of equality, fraternity, and liberty, the second world used state capitalism, totalitarianism, and centralism.[10]

For Sulak, social engineering, using ideology to change people from without, is not the answer. He feels the spiritual approach has something more powerful to offer. A Buddhist model of development begins with everyone truly practicing to understand oneself. In the Buddhist tradition, this is called *citta sikkha,* or the contemplation on mind. Meditation is important to attain insight and awareness. Critical self-awareness is crucial for personal empowerment; from this base a critical understanding of communities and society can be realized. To make real and lasting differences, strategies need to acknowledge and transform these unwholesome roots within individuals and societies. A two-pronged approach is required to work on practical social reconstruction and more deeply on the collective psyche or consciousness, where the hazardous lure of consumerism is deeply rooted.

When Asia confronted modernization in the last few hundred years, most of the intellectuals and thinkers, including the Buddhists, rationalized and justified their traditional philosophy to fit into modern concepts. By the time Asia gained independence from Western colonization, most of the Asian elite had lost confidence in their own cultural values. Most Thai elites are now educated in the West or receive Western-style education in Siam. They have come to feel that their society is intrinsically inferior to the West—so they have to adopt all the latest fashions of the West, even progressive Western thought. Buddhadasa and Sulak bucked the trend, and instead of using modernization as criteria for change, they used Buddhist wisdom teachings for their principles. They have offered important leadership in confronting this alienation from intellectual and cultural imperialism and gaining back self-respect for the Buddhist community in Asia.

Buddhist thought advocates that whether you are stupid or clever, man or woman, black, brown, pink, white, or yellow, rich or poor, powerful or powerless, believer or nonbeliever, you have intrinsic buddha nature within you. You do not have to be someone else to be valuable—hence the primacy placed on self-respect (*hiri-ottappa*). Any society with a structure that undermines this self-respect is an unhealthy society. You cannot be "more who you are" by rejecting what you are. This does not mean strictly adhering to traditional roles and responsibilities. It means rejecting the notion of belonging to a *lesser* race, class, gender, religion, culture, or civilization. Once one is firmly rooted in self-respect, it is possible to make healthy and critically aware choices from among the options offered both by what we inherit from our past and from Western modernity. Working for a sustainable future through political and economic structural change alone is not enough. A new kind of Asian cultural revolution is required to liberate Asia from Western cultural imperialism and from the colonized mentality. This kind of thinking of not being developed enough, and having to catch up with the West, is disempowering and must stop.

INITIATIVES ON THE PATH TO REDUCE SUFFERING

The Buddha prescribed the Eightfold Path of practice as the solution to the problem of craving; this is the Fourth Noble Truth. Buddhadasa and Sulak have both been instrumental in promoting alternatives to consumerism in Southeast Asia as a path to reduced suffering. Buddhadasa established Suan Mokkh as a monastery resisting the mainstream sangha and influenced many others through his writing. Sulak was greatly influenced by Buddhadasa and carried his ethics still further. Each has published hundreds of papers and books and given numerous talks criticizing the present system and proposing alternatives. As an organizer, Sulak has been a pioneer in starting modern nongovernmental organizations (NGOs) in Siam. In his forty years of committed engagement, he has built a network of small organizations based on engaged Buddhist teachings, working in collaboration with different groups. He and his colleagues have actively promoted translation of alternative visions from the West, introducing the Thai reading public to Mahatma Gandhi, E. F. Schumacher, Fritjof Capra, Thich Nhat Hanh, the Dalai Lama, Satish Kumar, Paulo Friere, Helena Norberg-Hodge, and David Korten. Through the Komalkeemthong Foundation and other publishing houses, these alternative voices from the West have strengthened the Thai engaged Buddhist movement. Sulak also took it as his mission to organize seminars and workshops among the progressive middle class, challenging the mainstream development discourse and arguing for Buddhist alternatives to consumerism. His influence in Thai intellectual and educated circles has been tremendous.

One of Sulak's first NGOs, the Thai Inter-religious Commission for Development (TICD), has been effective in supporting grassroots leadership among monks and nuns to promote sustainable development at the village level. Many of the monks and nuns in this network have become well known as initiators of sustainable community empowerment. For example, when modern development and consumerism came to the countryside around activist monk Luang Pho Nan's monastery, the villagers became the victims of middlemen and loan sharks and got into heavy debt. Luang Pho began a campaign of resistance and rehabilitation by using community meditation to raise awareness of the dangers of consumerism. At the same time, he encouraged villagers to form rice banks, community cooperative shops, and community savings groups based on Buddhist principles of participatory democracy (*vajji-aparihayadhamma*).[11]

Not long after Luang Pho Nan started this campaign, the work spread quickly to nearby districts and provinces. Now more than five hundred monks have joined this movement of community revitalization. Villagers can now gradually get themselves out of debt and aim at a self-reliant community life rather than joining the cash-crop economy. One community at Kutchum District, under the leadership of Phra Krusupajariyawat, even started its own community currency.[12] The work of TICD is so important because it helps monks and nuns to understand the structural violence behind the consumer monoculture.

The Spirit in Education Movement (SEM), started in 1995, is another initiative of Sulak and his colleagues'. Its mission is to develop a comprehensive educational movement to counter the trends of globalization and consumerism, using spiritual strength to empower individuals and communities to choose alternative ways of development with confidence and full awareness. This approach is rooted in cultural appropriateness and indigenous wisdom to confront the trends of cultural imperialism that inflict inferiority on people of non-Western origin. One SEM program, the Grassroots Leadership Training (GLT) program, has been ongoing for nearly ten years. The GLT works with marginalized communities in Siam, Burma, Laos, and Cambodia, running three-month training courses with follow-up sessions. The aim of the courses is to empower communities to be self-reliant in terms of basic needs while maintaining their cultural integrity and sustaining a healthy environment.

The empowerment education approach of GLT applies critical self-awareness in a far broader context. This starts with a community-needs analysis to highlight the structural injustices of the modernization process. Tools are given to help communities identify problems and develop sustainable solutions. The real "experts" are seen as those who know and care for their local environment. Staff facilitate problem analysis and reflection, especially in relation to the connection between local and global problems. GLT also offers study tours to innovative projects, introducing appropriate solutions such as sustainable technology and microcredit.

As communities begin to recognize the oppressive forces in society and how they are mirrored within themselves, they move beyond these trends, finding renewed belief in traditional wisdom and regaining their self-confidence and community confidence. This becomes a starting point for locally sustainable futures. GLT alumni are now involved in hundreds of small-scale appropriate development projects and training initiatives that focus on local production for local consumption. At best they hope to help traditional communities not yet marred by the consumer monoculture to protect themselves from the negative forces and make use of the positive elements to revitalize a healthy community life. The idea is to bypass the mistakes of other victimized traditional communities that opened up to modernization without critical awareness.

Though GLT works with participants of several faiths, encouraging spiritual practice according to their own beliefs, the content and process of the training reflect the basic essence of buddhist education (as in Sulak's practice of small *b* Buddhism)—the Eightfold Path. A large part of the training is to cultivate right view and right thought about internal and external development. Right thought is defined as unselfish, nonviolent, and free of hatred and excessive desire. In order for individuals and communities to develop properly, generosity (or sharing of wealth), power, and recognition are crucial. When conflict arises, a compassionate and nonviolent approach is encouraged.

To practice right speech, GLT students learn methods of reconciliation and mediation and develop understanding of the structural violence of the present media system. Right action refers to the five basic precepts for ethical conduct. The first precept, abstaining from killing, is applied to understanding the cruelty of the industrial production of meat and breeding of animals for consumption. GLT discussions also address the arms industry that supports powerful societies and is linked to many wars around the world. The second precept, abstaining from stealing, takes up the injustice of a national and international economic order that allows the rich to steal from the poor with legal and political legitimacy. GLT participants also learn about alternative economic systems. As for the third precept, abstaining from sexual misconduct, GLT courses investigate the global structure of male dominance and exploitation of women and how the structures of patriarchal greed, hatred, and delusion relate to violence in the world. To address right livelihood, GLT organizes exposure trips to self-reliant communities that practice cooperation to prevent exploitation, as well as sustainable agriculture and handicraft production.

The last three spokes of the Eightfold Path—right effort, right mindfulness, and right concentration—are related to meditation. In order to encourage these aspects, the GLT courses include a weeklong retreat integrating meditation, prayer, or puja practice into the daily schedule. Alumni are encouraged to do regular retreats and daily practice when they return to their communities. In the long term, the Spirit in Education Movement aspires to establish a residential college of sustainable communities for Southeast Asia. It is planned that courses will then devote about one-third of the time to practicing meditation and other serious spiritual practices.

Spirit in Education also works closely with the Assembly of the Poor. This is a wonderful example of a nonviolent grassroots movement challenging the mind-set of modernization and consumerism. Thousands of ordinary people who are victims of development projects work together to raise awareness and challenge the negative impacts of dams, large-scale farming and fishing, and industrial factories. For many years thousands of

Assembly members have gathered on a rotational basis to form a large protest village at Pak Moon Dam in northeast Siam. Up against the huge institutions of the World Bank, EGAT (Electricity Generating Authority of Thailand), and the Thai government, this is a story of real hope. The Assembly of the Poor protested the building of the dam to gain fair recompense, as it would drastically impact their traditional way of life. They also protested against wasteful use of electricity in air-conditioning and lighting hundreds of big department stores. However, the dam went ahead, and the lives of the local people, who were largely dependent on fishing and riverside gardens, changed beyond measure as more than two-thirds of the migratory fish disappeared. Undaunted, they campaigned to open the dam and return the river to its previous ecological state. In June 2001 the gates were ceremoniously opened, and very quickly the fish began to return and the people resumed their traditional occupations. But once again the government reneged and now plans to close the gates for eight months of the year.

In Siam, protests are traditionally seen as actions of the political left. Indeed, some of the Assembly of the Poor organizers are from the left movement and did not initially care about Buddhism. However, SEM workers introduced engaged Buddhist monks and nuns to support the movement as educators. The monks and nuns brought a new understanding of the Eightfold Path and also introduced chanting and meditation practice into protest situations. This worked miraculously. It became much more difficult for the police (also Buddhist) to beat or arrest people when they were chanting on the protest site. Once monks and nuns became involved, the Assembly of the Poor officially adopted Buddhist principles of nonviolent action, thus reducing the legitimacy of government use of violent oppression. Even the left-oriented leaders of the assembly now appreciate meditation and take it seriously. The persistent and extremely difficult protests for many years have influenced authorities to rethink and delay building other dams around the country.

Across these years of struggle, the Assembly of the Poor has been a huge conscientization exercise, gradually increasing awareness of the complex interconnected issues relating to consumerism, modernization, and globalization. It has also supported experiments with aspects of self-reliant and sustainable community. There are now initiatives advocating traditional health care and community businesses promoting fairly priced and environmentally friendly local production for local consumption. There is a new focus on using native resources and on self-reliance within families or villages to reduce the outflow from the community. This protest movement has awakened public debate on the differences between modern development and Buddhist values. Using dhammic wisdom to combat the prevailing ideology of consumerism has been very empowering for the protesters, as it shows how consumerism contradicts indigenous values and how dhamma, the base of their culture, can relate to their contemporary political struggle.

A FUTURE WITH LESS SUFFERING

Consumer monoculture is able to dominate contemporary society because individuals have become alienated from their buddha nature, from their culture, and from each other. Driven by greed, hatred, and illusion, we need to find ways to see this *tanha* to avoid destruction of soil, soul, and society. Empowerment education for grassroots communities and individuals from all social strata providing tools to counteract these trends is crucial. It must address both inner and outer landscapes in understanding *tanha* in order to give alternative thinking and behavior a chance.

In Buddhist society it is believed that every being embodies buddha nature, the potential to attain the highest understanding, and that we should all strive for this. The poor and marginalized are entitled to the same dignity as everyone else in their struggles. These grassroots initiatives are a light for the future, as they emphasize the importance of critical examination, localization of power, and economic activity growing from rather than deriding indigenous local wisdom. The GLT and other similar initiatives in the region are a vital proactive approach,[13] and the signs are that these will make a real difference to coming generations. The Assembly of the Poor in Siam has perhaps given people the most hope. As ordinary people start to understand the full impact of the situation on themselves and their societies, they gain the confidence not only to rise up in protest but also to find viable and sustainable alternatives.

How much healthier would all our societies be if they were based on value systems that truly advocated sustainability rather than unlimited growth! A society where people help each other out in hard times. A society with no concept of interest. A society where power is shared rather than fought over, that reveres and respects nature rather than controlling and using it as a resource. A society unsullied by the poisons of *tanha*. A society with values steeped in Buddhist wisdom.

Concrete steps are being taken to manifest this vision through initiatives inspired by Buddhadasa Bhikkhu and Sulak Sivaraksa. A good number of committed people are working on these initiatives. They do not have all the answers, but they have a clear awareness of the structural violence and a strong determination to work with the violence within the structures of their minds. They take the path of contemporary bodhisattvas confronting the suffering in themselves and in society in order to work for the liberation of all sentient beings. It is a very challenging yet enriching path—a combination of contemplation and activism, spirituality and politics, humor and seriousness. These committed people are returning to the very roots of the traditional Buddhist teaching and using this power to move toward a wholesome and sustaining future.

Taming the "I Want" Mind

Sunyana Graef

ONE SUMMER a Zen practitioner from Poland, who had never been outside eastern Europe, stayed at the Vermont Zen Center for a training period. She was an expert seamstress, and her first assignment was to repair a small sofa. When I asked her to have the work completed by the end of the week, she looked confused, then she became distressed. Why was she so upset? "It's impossible," she said, nearly in tears. "It cannot be done within the time I'm here." What could be the problem? "You don't have the fabric," she explained, "and it could take months to find." When I told her that we would go to a store that very day and get exactly what we needed, she was astonished. Before she returned home, she gave a talk to our sangha about the differences between Poland and the United States. She summed it up this way: in Poland if you need something—be it money, a piece of fabric, a car—you figure out how to do without it. In America if you need something—be it a house, a sofa, a new pair of shoes—you figure out how to get it.

At that time I was building a house, and I felt conflicted to the point of embarrassment about spending so much energy on the project. My parents had offered my husband and me the money to build a home so that we could have more space while our children were growing, and I wanted it to be large enough so that my parents would be comfortable should they ever decide to live with us. Yet I was unsettled about having made a decision to accept their money for what was, essentially, a matter of personal comfort. My preference would have been to live in a tiny cabin in the woods, but with two children and a husband, that was not an option. At one point I called my Zen teacher, Philip Kapleau, and asked his advice on the propriety of owning a large house. He said, "Your students would want you to have it." I wasn't so sure.

Now here was this woman—from a country where even the most common things were not taken for granted—holding up a mirror to our excesses. As our sangha reflected on her experience, we realized that, truth be told, we were spoiled, and we didn't even know it. We live in a land of plenty and have become so accustomed to the abundance surrounding us that we are oblivious to it. We are inundated by material goods to the point that we have become like someone whose appestat is no longer working properly. We eat until we're sick, we consume until we're drowning in . . . what? Things we don't really need or want. The fevered mind of entitlement reigns large in the West—if we want it, we feel we deserve it, and therefore we should have it—*now*! Discomfited by her words, I couldn't help but wonder if I had fallen into the very trap I had so often warned my students to avoid: the trap of misplaced need that turns into greed.

The unbridled consumerism of our culture fosters the belief that all we have to do to be happy is to satiate our desires. Consumerism is surely an addiction; long before we've left our childhood we've become consumerholics, addicted to the drug of *more*. We're a nation of hungry ghosts, wandering through life just like those pitiful beings in the preta realm who, owing to their inexorable greed, have condemned themselves to lives of wretched suffering.[1] Every time a hungry ghost tries to eat something, it turns to poison. Every drop of liquid they ingest turns to fire. Their lives are an unremitting circle of relentless desire followed by excruciating pain. Like poor hungry ghosts, each time we obtain a morsel of something—food, drink, sensory pleasures, consumer goods—we burn internally. Instead of being satisfied, our cravings increase. As our cravings increase, our distressing hollowness grows.

As with any addiction, the first step in overcoming it is to recognize it.

We need to see that, to paraphrase Gandhi, happiness does not consist in the multiplication of wants but in their deliberate and voluntary renunciation. The ideal of voluntary renunciation is well known to practitioners of the dharma. The fulfillment that comes through spiritual development does not lie in the realm of desire but in the purification and absence of desires. This is because desires simply cannot be quenched by feeding them. Rather, through capitulating to them, just the opposite happens: they proliferate.

Chasing after desires is like drinking saltwater, the Buddha said. Saltwater can never satisfy your thirst but only increases it. Likewise, desire builds upon desire, so we can never be satisfied. An ancient Hindu teaching describes the heart of a discontented, dissatisfied person as being like a bamboo basket riddled with holes. It is impossible to draw water from a well with such a basket. It will leak, and not a drop of water will remain to quench your thirst. Similarly, when you are suffering from the tormenting thirst of greed and yearning, your contentment leaks away even before your needs have been fulfilled. All that remains is discontent.

Unfortunately, it is not easy to transform habitual behavior and character born from greed and attachment. If it were, then all beings would be content with their rightful share in the bounty of this earth, and our planet would not be suffering from the effects of deforestation, pollution, and overpopulation. But there is a way out. While it is true that the small self is habitually and addictively drawn to objects, and while it is true that habit patterns are immensely difficult to eradicate, the practices of Buddhism provide a path through the morass of longing that surrounds us. Buddhist practice can be an antidote for the addictions of (and to) the spoiled small self with which we are masochistically enamored. It helps us recognize, unmask, and ultimately relinquish this small self, and in so doing we become less vulnerable to the ego's vocal, incessant demands.

Overcoming our firmly entrenched ego-feeding habit is an arduous undertaking; it requires strong measures. This the Buddha provided in the form of a potent medicine called "no-self." Through Buddhist practice we become less identified with the small self; the less self-identified we are, the less need there is to bolster the ego-I with "stuff." By gradually letting go of ego delusion, our sense of separation and alienation dissipates. Ultimately we see that we have everything; nothing is lacking anywhere. "The Buddha had only his begging bowl, yet he was the richest person on earth," said Hakuun Yasutani Roshi.

The foundation of the Buddha's teaching in every sect of Buddhism is the act of taking refuge in the Three Jewels, also called the Three Treasures or Refuges—Buddha, Dharma, and Sangha. In the Zen tradition, taking refuge is a daily act. Every morning begins with the repetition of the Three Refuges, as they form both the foundation and heart of one's spiritual life:

> I take refuge in Buddha, and resolve that with all beings, I will
> understand the Great Way, whereby the Buddha-seed may
> forever thrive.
> I take refuge in Dharma, and resolve that with all beings, I will
> enter deeply into the sutra treasure, whereby my wisdom
> may grow as vast as the ocean.
> I take refuge in Sangha, and in its wisdom, example, and never-
> failing help, and resolve to live in harmony with all sentient
> beings.[2]

By putting one's trust or faith in the Buddha (the ideal of awakening to our true nature of no-self), by following the dharma (which is the teaching of the Buddha), and by practicing within the context of a sangha (which is the community of followers of the Way of the Buddha), a radical reorientation of one's life takes place. Taking refuge is a powerful means for the transformation of selfishness into selflessness. Through this simple act of faith, one begins to understand how to live a life of wisdom, compassion, joy, and equanimity, free from the addictions of egocentric consumerism.

TAKING REFUGE IN BUDDHA— REALIZATION OF NO-SELF

One of the most effective tools of Zen training is sesshin, sometimes called a Zen retreat. *Retreat* is not actually a good synonym, implying as it does a peaceful, relaxing rest. That's not a sesshin. *Sesshin* literally means "collecting the heart-mind." Its purpose is to provide the framework for serious Zen practitioners to make the supreme effort to come to spiritual awakening, thereby realizing the truth of no-self—our buddha nature.

As practiced in the Harada-Yasutani lineage, sesshin is a three- to seven-day period of intense spiritual work centered around *zazen*, or sitting meditation (a minimum of ten hours daily), chanting (twice daily), and private interviews with the teacher (three times daily). There is also a *teisho* (Zen talk by the teacher), a work period, meals, and brief rest periods. There is no talking during sesshin. No one leaves the premises for any reason; even going outdoors is discouraged until after nightfall. At the start of sesshin the teacher warns participants to keep custody of body, speech, and mind by looking down at all times, by maintaining inner and outer silence, by eating less than normal, and by carefully guarding the thinking mind. In effect, once sesshin begins, everyone is in a cloistered monastery.

The simplicity of life during those days of intense training is refreshing and liberating. This is one of the things I love most about sesshin: everything is reduced to the essential. I open my closet: there is a robe, an underrobe, a set of work clothes. That's it—nothing else! You have a bed, toiletries, and a set of eating bowls—complete freedom from the tyranny of objects. The food is vegetarian, simple, and similar every day. Paradoxically, eating less, you feel more full.

In such an environment, wants, needs, and desires virtually melt away. I've never heard of anyone spending time at sesshin thinking about clothes, computers, or cars, though there are undoubtedly those who crave sensual pleasures—a soak in a hot tub and a massage around day three would be heavenly! And there is always going to be someone who is struck with a powerful longing for pizza or ice cream. Nonetheless, since there's nothing you can do about it, eventually the desires dissipate.

Sesshin changes your priorities, your perspective, and your life. As you work on letting go of the ego-I, the triggers that set off urges to buy become less compelling and therefore less operational. Where does consumerism come from if not the need to feed this nonexistent self in order to bolster the false image of who and what we are? As you would expect, the deeper the experience of no-self, the more dramatic the change. But even with one or two sesshins, people often experience a subtle dropping away of attachments. Taking refuge in the Buddha, our true nature of no-self, makes this possible.

There are many cases of people who found that their need for such consumer addictions as cigarettes, alcohol, junk food, and passive diversions such as television, movies, and computer games radically diminished or even disappeared completely after sesshin training. Things that seemed important, even essential, before sesshin oftentimes have less appeal at the end of seven days of deep spiritual work.

Sometimes people are bewildered when this happens. We've become so passive about our addictions that we don't realize we have the power to overcome them. For example, a young Zen student called me a few days after her first sesshin. "I haven't smoked in two days," she said. "Is this okay?"

Perplexed, I asked, "What do you mean? Why wouldn't it be okay?"

"Well, it seems strange that I don't *want* to smoke anymore."

"It's not strange at all," I said. "It's wonderful! Don't smoke!" And just like that, she stopped smoking and never again picked up a cigarette.

More often the letting go is a gradual process. A middle-aged man had been attending sesshin sporadically for close to twenty years. To all appearances, everything in his life was in order. He had a high-powered, well-paying job, a loving, supportive wife, well-adjusted children. But he was also unhappy and a workaholic. No matter what he did, something kept pushing at him, an inquietude, a sense of alienation. One day he called me to say that he was taking early retirement in order to devote as much time to Zen training as possible. He began attending eight to ten sesshins a year. Within three years, his life had changed completely. He became a vegetarian; he felt more at peace with the world and with himself. His devotion to the dharma was a model for younger students, and his generosity supported the Zen center and helped people attend sesshin and go on pilgrimage. It was as if his intensified training had opened his heart and enabled him to let go of his need to possess and consume.

When you are in sesshin focusing on your spiritual practice, bit by bit you deconstruct and loosen your attachments to the false ideas of self and other. Eventually you come to the realization that there is no thing, no entity, called I. There is no *me* for things to be *mine.* "It's like robbers breaking into an empty house," an ancient master said. Your identity becomes the whole universe, and you clearly see that "heaven and earth and I are the same root. All things and I are of one substance." You have everything—what is lacking anywhere? When you know this in your very guts, then you never have an urgent sense of want or need. This is taking refuge in Buddha, and with it comes a profound feeling of contentment, equanimity, and joy.

TAKING REFUGE IN DHARMA—
CAUSATION AND THE PRECEPTS

Sesshin plunges you into the world of emptiness in which there is no self, no other. Returning to everyday life, you are deposited back into the world of form. The self and all things instantly reappear. Although "form is only emptiness, emptiness only form," it can be a jarring experience to move from the rarefied sesshin realm of emptiness, selflessness, and thinglessness into the discordant samsaric realm of ego, form, and desire. Children want attention, the house needs cleaning, mail is waiting to be answered, there's grocery shopping to be done. Phone calls, disturbing headlines, piled-up work, dirty laundry . . . in less than an hour, the fruits of seven days of cultivating wisdom, compassion, and equanimity seem to fly out the window.

Practicing Zen means being fully engaged and present in the here and now, not separate from the messiness of life. Given that, it must be said that sesshin training by itself is not of much use in ordinary life. After all, we don't go through our days in silent meditation, with downcast eyes and minimal interaction with others. Moreover, during sesshin it is easy to resist the temptation to consume—the only temptations are mental ones, and the only things to consume are the food at mealtimes and sleep (but that's another story). Outside of sesshin it's a different matter. What we need is a way to deal with the commotion and challenges, confusion and pressures of daily existence, not the least of which is the lure of excessive consumption.

Taking refuge in Dharma, the teachings of the Buddha, provides a path that shows how to live a balanced, sane existence amid the uncertainties and seductions of everyday life. The Buddha's teachings are vast, but they can be expressed simply:

> *All things are produced by causation.*
> *The Buddha has explained their cause and the way to*
>   *eliminate them.*
> *This is his teaching.*[3]

It was this explanation of the dharma that was given by the monk Assaji to Sariputra, who had long been searching for the supreme teaching. Upon hearing these words, Sariputra immediately gave up his search and took refuge in Buddha, Dharma, and Sangha.

Another monk, famous for doing zazen in a tree, was perched on a branch when someone asked him, "What is the essence of Buddhism?" He answered:

> *Not to commit wrong actions,*
> *But to do all good ones*
> *And to keep the heart pure—*
> *This is the teaching of all the buddhas.*

His questioner said, "Even a three-year-old child knows that." The monk replied, "Yes, but even an eighty-year-old man has difficulty doing it."

These teachings—the law of causation and the basic precepts of moral behavior—are an inseparable continuum. Belief in the law of cause and effect is a powerful impetus for living an ethical, pure, and compassionate life. Moral behavior, in turn, leads to the elimination of pain-producing karma and thus shows a way to end confusion and suffering. Since so much suffering is caused by greed and desire, it follows that observing the precepts and accepting the principle of causation would naturally lead to a reduced need to consume. And indeed they do.

The ten cardinal precepts are all concerned with avoiding volitional actions stemming from greed, anger, and ignorance, which lead to painful karmic effects. They are, as Zen master Bassui said, "a shortcut for entering the Buddha Gate."[4] Interestingly, fully half of them deal directly with consumption: the first, second, and third, the fifth, and the eighth.[5] For example, the decision to follow the first precept will necessarily mean avoiding engaging in any occupation that causes the suffering and death of sentient beings. It means that you will not eat (or cook or purchase) meat, fish, or poultry. It means you will not wear (or buy) leather, fur, down, or silk. In like manner, every single precept can be looked at as a guidepost for living simply, without consuming excessively or unnecessarily. Even the precepts dealing with speech are pointing to a type of mindless consumption: the consumption of other people's time, happiness, and sense of well-being.

The third precept, not to misuse sexuality but to be caring and responsible, is particularly important in this respect. Most obviously, the precept means not to enter into adulterous relationships. It also means not to engage in any sexual relationship in which there is a wide disparity in power, such as teacher-student, adult-child, supervisor-employee, or in which there is a lack of respect or violence. And it means not to use pornography. All consumer addictions are major obstacles to spiritual development; addictions to alcohol and pornography are undoubtedly the most disruptive to serenity of mind.

If any students have the courage to tell me they are indulging in pornography, they do so because they are feeling powerless over this addiction. They desperately want to break free of their lust, as they are deeply ashamed of what they are doing. We discuss the fact that an addiction to pornography violates not only the precept of abusing sexuality but also that of killing, lying, and stealing. Everything we do affects others, including looking at degrading pictures of men, women, or children who were certainly at some point in their lives mistreated, abused, neglected, or were, at the very least, suffering from abysmally low self-esteem. To look at such pictures robs not only them of their dignity but also the one who is looking at the pictures. Thus it is a kind of killing as well as stealing. Then, too, many people who compulsively use pornography lie to their partner about it.

If I ask people how this addiction is affecting their life, they invariably say their partner hates it, they'd be mortified if people found out about it, and they definitely want to stop. Fortunately, if they have taken refuge in the dharma, they already have a powerful tool for overcoming this addiction. They see that the consequences of their actions are painful to themselves and others and that by abandoning that which causes suffering, they can be happier and in a better position to help others. They see that any obsessive behavior keeps them from living freely in the present moment. Instead of being fully aware, they are distracted by intruding fantasies and daydreams of getting the next fix; their mind is not at ease.

I suspect that for Buddhists in particular, with this as with other consumer addictions (drinking, gambling, compulsive eating, excessive shopping), there is a very strong element of shame and secretiveness. I tell my students that if they have secrets, they are protecting their ego. When you protect your ego, you hold yourself back spiritually because so much energy is going into maintaining a facade. One of the principles of twelve-step programs—which are a good model for Zen practitioners trapped in addiction—is to be fearlessly honest. Those students who can admit their powerlessness and call out for help find that this is the first step in freeing themselves from their addiction and changing their life. The courage to do this often begins with taking refuge in the Dharma.

In my own life, it was not addictive behavior that caused problems as much as an oppressive feeling of separation from everyone and everything. As my practice developed, I gradually came to see that my feelings of separation were just that: feelings, and that in fact I was not separate from anyone, anything. Slowly the understanding dawned that everything I did had far-ranging implications, since I was not apart from the world. I began to look more closely at my speech, behavior, and even thought patterns and to consider how they might affect others. It became clear that any choice to consume excessively, be it clothing, food, paper, water, or consumer goods, would have a negative impact on me—it was wasteful, unnecessary, and selfish—and by extension a negative impact on others. I began to take responsibility for my actions in a way I had never done before. I had to admit that my difficulties were not due to fate or someone else or anything else but rather that I myself had made my life the way it was and was continuing to shape my future life.

This realization filled me with a sense of tremendous power—and tremendous dread. There was a feeling of wonder and freedom that came with the understanding that I absolutely had the ability to change my life, but with that came onerous and inescapable responsibility. It was impossible to ignore the effects of my actions or to flippantly say, "It doesn't make any difference," when it manifestly *did* make a difference, especially in actions involving selfishness or generosity, consumption or renunciation.

In "Deep Faith in Cause and Effect" (*Shinjin Inga*), Zen master Dogen speaks of the importance of understanding causation for one who is practicing the dharma:

> Those who study Zen in the Buddha Dharma may wish to start by arousing the thought of enlightenment and repaying the kindness of the Buddha and patriarchs, but first of all they should clearly understand the principle of cause and effect.[6]

Cause cannot be separated from effect, no matter how long it takes for the effects of an action to bear fruit. If we see this clearly, then the palpable sense of the weightiness of our volitional actions and conscious choices causes us to be more aware of the way we live. Awareness in our life leads to awareness of the consequences of our actions. We see that some choices inevitably generate suffering for ourselves and others, while other choices produce happiness. Furthermore, we see that overcoming excessive desire and unrestrained consumerism is directly connected to leading a more joyful, serene existence. The more thoroughly we understand that it is a matter of causality, the harder we will try to avoid evil and do good. In such a way we begin to actualize the Dharma in our everyday life.

TAKING REFUGE IN SANGHA— FAMILY AND COMMUNITY PRACTICE

Living the Dharma gives rise to a better understanding of taking refuge in Sangha. The sangha, a community of practitioners of the dharma, serves as both a foundation and a support for others on the spiritual path. It is encouraging to see how people with many years of dharma experience live their lives. The careful way they use the earth's resources, the simplicity of their everyday life (sometimes even in the midst of wealth and luxury), their generosity, devotion to practice, discipline, patience, energy, virtue, compassion, wisdom, and warmth—all this is inspiring and motivating. It is also a wonderful boon when raising a family to be among such mature people.

At the age of twenty, when I began practicing Buddhism at the Rochester Zen Center, I was not a mature person, nor did I possess any of the virtues that come from steady practice. I was emotionally ungrounded and immature and quite sure that having a child in my state of confusion—never mind the fact that I wasn't yet married—would be tantamount to child abuse. Fortunately for my two daughters, I waited until I was married and in my thirties before starting to raise a family. With greater spiritual maturity, it is easier to make decisions and there is somewhat less angst around child rearing, though you basically have no idea whether or not you are doing well by your children until they are grown, and maybe not even then.

It seems that it is almost impossible to protect children against the aggressive consumerism and peer pressure associated with substance abuse and early sexuality. Being part of a sangha and associating with spiritually developed people provides a bulwark against some of those pressures. All the same, no matter how simply Buddhist parents want to live, no matter how free of acquisitiveness they are, no matter how much they wish to protect their children from the pressures of consumer culture, children have their own needs and their own karma.

Years ago I saw a pertinent article in the *New York Times* magazine in the "Lifestyle" section. The writers had gone to the apartment of a Zen Buddhist woman in Manhattan and photographed various rooms to show the "Zen style." Looking at the pictures, my jaw dropped, my eyes grew wide. Incredibly, there was practically nothing in her house! Her young son's room was bare except for a bed; the walls were devoid of a single picture, poster, or decoration. No books, no toys, no sports equipment, no musical instruments—there was no sign of life anywhere. And this was supposed to be Zen?! Looking at the pictures, I thought: *This is not Zen; this is bizarre. People don't live like this; kids especially don't live like this.* I wondered if she thought that in order to be a Zen Buddhist you had to live in an empty shell, foregoing all possessions. Maybe she thought that if she didn't have anything, her son wouldn't become attached to consumer objects. It made me think of Layman P'ang, a deeply enlightened ancient worthy who felt so strongly about the corruptive influence of wealth that he threw all his money into a deep river. He did this despite the fact that he had a family to support. (His wife's reaction was not recorded.)[7] If you are single and want to live like that, that is your choice. But it is misguided to impose such an austere lifestyle on children no matter how enlightened you may be. It is important to stimulate children's creativity with books, toys, music, and art. This is not the same as catering to every whim of your child—limits are important. The difficulty is in finding the middle way. So, what's a Buddhist parent to do?

While you might want to deal with the pressures of consumerism by living in an empty house or throwing away all your wealth, there are other, more practical ways to approach this challenge. Children need a certain number of possessions in order to learn about sharing, taking care of things, and respecting property. But even more important, they need the example of their parents. Take, for instance, the problem of drinking, something most parents face with trepidation as their kids enter adolescence. As a point of spiritual practice, if parents strictly follow the fifth precept and don't drink, they will effortlessly communicate to their children the messages of sobriety and clearness of mind. If parents consistently pick up a glass of wine for relaxation or enjoyment, it is only natural that their children will associate drinking alcohol with having a good time. What better thing can parents do than practice what they preach? If as Buddhist parents we drink alcohol, including wine and beer, and yet are trying to get the message across to our children not to drink, it is hypocritical or at the very least confusing. It is much cleaner and easier to just not drink. Of course, not every parent who drinks is going to have children who drink, nor is every parent who doesn't drink going to have children who abstain, but by setting an example you can increase the odds.

In our family the precepts were part of our daily life. Discussing the meaning of the precepts with our daughters and engaging with the questions that came up around them seemed quite natural, and it was excellent training for dealing with consumer issues and moral dilemmas. For me the precepts were a tremendous gift in that they provided impeccable guidelines for daily life. By the time I had a family, I could think of nothing better to do for my children than to follow the precepts to the best of my ability. Now my daughters are grown, but it is a special joy when I see parents bringing their children to the precept ceremonies we hold each year.

Along with following the precepts, I firmly believe that the single most important step parents can take to avoid the excesses of consumer culture is to banish television from the home. When people ask me for child-rearing advice, I tell them just one thing: *Get rid of your TV!* True, there are some excellent, worthwhile programs on public television, but I honestly do not think the risk is worth it. Television is a dangerous intoxicant, in its own way as destructive as alcohol and drugs. It erodes communication within the family, promotes base values, exposes children to foul language, sex, drinking, and drugs at far too early an age, and interjects destructive, disturbing, violent imagery deep into the mind. Of equal importance, the barrage of commercials on television encourages greedy consumerism. The advertising industry creates desires for unnecessary things by convincing hapless people that they are *worth* it, they *deserve* it, they *ought* to have it. Is it any wonder we grow up believing that in order to be happier, sexier, prettier, more fulfilled, we need the latest . . . whatever? All in all, I cannot imagine why any parents who are practicing the dharma would want their children to ingest the toxic waste they are bound to see on television.

Without TV my children were not exactly clueless about trends—they did attend public school—but they certainly were not much influenced by them either. Instead of spending their time watching junk, they played sports, visited with friends, practiced musical instruments, read books, painted, danced, spent time outdoors, did homework, goofed off, and attended events at the Zen center when they wanted to. My daughters did think that we were a weird family—vegetarian, Buddhist, mother a priest, dad on the school board, no TV, no alcohol—but they weren't angry, resentful, or friendless. In fact, they rather liked our unique strangeness. Our household was exceptionally harmonious, and I am convinced that the absence of television had as much to do with it as anything else.

When you take refuge in the wisdom and warmth of the sangha, the teachings of the Buddha can more easily take root in your life. In time they inform daily interactions with family and community. I have found that taking refuge and following the precepts are ways of working with the forces of entropy on both a personal and a parental level. Our society, with its pressure to consume excessively, pulls us away from our center. This powerful centrifugal energy is unsettling. Always looking outside ourselves, we feel unbalanced, disorderly. The blessing of raising a family with people who are seriously practicing the dharma is that just the opposite energies are at work. Rather than being pulled outward, the centripetal forces of zazen bring one, day after day, back to the center. There is order, and with it comes tranquility.

The values of family and sangha are reflected in each other because sangha is actually an extension of one's family. In our spiritual community, as in our family, we face difficult issues, consumer or otherwise, in much the same way: through respectful discussion and careful listening, trying to maintain virtue, harmony, and equanimity. The sangha of the Vermont Zen Center began with only four people. As a tiny sangha, what was important was the way we conducted our lives and not the things we possessed. Besides, we possessed almost nothing. For close to fifteen years we managed to keep everything on a small scale—no staff, a little house, a tiny budget. But over the years our membership grew, our activities increased, and we developed a pressing need for more space. This became a dilemma for us: Do we limit our growth or raise money to expand our facility?

It was not an easy question to answer. If we were to build new facilities, we faced questions about building materials, scale, design, and ecological impact. Additionally, we would need to borrow money. Part of our practice had been to keep free of debt; Vermont Zen Center has no credit cards. We had worked hard to retire our original mortgage in ten years and had never before purchased anything we could not afford. Suddenly we were considering incurring a huge expense, way beyond our current means. Over and over we asked ourselves: Is this truly need or is it greed? We thought, with so many people suffering from poverty and hunger, do we have the right to ask for contributions and spend this kind of money?

As we debated the merits of expansion versus staying small, we agreed that the only reason for expanding was to increase our ability to help rid the world of suffering. We looked at the root of suffering: greed, anger, and ignorance, in other words, addiction to the ego-I. We concluded that there is no more effective antidote to greed and consumerism, nor is there a better way to help people overcome ego addiction and lead lives of wisdom, compassion, joy, and equanimity, than to expose them to the dharma.

After much discussion, we decided that we would expand. There was a demand for the dharma, and we could better serve people with a larger Zen center. Through the long process of planning and building, we tried to keep costs down, build as "green" as possible, use recycled materials and solar principles, and have a low impact on the environment. While we haven't been able to meet all our goals, we have done our best to build in a responsible way.

I still find it painful to think about the money we have had to spend to expand our center—thousands of dollars for the permitting process alone. But every time I despair, I am immediately filled with the deep conviction that what our troubled world needs now more than anything else is places of spiritual practice. When I was in Japan and saw temples where people had trained for centuries, temples like Ryoanji and Sanjusangendo, Bukkokuji and Sogenji, I had a visceral reaction: *This* is why the world is still here! If such places did not exist, the world would surely be destroyed. We might not see that or feel that or know that on a conscious level. Nonetheless, I am certain that our planet is intact only because of the efforts of people who let go of their ego delusion, who care more about the welfare of our planet than their right to consume, and who devote themselves to living a wise and compassionate existence.

Part of Vermont Zen Center's mission is to give back to the community through outreach. For example, we open our gardens to the public, raise funds for food shelves and the homeless, work with prisoners, and hold services dedicated to world peace. Some of our fundraising goes toward supporting Oxfam's community programs and paying for the education of a Tibetan child in India. Many sangha members feel inspired to become involved with hospice work, human rights activities, and environmental issues. By making community service an integral part of our practice, we cultivate compassion and selfless giving. It is our hope that the new center will greatly enhance our ability to serve the community. Since generosity and an awareness of the needs of others are remedies for greed, our outreach activities help us as a sangha overcome our consumer addictions.

RENOUNCING DESIRE

The first major ceremony we will observe in our new center is Jukai, the ceremony of taking the Three Refuges, the Three General Resolutions, and the Ten Cardinal Precepts. Twice each year we conduct Jukai; every five years we have Great Jukai. In the expanded ceremony of Great Jukai, participants move through the Center past vivid depictions of the six hell realms.

Participants start with the lowest realms of hell and travel through representations of the hungry ghost, animal, titan, human, and deva realms in turn. At the start of our journey, each person is given a drawing of three animals in a circle: a pig representing ignorance, a cock representing greed, and a snake representing anger. Each animal is biting the tail of the one before them, just as we devour ourselves when we give way to consumer excess. As we walk slowly past the sights, smells, colors, and images of the six realms—some of them frightening, some exquisite, some eerie, some unnervingly familiar—we reflect on the causes of being reborn as a person in war-torn lands or as a starving person, as a dog or a human child, a general or a princess. The consequences of acting on uncontrolled desires stand vividly before us. What a powerful antidote to the forces that drive us to consumerism!

The last realm we pass through in Great Jukai is filled with seductive material comforts and temptations. This is the sweetly scented, beautiful world of the devas. There we linger perhaps a moment longer than in the other realms, enticed by the pleasurable sights and smells. Just beyond is the zendo, where we hear the words of the dharma being chanted by those who have crossed the realms before us. We pass into that tranquil space and, with utmost gratitude, bow down before the Buddha, taking refuge in Buddha, in Dharma, and in Sangha, knowing that this is the path to liberation.

Traveling through the six realms, with body and mind we absorb the teaching on the interrelated causes of being reborn in realms of suffering. We see how our craving and desire in the form of attachment to consumer objects and sense pleasures bind us to the wheel of rebirth. Zen master Dogen's forceful words echo the teaching that has been passed down for twenty-five hundred years: "Do not idle away the time needed for practice, but rather practice in the spirit of a person trying to extinguish a blaze in his hair." Dogen admonishes us to abandon all thoughts of fame and desires, get rid of material goods, part with fields and gardens, renounce everything. "You should renounce them even if you do not possess them. What should be clear in this matter is the principle of being free from them whether you have them or not."[8]

In Tibetan thangka paintings of the Wheel of Life, there is a graphic image of a man with an arrow piercing his eye, depicting the powerful impact of objects on the senses. This impact generates the overwhelming feelings of desire and craving, wanting and greed, which afflict us all and lead to the disease of consumerism. For those who long for freedom from this illness, the Dharma provides a refuge where greed, anger, and ignorance can be relinquished through concentrated effort. The best antidote, therefore, for taming the "I want" mind is the Buddha's teachings, the emphasis on no-self, and the way this no-self is actualized through Zen training.

Anyone who takes up the challenge of walking the path commits to diminishing the "I want" mind. The process is difficult and challenging because it goes against the grain of the "more" ethos of Western society. But ultimately it is transformative and worthwhile. And, really, if we wish to grow in wisdom and compassion, what other choice do we have?

10

Penetrating the Tangle

Stephanie Kaza

GOING SHOPPING can be a perilous mental activity these days. As I wander through the department store, I am barraged not only by a daunting array of goods but also by virtually nonstop moralistic thoughts. A new bedspread—*you don't really need this, the old one's good enough.* A stylish dress—*why would a Zen person need this?* A stunning carpet—*was this made by enslaved children?* It goes on and on. The critical voices are all too familiar. As a professor of environmental studies, I am especially plagued by environmental critiques—*if it's not organic, it must be laced with toxic pesticides.* Or *Who knows how far this wood has been shipped and from what decimated forest?*

The koan of consumerism is vast and deep, a tangle within tangles, impossible to completely untangle. Part of the tangle is the resistance, the questioning mind, the nagging thoughts that add up to moral engagement. Sometimes I find myself paralyzed in the co-op, staring at the bounty on the shelves, lost in thoughts of fair trade, farmworkers, and food security. Critiques of consumerism are not new, but as the deluge of products becomes a flood, more and more voices are shouting their concerns.

Some of my own questions come from early training in self-sufficiency in the 1970s; others stem from painful exposure to increasing environmental assault on beloved forests. Still other critiques seem to be part of the social fabric of being American—a puritanical righteousness, a stubborn resistance to corporate control. Can a Buddhist perspective shed any light on this mix of critiques? As in any mindfulness practice, it helps to be able to identify what is going on. *Resisting, resisting, judging, judging*—these activities of the mind are part of a much bigger historical pattern of moral response to consumerism.[1]

Sociologist Michael Schudson lists five traditional critiques, which provide a preliminary taxonomy of consumer resistance.[2] The first of these is the "Puritan" critique, referring to the early New England colonists who believed people should invest less meaning in material possessions and more meaning in religious pursuits. Puritans felt goods should serve practical human needs but should not be ends of desire themselves. Consumerist attitudes were thought to corrupt people, impairing their capacity for spiritual development.

The "Quaker" critique focuses more on the wasteful nature of the goods themselves. From this perspective, excessive choice and pointless proliferation of products is seen as extravagant and unnecessary. Planned obsolescence, as in the annual new models of cars and computers, is particularly objectionable. If goods cannot be made to endure, keeping the limited resources of the earth in mind, then they should not be made at all. The Quaker critique challenges a core value of consumerism—that more choice is good for consumers and good for the economy.

What Schudson calls the "republican" critique addresses the impact of consumerism on civic society as a whole. In this view a consumerist approach replaces public engagement in politics with private involvement in personal goods. It also shifts a person's identity away from work (what one does) and toward lifestyle (what one owns), promoting individual pleasure over social justice. Historically, the increasing orientation to consumerism has turned people away from social activity. "People abandoned the town square for the front porch, and then later the front porch for the backyard or the television room."[3] This trend is corroborated in the *State of the World 2004* report with studies showing that overall social health has declined in the United States in the last thirty years despite higher levels of consumption.[4]

The "Marxist," or socialist, critique objects primarily to the exploitation of workers in the capitalist economic system. The production of a common cotton T-shirt, for example, means farmworkers are exposed to intensive toxic pesticides and garment workers in sweatshops work long hours for low wages. From the Marxist perspective, consumerism can also be seen as a distraction or opiate, leading workers to seek satisfaction in goods rather than improve the abusive profit-driven workplace. The last of Schudson's list, the "aristocratic" critique, focuses more attention on aesthetics, attacking mass-produced goods as ugly. That which is rare or exclusive holds the greatest value, thus generating a classist sense of privilege.

Perhaps the strongest critique of consumerism today is being mounted by environmentalists. Thirty years ago concerns about population growth and the earth's limited resources were the primary topics of environmental debate. But since the 1992 Rio Earth Summit, the global South has made it clear that the wasteful consumption of the North is of equal concern. It points out that the North is generating far more significant ecological damage with its high use of water, oil, minerals, and timber. Some have described this as casting an "ecological shadow" on the middle-income and poor classes who bear the burden of the hidden economic and moral costs to the environment. Environmentalists point to industrial nations' oversized ecological footprint. This is the land necessary to sustain current levels of resource consumption and waste discharge. The average American has a thirty-acre footprint—if everyone lived like this, we would need five more planets to support human existence. Though world population may level off by midcentury, environmentalists are concerned that consumption will only keep growing as more and more of the world's population enters the consumer class.[5]

BUDDHIST CRITIQUES

What can Buddhism contribute to these critiques of consumerism? Are Buddhist critiques simply a variation on the commonly expressed critiques above? Or can Buddhism offer a new approach that is helpful in today's galloping rush to consume the planet? Reflecting on this from my own perspective as a Zen student committed to environmentalism, I believe Buddhism offers something distinctive and very useful. As a new religion in the West with growing popularity, Buddhism holds the potential for not only challenging global consumerism but also for offering a practice path to liberation through the very thick of the tangle.

Sorting through my own questioning voices, I find three critiques that clearly derive from a Buddhist orientation.[6] The first critique focuses on the role of consumerism in the process of personal identity formation. The usual idea of self is seen as a significant delusion in Buddhist thought. Consumers in today's marketplace are urged to build a sense of self around what they buy. Consumer goods are symbols of status, political or religious views, social group, sexuality—all of which solidify a sense of self. "I am what I have" has become the operative slogan, using shopping to define identity. Advertising aggressively promotes self-involvement, playing on people's needs for security and happiness. When self-identity depends on products, the need for social acceptance can fuel addictions to brand names, to styles, and even to shopping itself. Consumerism can actually have a negative effect on self-identity, preventing the mind from engaging in more positive life-affirming activity.

From a Buddhist perspective, ego-based views of self are fundamentally mistaken, promoting ignorance and suffering. Deep identification with the separate self as autonomous and fixed prevents us from experiencing the world as relational and co-creative, always in dynamic flux. Material accumulation strongly reinforces this mistaken view. The more we relate to material objects as real and permanent, the more deeply we tend to think of ourselves as a fixed self with specific identity. More attachment, more need for consumer goods to prop up our identity. Or you could take the (false) position that *nothing* is real or permanent. If nothing is real, then nothing matters, so why not indulge in whatever momentary pleasure you like? With this logic you can successfully avoid engaging the actual relationships of the world that shape and condition your life. If nothing matters, why be concerned about the suffering behind consumer products?

A second Buddhist critique is that consumerism promotes, rationalizes, and condones harming. The foundational principle behind all Buddhist ethics is nonharming, or *ahimsa*, expressed as the first of the five precepts: "do not kill," or "do no harm." Monks were taught not to destroy "the life of any living being down to a worm or an ant."[7] This precept reflects the Buddhist understanding of interdependence—that the flourishing of life is a complex and ever-changing web of relationality. Killing or harming another being in the web has serious consequences, especially if you do so with the intention to harm. Such an act would show obvious disregard for the true nature of reality.

While consumer good manufacturers may not intentionally choose to cause harm, their actions nonetheless often leave death and injury in their wake. In some cases the choice is deliberate—to clear-cut forests, to pollute waterways, to abuse workers on the production line. Producers justify tremendous harm to many forms of life to meet the bottom line of profit and gain. Slavery is not uncommon even today.[8] Harmful actions produce negative karma, leading to lower rebirths and increased suffering, while minimizing harm leads to positive karma and less suffering for self and others.

Perhaps the strongest Buddhist critique is that consumerism promotes desire and dissatisfaction, the very source of suffering, as explained in the Four Noble Truths. The state of dissatisfaction—clinging, craving, impulse, thirst, attachment, compulsion—could not be more opposite to contentment and equanimity. Craving in its most fundamental sense is the desire for existence. Just to want to exist or be alive is a basic biological drive. Often identified in terms of karma and rebirth, craving is the "thirst that gives rise to repeated existence." Marketers play on this strategically, stimulating this desire to be alive through delicious foods, powerful cars, and exotic vacations. Craving also includes aversion, the desire for *non*existence. In this case one craves relief or escape from what is unpleasant or undesirable—mosquitoes, for example, or a heat wave or maybe just bad body odor. Marketers take advantage of this too, offering a parade of products that profess to relieve almost any form of human suffering.

Early Buddhist teachings describe the results of desire in terms of four types of clinging or attachment.[9] The first is clinging to sensing and sense objects. Graphic examples are consumer addictions such as tobacco or alcohol and their attendant sensory pleasures. The second is clinging to views and values that reinforce a sense of self. The desire to promote one's views or sense of what is "right" can afflict consumers (as well as their critics). The third result of desire is clinging to actions. Attachment can develop around behaviors necessary to support consumer values. Choosing what to wear, what and what not to eat, and who to please all become part of the consumer's identity, carefully analyzed by market specialists. The fourth, self-clinging, means literally clinging to one's own sense of identity as subjectively experienced. This is the attempt to bridge the sense of fragmentation that arises from experiencing things as separate. Paradoxically, identity building exacerbates the gap it is trying to eliminate and thus can never bring satisfaction.

Of the three Buddhist critiques, we can see that some overlap with traditional critiques yet also offer distinctive contributions to this discussion. The Buddhist critique that consumerism promotes a false sense of self might parallel the Puritan critique of material goods as distractions from spiritual development. The Buddhist concern for nonharming would reinforce the Marxist critique regarding worker exploitation. But the Buddhist focus on desire in promoting an endless cycle of suffering may be the most penetrating critique. Awakening or enlightenment rests on realizing the all-pervasive nature of this existence-based drive. Taking up the study of desire in the form of consumerism offers an endless field for spiritual practice. With the structure of this critique firmly in mind, the consumer beset by desire can plunge into the tangle, seeking insight in the midst of confusion.

BUDDHIST METHODS FOR LIBERATION

What, then, are some useful liberative methods to relieve the suffering of consumerism? Taking consumerism as the context, we can look to traditional methods of insight and practice for cultivating enlightenment. Here I offer one approach for each Buddhist critique of consumerism. The first provides exposure to the process of identity formation; the second offers guidelines for nonharming; and the third describes the specific links that perpetuate desire.

Exposing Identity Formation

The first Buddhist critique points out that the problem with consumerism is its constant reinforcement of ego identity. Misunderstanding the self as either fixed or insubstantial misses the empty nature of self. This is almost impossible to grasp through armchair reflection. You need a more vigorous method to challenge the false views of the consumer self.

In Dogen's well-known verse from the *Genjokoan*, we find one approach to dismantling these false views:

> *To study the Buddha way is to study the self*
> *To study the self is to forget the self*

> *To forget the self is to be confirmed by the myriad things*
> *To be confirmed by the myriad things is to drop off*
> *body and mind of self and others.*[10]

Zen priest Shohaku Okumura explains that the original Japanese word for "study" in Dogen's text was *narau*. This derives from *nareru*, which means "to become familiar or intimate with."[11] Dogen approaches this in the biggest sense—studying one's mind, body, sense organs, speech, and social relations as deeply conditioned by self-centered needs. Studying and forgetting the self, in Dogen's view, is fundamental to becoming authentically human.

How does one study the consumer-constructed self? Suppose I really love drinking tea. (I do.) I can study how my self is constructed around drinking tea. I can observe my preferences for a certain brand or tea shop. I can study my pleasure: What delights me about the act of drinking tea? Is it the flavors, the stimulation, the social company? (All of the above.) I can study my memories of drinking tea and see how they add up to a specific subjective identity as a tea drinker conditioned over time.

Looking closely at any one of these aspects of my self as a consumer of tea, I see how dependent my idea of self is on conditions outside my "self." Time of day, quality of tea, source of the water, mind of the tea preparer— all of these contribute to my experience of tea. There is no such thing as my separate self enjoying the separate tea. It is all happening at once. Observing the endlessly connected web of tea conditions and relations, I go beyond the small self. I see myself as part of the co-creating universe, my inflated self-identity as tea drinker busted. The delusion crumbles.

"Self and all others are working together. The working done by self and all others are called our actions."[12] Okumura points out that we think "we" are "driving" a "car." But actually the "car" is "driving" "us." The car we drive is being driven by the oil economy, its parts produced across the globe. Our driving is the action of highway builders, car designers, city planners, and congressional policy makers. All these beings contribute to our existence, poking us to let go of confused views of a separate self.

But how is this "dropping off body and mind?" Dogen's teacher Nyojo said, "Dropping off body and mind is zazen. When we just practice zazen, we part from the five desires and get rid of the five coverings."[13] The five desires come from contact with the five sense organs, generating a false sense of self that is attached to the pleasures or aversions we experience with our senses. The five coverings are the hindrances of greed, anger, sleepiness, distraction, and doubt that keep our minds from functioning in a healthy way. Discarding sensory attachment and hindrances is one path to deflating the consumer self. Studying deeply the myriad aspects of my consumer identity, I see into the delusion of self as consumer, of self as anything separate from anything else.

The insights from studying one type of attachment can be applied from one context of consumerism to another. Studying my self as tea drinker gives me practice experience to study my self as consumer and producer of knowledge, for example. (I am quite attached to my books.) Seeing how self-construction works, I am less gullible to the consumer industry and its endless hooks (including the hooks of books). I can check my psychological conditioning as I lean toward various book purchases. But this self-examination is not in itself the experience of enlightenment. Zazen provides a deeper ground for awakening to the actual experience of the selfless state. This more profound level of insight only strengthens your capacity for seeing through the lures of the consumer self.

Practicing Nonharming

The second Buddhist critique of consumerism is that it promotes harming. This critique raises questions of right and wrong—how do you decide what is harmful in the realm of consumerism? The Buddhist texts on ethical behavior offer specific guidance in the form of the Five Precepts: not killing, not stealing, not abusing sexuality, not lying, and not using or selling intoxicants. The precepts represent practices of restraint, calling for personal responsibility for reducing environmental and human suffering. Taken together they indicate choices one can make to avoid harming others.

I will work primarily with the first precept here, though each precept can apply to aspects of consumerism. The first precept is the practice to abstain from "destroying, causing to be destroyed, or sanctioning the destruction of a living being."[14] A living being is anything that has life, from a small insect to a complex forest. Clearly, every act of consuming raises the issue of harm—just to stay alive we have to eat food that has been killed or harvested. Accepting this paradox, we nonetheless can choose *how much* harm we want to be responsible for. For example, many people practice vegetarianism because they don't support the harming of animals from industrial agriculture.[15] Others eat organic fruits and vegetables to reduce harm to soil from chemical fertilizers and pesticides. Some avoid fast food because of labor exploitation and human health impacts.

Consumer awareness movements are now promoting "chain of custody" verification that can document the source and treatment of material goods. Forest certification and green building are two arenas where knowledge of production processes have given consumers the option to choose more ethically produced goods. Buying locally often shortens the chain, making it easier to track harmful impacts. Under pressure from students and the Environmental Council, my campus at the University of Vermont is now including green building standards in new capital projects. Our neighboring campus at Middlebury College has used locally certified wood products throughout its new science building.

The precept of nonharming can also be stated as a positive commitment to practice metta, or lovingkindness. One version of the metta verse is:

> *May all beings be free from enmity, affliction, and anxiety, and*
> *live happily.*
> *May all breathing things, all who are born, all individuals of*
> *whatever kind be free from enmity, affliction, and anxiety—*
> *may they live happily.*[16]

Actively holding this wish for all beings makes it very difficult to participate in their harm. Quite the opposite—you want all beings to flourish and thrive and be free from the impacts of human excess. I think of the blunt checkerboard of clear-cut forests in my home state of Oregon: it has been so painful to witness the fragmentation of the Northwest forest. Offering the metta verse, I wish for kindness to these forests—may they be free from profiteering and politics, may they live happily.

Traditionally the precepts, including nonharming, have been oriented toward individual conduct; the Buddha did not offer a counterpart set of moral guidelines for institutions. Because social structures (governments, schools, churches, and so on) contribute to consumer-related harming, ethical guidelines for social structures would also be useful. Individuals and institutions influence each other. More conscious standards of restraint in public arenas (such as no advertising in schools) can encourage greater personal practice of nonharming, and the reverse can also happen. This means holding social or institutional agents accountable for the impacts of their actions. By taking the initiative here, consumers could reclaim moral integrity that has been eroded by consumerist agendas. It is not necessary for one to have perfected moral practice before asking others to consider their own actions. The point of the precepts is to reduce suffering and to practice interrelationship rather than self-interest.

Breaking the Links of Desire

The third Buddhist critique is that consumerism promotes desire and dissatisfaction, the cause of suffering. A classic method for working with desire is the teaching of the *nidanas*, or causation. The Twelve Limbs (or Links) of Co-dependent Origination are sometimes portrayed as a wheel of becoming describing the process of reincarnation and rebirth.[17] But these can also be used to describe common patterns of causation that arise in each moment of desiring or grasping. Consumerism utterly depends on this process, reflecting its completely human nature.

The twelve links follow each other in order: ignorance, karmic formations, consciousness, name and form, six sense fields, contact, feelings, craving, grasping, becoming, birth, death, then on to ignorance, and the cycle continues. The pull of each link, based on the strong experience of the one that precedes it, is so powerful that we are continually in the grip of this metapattern. Release from this cycle of grasping and suffering is what the Buddha called nirvana. As consumerism is a never-ending field of desire, it offers an ideal platform for studying the twelve links.

We can start our study at any point in the cycle; for this discussion, let's begin with *craving*—for the latest Dalai Lama book, for instance. Craving is the experience of being hooked by an object, a thought, or a need and then yearning to grasp it. In the twelve-link cycle, craving depends upon *feelings* that arise following contact with objects in the sense fields. *I see the book, it feels good in the hand, the words feel good in my mind.* Feeling states in Buddhist psychology are categorized as pleasant, unpleasant, or neutral/indifferent. It doesn't matter so much whether one is happy, afraid, tender, or irritated; for each feeling, one either wants to perpetuate it (usually the pleasant feelings) or get rid of it (usually the unpleasant feelings). Since feelings are impermanent, advertisers or sales agents continually restimulate potential buyers to keep pleasant and unpleasant feelings going. This is done by generating a barrage of *contact* points for the sense organs, such as colorful displays, flashing signs, tantalizing café aromas. The point of contact is where the object of perception (book), the sense organ (eye and hand), and the sense consciousness (sight perception) come together. The bookstore provides the object; I, as consumer, provide the already conditioned sense organs and consciousness. To slow the production of feeling states and the craving arising from feeling, we can reduce the points of shopping-related contact.

The six *sense fields* of eye, ear, nose, tongue, body, and mind include both perception and consciousness shaped over time by *name and form*. This is the material form of a being—that is, your body, including your physical sense organs. What you perceive through your sense fields is completely conditioned by your experience. How I read the Dalai Lama's book is conditioned by hearing him speak, seeing his picture, even the memory of meeting him once. Considering the power of the sense fields, I wonder about young children watching hours of television—does their consciousness become dominated by products and brand names?

Name and form are conditioned by previous experiences that mold *consciousness* and the material form it takes. Such conditioning is well documented for alcoholism and other addictions. Repeated use of alcohol changes people physiologically so they are more attracted to the states induced by alcohol. Apply this conditioning to other forms of excess consumption and you can extend the addictive cycle to luxury foods, designer clothing, and television serials. Advertisers do their best to capture teenage consumer consciousness by imprinting brand-name loyalties for cigarettes, beer, and hygiene products at an early age. Teen product companies even hire teen trendsetters, passing out free samples to establish brand loyalty. Resisting the slogans of consumerism becomes one way to break the conditioning that is being so aggressively promoted.[18] Culture-wide consumer consciousness eventually results in long-term *karmic formations*, which will require culture-wide attention to transform.

Turning back to craving, we can see how craving perpetuates the other limbs. In craving pleasant experiences, one grasps after their continuation; in craving the absence of unpleasant experiences, one grasps after their cessation. These forms of grasping are especially strong where the ego or sense of "I" attaches to what is craved or avoided. Marketers are masterful at using human grasping to create specialty niches; even green consumers and dharma practitioners are now well-established market groups.[19] No one is immune from having his or her identity needs worked for profit. Breaking the energy in this part of the cycle is especially challenging. *Grasping* generates *becoming*: the more one grasps after consumer goods or values, the more one becomes a consumer, leading to "*birth*" of the self-identified ego that defines life primarily as consumption. Thus we have the phenomena of suburban "mall rats," Tupperware queens, and eBay treasure hunters.

Eventually, of course, the consumer must confront the twelfth limb—*death*—when the self can no longer be propped up by possessions. Fueled by *ignorance* of the nature of dependent origination (compounded by massive denial in consumer culture), karmic traces carry over from previous actions or lifetimes. Consider the alcoholic father who models the pattern of alcohol abuse to his son, or the shopaholic mother who fosters an appetite for fashion in her daughter. From generation to generation, consumer consciousness flourishes, feeding the cycle of causation driven by desire.

Observing the nature of co-dependent origination can provide a penetrating tool for analyzing consumerism. The cycle can also be studied in terms of cessation as well as origination. Breaking the driving energy from one link to the next slows down the desire-generating cycle. If you reduce contact with consumer stimulants such as television, your sense fields are less flooded with product messages. If you overcome a debilitating addiction, that craving has less impact on your consciousness. The point here is not that the cycle of causation can be brought to a halt, since beings keep taking form and are conditioned just by existing. But by applying mindfulness, one can observe the process and even learn to unhook from the craving. Each moment of consumption can thus be an opportunity for insight, tasting, if only in a small way, the freedom from grasping and dissatisfaction.

PRAGMATIC RELIEF

The Buddha told his followers that his teachings should offer pragmatic relief for their suffering. If they weren't useful in everyday life, then the teachings were not of value. It seems to me that Buddhist methods of working with consumerism offer very practical methods to address the suffering it generates. Consumerism is a dominant practice field of our times; if the Buddha's teachings have merit, they can be applied to untangle the complex web of all-consuming relations.

For me, this work is an ongoing personal experiment in resisting the invasion of consumer economics and consciousness. Does Buddhism help relieve the suffering of consumerism for me personally? The critiquing voices are never far away, but now I see them as wake-up calls, each one an opportunity for liberation. Hearing about slavery on cocoa plantations, I vow to practice nonharming and reduce my desire for chocolate. Reading about pesticides on strawberries, I vow to support my local organic farmers in the interdependent web. Studying the privilege that comes with first world status, I vow to study the twelve links that perpetuate global poverty.

Practicing deeply with consumerism may provide a very wide Dharmagate to awakening. Endless desire, endless suffering, endless cycles of consuming. The tangle fills the whole universe—how far into the tangle can the Buddha eye see?

Form and Elegance with Just Enough

Rita M. Gross

ASK FOR BUDDHIST ADVICE on almost any topic and you might well receive the answer, "Follow the middle way—not too much, not too little." Western appropriations of this advice almost always focus on the "not too much" component, for good reason. Excessive consumption and runaway greed are extremely evident in many Western contexts. Many sensitive commentators and thinkers struggle with the issue of how to encourage moderation in the face of the relentless message, "Happiness (or safety or security) is just ahead, if only you buy our product." This message is beamed at us nonstop by advertisers hired by multinational corporations seeking to maximize their profits. The quest for moderation in the midst of excess is especially poignant and urgent because so much of the world lives with far, far too little.

However, the Buddhist slogan also contains the phrase "not too little," which is rarely applied in discussions of how to encourage moderation rather than overconsumption. Could guidelines about what constitutes "too little" actually help rein in excessive consumption? This essay will explore such a counterintuitive proposition.

My contemplations of this possibility are taken up in the context of the Buddha's life story, of how he discovered each guideline in turn. What could otherwise seem like abstract speculation becomes concrete when we think about his life and how it unfolded. The canonical stories tell us that as a young man from a wealthy family, the future Buddha enjoyed a life of luxury. Many accounts spare no effort in detailing this luxury: the three palaces—one for each season—the women at his beck and call, even the culture of music and dancing readily available. The young prince was the best at everything he tried—the best archer, the best wrestler, the best charioteer—learned and cultured in all the arts of his day. The stories also say that Siddhartha was protected from any awareness of certain basic facts of life such as illness, old age, and death by his ambitious father, who wanted to ensure that his son *not* be interested in seeking another way of life.

Siddhartha's curiosity led him to leave his palace, whereupon he saw in succession a sick person, an old person, a corpse, and a world renouncer, the last of whom seemed more serene and contented than anyone he had ever seen. The future Buddha realized that his lifestyle, which could be seen as the epitome of modern pleasures, brought him no real happiness or satisfaction. He decided to leave his life of privilege and set off on a quest for understanding. His lifestyle then swung to the opposite end of the spectrum. He practiced severe asceticism in an attempt to starve himself into true awakening, seeing everything that had formerly promised satisfaction as an enemy to be overcome.

The textual accounts of this phase of the Buddha's life are also quite graphic. He starved himself until, pushing his hand against his stomach, he could feel his spine; he sat between several hot fires on a torrid day. After years of extreme austerity he saw that such a course of action was equally futile, that self-denial was not bringing liberation, contentment, and happiness either. He suddenly realized that a sensible middle path between overindulgence and self-torture would be far more productive. Deciding to bathe and eat food again, the future Buddha endured the scorn of his fellow ascetics but attained enlightenment very shortly thereafter.

It is just as significant that the Buddha found no real peace while practicing extreme self-denial as that he found no real satisfaction in his luxurious palace life. Self-denial is no more effective than self-indulgence in solving the problems of greed and grasping leading to suffering. Suffering due to hunger, thirst, and lack of shelter does not promote spiritual well-being; it only increases attention to the suffering self. And when the deprivation is not self-chosen, the focus on the suffering self becomes all-absorbing, making genuine detachment and tranquillity very difficult. Furthermore, voluntary self-denial often leads to self-righteousness, sometimes based on religious views of the body and material world as unimportant or problematic and therefore to be minimized or avoided. Such a view is simply not compatible with Buddhism as I understand it.

Undue emphasis on not consuming too much can be ineffective and therefore may not be the best course of action. People tend to respond to lectures about the need to cut consumption more often with resentment or guilt than with any actual change in lifestyle. In my view, real lifestyle changes are more likely if the changes lead to a greater sense of well-being rather than a continual sense of restraint and deprivation. Because of this psychology, I suggest that exploring the "not too little" component of the Middle Path has a great deal to add to the commentaries on "not too much" in regard to excessive consumerism. The Middle Path involves not consuming too much, but it also involves a proper appreciation of form, of the phenomenal world, and an accurate understanding of how to work with our embeddedness within that world. That is part of the "not too little" component of the Middle Path. This delicate balance, I suggest, is one key piece of a Buddhist understanding of issues of consumption and overconsumption that may not often be noticed. People may well consume too much precisely because they lack techniques for appreciating the phenomenal world, the world of form. Their greed may well be tamed by learning how to appreciate deeply what they do consume or what needs to be consumed to maintain a dignified life. Greed may be much more effectively tamed by such appreciation than by struggles to curb consumption based on guilt or feelings of obligation.

This insight comes to me from the teachings of my root guru, Chögyam Trungpa, and Buddhist practices I have observed in Asia. At a certain point in his work with Western students, Chögyam Trungpa Rinpoche began to train us in many practices that involved working with and appreciating the phenomenal world. These teachings are especially connected with the Shambhala vision that he began presenting after 1976, but they are also consonant with the general view and practice of Vajrayana Buddhism. He emphasized precision in arranging and placing objects, elegance in decorum and decoration, and concern for whatever would generate a sense of upliftedness. Some of these practices, such as beautiful shrines and shrine rooms, precise shrine room decorum, and treating teachers with respect and care, are traditionally Buddhist, but they had not been emphasized so much in Trungpa's early years in North America. Japanese-style flower arrangements were part of the new wave of material appreciation. Virtually no Shambhala Buddhist program will occur now without beautiful flowers, especially on the shrine and the teacher's side table. Creating and caring for the flower arrangements is part of the rota of work assignments at many Shambhala Buddhist centers. Colorful banners are also common at most events; for newcomers, they just add a sense of elegance, but for older students, each banner has symbolic significance and embodies certain Shambhala teachings.

Some of the other practices seemed less characteristic of traditional Buddhism and have often raised questions from other (Western) Buddhists. Advice about how to dress and how to eat, even how to arrange furniture in one's home, began to appear. Trungpa emphasized dressing well, eating good food, and upholding a general sense of personal decorum and elegance. Jewelry, too, became important, and now the Shambhala community has adopted a whole repertoire of pins that signal something about their bearers to other members of the community. At the concluding ceremony of Level Five of the Shambhala Training program, for example, participants are given a pin, which they are expected to wear especially at Shambhala events.[1] Another pin is given to those who complete Kalapa Assembly, the final program of the Shambhala Training sequence. Part of the etiquette of teaching the various levels of Shambhala Training involves remembering to wear that pin. Though I am somewhat casual about this etiquette, I am careful to remember to pack the appropriate pin when I am preparing to teach a Shambhala level.

Trungpa always emphasized that he was not talking about people spending a lot of money to present a more elegant appearance. Repeatedly, he stated that if one had developed a sense of dignity and style, one could put together beautiful outfits from used clothing. One does not need a lot of beautiful or elegant things; a few such things are far more satisfactory than a large closet full of ill-fitting, garish clothes. The same kind of advice was given regarding food and drink. Enjoying good food and eating with proper table manners was highly recommended. As part of this training, people were also taught how to serve formally both visiting teachers and each other. I have fond memories of programs at which I would be a server one evening and be served the next evening. I also became much more confident of my appearance without worrying about fashion or size. I did find some of the recommended forms, such as Viennese waltzing, rather stiff and unattractive, but by and large I found this training intriguing and helpful. My insight into the wisdom of this advice has grown over the years, until I now think that appreciating form properly is central to undoing habitual greed and overconsumption.

As people took this advice to heart and began to practice it, an aura of wealth began to develop in the Shambhala community. People looked good, even if they were not conventionally attractive, and they also seemed more content. There was less need for more and more. If one truly enjoys, with elegance and dignity, what one needs to consume, there is no need for more. Conversely, if that appreciation is lacking, one will never have enough, no matter how much one has.

Looking around the traditional Buddhist world, I see this aspect of the Middle Path that emphasizes appreciation of the phenomenal world and "not too little" being lived out in many ways. As I have had more experience living with Tibetan Buddhists in India, I have come to wonder if, in fact, Trungpa's advice about elegance and good appearance might not be rather traditional. I now suspect that North Americans who find his advice odd represent North American casualness and informality rather than a cogent interpretation of Buddhist values. On several occasions I have been with a group of pilgrims traveling in India with Khandro Rinpoche.[2] Gently but repeatedly she asks people to dress well, and her helpers explain that the local people make judgments about her based on the appearance of her Western students. On my most recent trip, she really wanted all the women to wear traditional formal Tibetan *chubas* (a woman's dress) and even directed a local tailor to make a number of *chubas* that the women could purchase as soon as they arrived. (She had even correctly figured out everyone's size.) Unfortunately, some of the women (not students of Trungpa's) insisted on wearing pants anyway on ideological grounds.

It is very common to look at traditional monastic lifestyles and notice the many practices of renunciation. But equally, one could notice aspects of monastic life that carefully delineate the "not too little" component of the Middle Path. One could note the dignity and elegance of traditional robes, perhaps made of patches sewed together, but also made of good fabric appropriate for the climate. In the Tibetan context, bits of brocade on the upper garment worn under the robes are not uncommon, and some are made entirely of brocade. Monastery grounds are well kept, often with beautiful gardens. The buildings are often impressive, adorned with artwork that expresses the vision of the form of Buddhism to which the monastery belongs.

Mindrolling Monastery, in Dehra Dun in northern India, the seat of Mindrolling Trichen, an important Nyingma lineage holder and the father of Khandro Rinpoche, is such a place. The centerpiece of the compound is a 180-foot-tall stupa with four levels inside.[3] Each level contains shrines to different figures important to Tibetan Buddhism and the Mindrolling lineage, including Shakyamuni Buddha, Padmasambhava, and the founder of the Mindrolling lineage as well as all his successors. The walls are covered with detailed murals depicting life stories of important teachers and various mythological figures important to Tibetan Buddhism; statues of buddhas, bodhisattvas, gurus, and *yidams* (meditation deities) are everywhere. A short distance from the stupa is a comfortable guest house for visitors, with a lovely view of the monastery complex. Perhaps most notable, however, are the grounds, with their many potted flowers and well-kept lawns, a great contrast to the crowded, dirty, and noisy streets just outside the compound. One group of plantings sets off a large pond with a fountain, which is turned on for a few hours in the evening. The entire setting generates a feeling of peace and serenity. Local people, both Buddhists and non-Buddhists, also appreciate the appeal of the compound; it is open during the day, and many local people come to rest, to pray, and simply to enjoy the place.

Clearly these and many other forms go well beyond merely functional needs. One does not need a 180-foot-building to house the ongoing ritual life of the monastery (for which the first floor is used extensively). A pond and a fountain are completely unnecessary from a purely functional point of view. Brocade on the top garment worn under the robes is likewise not necessary. Why does the Middle Path, as expressed in monastic institutions, consistently involve consuming *more* than the barest functional minimum? There must be some clues embedded in these practices that tell us how properly consuming "not too little" helps us overcome grasping and greed.

Such elegance and beauty in the monastic lifestyle, indeed in religious forms altogether, could be and have been criticized as unnecessary, as

somehow inimical to the spirit of Buddhism, with its emphasis on renunciation. Anticlerical and antireligious movements and ideologies, including
socialist movements, have made such criticisms of all religions, not just
Buddhism. They claim that the buildings and artwork are merely ways to
hoard wealth and that such practices demonstrate the hypocrisy of religions, especially those whose founders lived in relative poverty. The money
could better be spent on various relief projects, they say. While it is possible
to argue that such displays sometimes go beyond the guidelines of the Middle Way into "too much," I would argue that usually they express instead
the "not too little" aspect of the Middle Path. The minimum for sheer physical survival is "too little," and trying to live with too little does not lead to
peace and freedom. An aesthetic dimension, a way of working with form
that expresses elegance and dignity beyond sheer physical survival, does
seem to promote true peace, given that such aesthetic practices recur over
and over throughout the Buddhist world. But before this point can be fully
developed, it is necessary to return to the Buddha's life story and the practice of "not too much."

NOT TOO MUCH

The Buddha's life story provides further clues about the Middle Path. First
he discovered that "too much" wasn't satisfactory; then he discovered that
"too little" was equally problematic. I think the discoveries have to be in
that order, and also that the sequence is especially important for those of us
who have plenty of opportunities to consume too much. According to Buddhist psychology, humans have a deeply ingrained habitual pattern never to
be satisfied and to always grasp for more. That is the nature of samsara, the
ultimately unsatisfying way of dealing with life, which the path of Buddhist
practice seeks to remedy. With little advice on how to appreciate form and
the phenomenal world, it is not surprising that the religion of the marketplace,[4] the practice of consuming as much as possible in an attempt to allay
existential anxiety, is so successful. It appeals to deep-seated habitual patterns that have been ingrained over countless lifetimes, according to the
traditional Buddhist perspective. This "religion" features the cultivation of
desire and promises that the right car, the fastest Internet connection, and
the most convenient loan to cover those purchases will make people feel

better. Competing visions of fulfilled desire are offered to consumers, at-tempting to assure them that if one version of salvation through consump-tion fails, there will always be another one that might work.

From a Buddhist point of view, this logic is completely and fatally flawed, of course. The cultivation of desire is the problem, not the solution, both because desire is insatiable, as new desires immediately arise to replace those temporarily satisfied, and because the state of being filled with desire is itself painful.[5] It is difficult to imagine how genuine satisfaction could be built on a foundation of denying Buddhism's Second Noble Truth, which states that the cause of suffering is ignorance rooted in desire—exactly what the religion of the marketplace promotes.

Nevertheless, it is difficult even for long-term practitioners to fully grasp the futility of trying to satisfy desire completely, once and for all. The siren song, "next time it will work," is extremely alluring. Without alterna-tive training in renunciation and appreciative consumption, the habitual patterns of mindless and excessive consumption will prevail. Like us, the future Buddha had many opportunities to consume too much, so it is not surprising, and probably necessary that the Buddha first discovered the un-satisfactory quality of consuming "too much" before he could learn the middle path and recognize that "too little" is also a problem.

As is often observed about swinging pendulums and major shifts in be-havior, it is usually necessary to go to the other end of the spectrum before things can settle into the Middle Way. Thus, in Vajrayana Buddhism, espe-cially as taught in Shambhala Buddhist centers, the path is regarded as a progressive unfolding, the first stage of which is about renunciation, sim-plicity, and slowing down so that one can see one's situation more clearly.[6] First, opulent consumption must be renounced. Such renunciation is the necessary foundation for going further, for having the ability to enjoy beauty and elegance without grasping and attachment. If beauty and ele-gance result in attachment rather than uplifted peace and dignity, then one can hardly claim to be practicing the middle path and not erring on the side of "too little." Rather, one still needs to reach a point where attachment is not the ruling passion and "too much" no longer seems attractive. Given that grasping and greed are endemic habitual patterns ingrained over many lifetimes, such a stage of practice is seen as necessary for most people.

In this initial period of practice, one works especially to see how coun-terproductive attachment is, how attachment and greed never bring any lasting peace but only increase the amount of pain one experiences. At this stage, learning how to renounce the feast of discursive thoughts, wandering mind, and attachment to one's own opinions is especially important. Though one may renounce things or activities in order to spend time in meditation practice, attachment itself is the primary thing to be renounced. As the Kagyu lineage chant used by Shambhala Buddhists says:

> Renunciation is the foot of meditation, as is said
> To this meditator who is not attached to food and wealth
> Who cuts the ties to this life
> Grant your blessing so that I have no desire for honor and gain.[7]

Notice that food, wealth, honor, or gain are not the problem, not what needs to be renounced. Rather, attachment and desire are what must be given up. Though renunciation of attachment and desire can be fostered by a simple lifestyle, the main point is to develop a state of mind that is not so consumed by attachment and greed.

This first level of training provides a foundation that is never left behind in the practice of later stages of the path. In fact, one cannot successfully practice later stages of the path without this foundation of renunciation. Most people probably do not take their renunciation to the stage of severe starvation practiced by the Buddha. Nevertheless, things can be appreciated and enjoyed *only* if they can also be renounced; only a mind familiar with renunciation offers the peace and calm necessary for appreciating elegance and beauty without becoming attached to them. Otherwise one can still be hooked by neediness, and thus the religion of the marketplace continues its reign.

With genuine renunciation in place, the Buddhist alternative to the religion of the marketplace and the need for endless consumption can arise. This is the development of genuine peace, contentment, and happiness, rooted in detachment and equanimity. Sometimes it is not well understood that Buddhists seek genuine happiness rather than some grim stalemate in which desires are held at bay. For Buddhists it is not the case that the best we can achieve is desireless resignation to an unsatisfactory status quo, though Buddhism has been portrayed that way in older accounts. Some Buddhist discourse is suspicious of positive language, which makes it difficult to use terms like *contentment* or *happiness.* Nevertheless, such terms must eventually be used; the difficulty is to communicate the difference between trying to find happiness based on the satisfaction of desire, which is impossible, and happiness arising from living in the present without expectations and desires. Though these two may sound the same with only superficial acquaintance, they are quite different. Happiness based on the satisfaction of desire is always subject to disintegration, whereas happiness free of attachment can accommodate difficulty and disappointment without disintegrating. Buddhism can never be understood nor can its response to consumerism be fully appreciated if one ignores the central importance of genuine delight and pleasure, contentment, and peace of mind in the overall Buddhist vision of release and fulfillment.

At some point the student on the path does become somewhat detached, somewhat less driven by attraction to phenomena and the consequent grasping and attachment. It becomes clear through experience that the problem has always been the mind that is attached, not the phenomena to which it attaches. This fundamental point is often missed in discussions of attachment and detachment. The phenomena are neutral, not really the cause of grasping at all. Giving them up physically, though, is no guarantee of detachment; yet to a mind that is fundamentally detached, living in their midst does not threaten one's equanimity. This point is especially elaborated in Mahayana teachings, the second stage of the unfolding path of spiritual development as taught by Shambhala Buddhism and other forms of Vajrayana Buddhism.

The Mahayana bodhisattva or the Shambhala warrior[8] is pictured ideally as living in the messy and attractive world rather than in a safer, more isolated place. The attractions and woes of such a lifestyle no longer distract such a warrior as he or she goes about the fundamental task of trying to be of service in such a world. The bodhisattva's ability to live in the world without attachment is expressed in Mahayana art by the crowns and jewels they wear, in contrast to buddhas, who are always pictured wearing monastic robes. The image of the Shambhala warrior goes even further. Although the task of warfare is usually thought to be completely inimical to spiritual practice and attainment, these teachings use the image of the warrior to signify someone who is brave enough to look directly into all experiences, including fear. For the bodhisattva and the Shambhala warrior, things that normally involve intense attachment—wealth and warfare—are transformed through detachment into tools for living in the midst of ordinary people, providing help and comfort.

Vajrayana teachings and practices continue this trajectory. The lushness and sensuality of Vajrayana art and liturgy often seem quite discordant with other forms of Buddhism. Bejeweled "deities" dwelling in palaces of jewels and flowers, often portrayed in sexual union, might seem shocking as representations of enlightenment in many parts of the Buddhist world. Indeed, I have been in Buddhist-Christian dialogues where other Buddhists felt secure enough to voice their skepticism about Vajrayana sexual imagery, saying in effect, "Why *that*? It's so embarrassing! Couldn't you think of some other way to express what you Vajrayanists are trying to say?" The Vajrayanist would answer that it is helpful to use the most striking and startling imagery to express a fundamental teaching of Vajrayana Buddhism—that seen as it is, free of the distortions brought about by grasping and attachment, the world is sacred, delightful, and enjoyable. Such images express the fact that the beautiful, appealing, sensuous phenomenal world actually becomes an aid rather than an impediment to awakening when it can be viewed as sacred rather than as a potential trap filled with desire-producing objects. The caution with which phenomena and pleasure must be approached when the mind is still easily seduced by attachment is no longer necessary. Mahayana Buddhists, and Vajrayana Buddhists to an even greater degree, suggest that once renunciation and detachment as states of mind are well in place, it is not necessary to avoid phenomena; indeed, worldly phenomena may even be helpful to the practitioner.

NOT TOO LITTLE

At this point in the unfolding path of spiritual development, the focus switches from "not too much," which is now an intuitive discipline rather than a self-conscious effort, to "not too little." On one level of understanding, this principle is rather straightforward. Buddhists have always recognized that minimal standards of physical and emotional security are nec-essary prerequisites for the successful pursuit of spiritual discipline. For example, in its discussion of the paramita (virtue) of generosity, the well-known Mahayana training manual *Gems of Dharma, Jewels of Free-*

dom states that gifts should be given in proper order: first the gift of material well-being, next the gift of emotional well-being, and finally, the gift of dharma.[9] This point seems rather straightforward; people cannot be expected to practice meditation when they must spend all their time trying to make a living, and it is difficult for all but the most advanced practitioners to appreciate emptiness in the midst of emotional suffering and turmoil. However, it helps explain why Buddhism is initially more attractive to well-off people, not only in North America, but in all situations in which Buddhism has been a new religion.

This suggestion that we must first meet peoples' material and emotional needs before dharma practice can be relevant also serves as a dharmic justification for the engaged Buddhist movement. This movement is regarded with skepticism by some Buddhists, who claim that political and economic concerns are irrelevant to Buddhists. Therefore it is important that the justification for engaged Buddhism be based on traditional dharma teachings rather than values purported to be non-Buddhist.

However, there may be more subtle and radical aspects to the guideline "not too little." To access these dimensions of the guideline, we need to return to contemplation of the practices discussed earlier. Why did Chögyam Trungpa advise his students to dress and eat well? Why did he encourage so much attention to precise and elegant forms? The answer may be found in one of the protector chants of Shambhala Buddhism, done especially in times of turmoil and negative influences.[10] The chant speaks of "the end of the five-hundred-year dark age,"

> *When sons do not listen to their father's words,*
> *An evil time when relatives quarrel,*
> *When people dress sloppily in clothes of rags,*
> *Eating bad cheap food,*
> *When there are family feuds and civil wars.*

The chant goes on to say that these activities provoke the wrath of certain negative forces, which then send turmoil, war, disease, and other calamities to fill the earth.[11] This is an extremely interesting assertion of cause and effect: because of undignified, depressing activities such as eating bad cheap food and wearing clothes of rags, negativity increases. Conversely, acting in a more dignified and uplifted fashion reverses that negativity, which is why

Chögyam Trungpa encouraged his students to eat and dress well (but not expensively).

How can the phenomenal world, the world of form, become an ally in the path of spiritual development? What might working with the phenomenal world, the world of form, and paying attention to the "not too little" component of the Middle Path have to do with consumerism? What's the problem with dressing sloppily in clothes of rags and eating bad cheap food? What would its opposite have to do with spiritual development?

The answer has to do with the effect that elegant, beautiful things have on the mind. In Shambhala Buddhist programs a great deal of attention is paid to the environment in which the teachings occur. In fact, the environment is thought to be almost as important as the quality of the dharma talk. It is often said that people usually remember very little content from the first talk they hear. But the overall environment, its dignity and aesthetic quality, along with the friendliness of the staff, are remembered and have a great deal to do with whether people return to the center. Flower arrangements and banners are especially prominent in setting the tone, but much attention is also paid to how various objects are placed in space and how they relate with each other. The Shambhala aesthetic calls for enough space between objects, with the whole pattern being coherent and harmonious. The result is a palpable sense of upliftedness and confidence that contrasts significantly with the depressed feeling that results from a dirty, sloppy, ill-arranged environment. Such an uplifted state of mind is much more conducive to spiritual growth and development than the depression brought about by lack of attention to the quality of one's environment. People may not be consciously aware of the impact of their environment on their state of mind, but the impact still occurs. Buddhists throughout the ages in all Buddhist cultures seem to be keenly aware of the relationship between beautiful, elegant forms and a more uplifted, serene, spiritually developed state of mind. Buddhist art and architecture across continents and traditions offer a potent testimonial to this understanding.

One might ask: "Are sloppy clothes and bad cheap food insurmountable obstacles?" The answer, of course, is no. For various reasons, one may be in a situation in which there is no possibility of clean, attractive clothing and good nutritious food. Then one practices equanimity, the one taste of the fundamental equality of all phenomena, so as not to be thrown off course by such negativities. But when there are alternatives, it is counterproductive not to use the beauty and delightfulness of the phenomenal world as an ally, drawing on its ability to encourage states of mind more in tune with enlightenment. Refusing to take advantage of such aids to enlightenment embedded in the phenomenal world or not knowing how to do so errs on the "too little" side of the Middle Path.

Such practices land us precisely in the middle of the Middle Path—not too much, not too little—and this is very relevant to consumerism. Usually consumerism is thought of as "too much," as erring on the side of overdoing, and in a superficial way that is correct. But why is there so much temptation to overdo? I think it sometimes results from too little appreciation of appropriate forms, of elegance and beauty. We are buried in a mountain of material goods with little sense of how to enjoy what we consume, because we have never been taught etiquette and elegance, because we do not have the practices and forms that would allow us to enjoy phenomena without being tempted to overindulge. As a result, we always want more. With a real understanding of how to work with the phenomenal world, one knows when enough is enough and knows how to enjoy what is enough.

One potent example is that of a flower arrangement. If one tries to put in one extra flower, the whole arrangement can be ruined. Likewise, an arrangement may need one more branch or flower. To enjoy it, to have the flower arrangement work to promote peace and contentment, it must be just right, just enough. But more important, unless one understands the form or guidelines for making a flower arrangement, one will probably not arrive in the middle of the Middle Path. Too little appreciation of beauty and elegance is counterproductive, and, in a situation in which material goods are abundant, underappreciation actually encourages consumerism and overconsumption. Thus, counterintuitively, one of the ways of discouraging consumerism may well be to encourage love of beauty, elegance, and dignity, so that we know how to enjoy the right amount. And I suspect that in many ways such a strategy is more effective than urging people to consume less out of guilt about the effects of their consumption on the rest of the world.

Consuming Time

David Loy and Linda Goodhew

The odd thing was, no matter how much time he saved, he never had any to spare; in some mysterious way, it simply vanished. Imperceptibly at first, but then quite unmistakably, his days grew shorter and shorter. . . . Something in the nature of a blind obsession had taken hold of him, and when he realized to his horror that his days were flying by faster and faster, as he occasionally did, it only reinforced his grim determination to save time.

—Figaro the barber, in Michael Ende, *Momo*

TODAY MR. FIGARO'S COMPLAINT is all too familiar. Even with so many labor-saving devices and efficiency measures, how is it that we seem to have so much less time? What social scientists call a "time-compression effect" contributes a manic quality to much of daily life. Increased stress at work and school, sleep deprivation, up to half the U.S. work population suffering from burnout, workaholism (and sometimes death from over-work), no time for family and friends, children left by themselves . . . it's not a pretty picture.

A 1992 survey by the U.S. National Recreation and Park Association found that 38 percent of Americans report "always" feeling rushed, up from 22 percent in 1971. More recently Joe Robinson in the *Utne Reader* claims that the United States has now passed Japan as the most overworked country in the industrialized world.[1] He reports that the husband and wife of an average U.S. household are now working five hundred more hours a year than they did in 1980. Lou Harris public opinion polls have shown a 37 percent decrease in Americans' reported leisure time over a twenty-year period, leading Harris to assert that "time may have become the most precious commodity in the land."[2]

But could commodifying time itself be the problem? Perhaps our problem with time is not so different from our problem with everything else we consume. By commodifying we convert things into resources for buying and selling. Today the earth and all its beings continue to be commodified in new and ingenious ways, such as the trading of carbon emissions and manipulating the genetic codes of biological species, including our own. With the profound impact of the industrial revolution, life was transformed into labor—work time—to be bought and sold, and hence also valued according to supply and demand. Our accelerating postmodern world has aggravated this development. Because we can never consume enough of it, the most precious "resource" of all has become time.

This suggests that if we want to understand consumerism, we need to understand how and why we consume time. This paper will examine time consumption with the help of the Japanese Zen master Dogen Kigen (1200–1253) and the German novelist Michael Ende (1929–1995). Dogen's classic text, the *Shobogenzo*, includes some of the most profound Buddhist reflections on time, more precisely, on the delusive duality we usually experience between ourselves and time, between events and the time they are "in." Michael Ende wrote many books apparently for children, including *Momo* and *The Neverending Story*. *Momo* is a provocative fantasy built on an insightful conceit: What if time *could* be saved, just like money? By exaggerating our preoccupation with time-saving, Ende reveals why time cannot be saved or consumed and why people who try to do so lose sight of what life is all about.[3]

Dogen's obscure and epigrammatical reflections on time are as incisive today as when he wrote them. *Momo* was published in 1973, presciently, for only since then has the temporal nightmare it depicts (or predicts?)

become our reality. Together Dogen and Ende can help us understand how we consume time today and how we might realize a more healthy alternative.

TIME COMMODIFIED

> Life holds one great but commonplace mystery . . . time. Calendars and clocks exist to measure time, but that signifies little because we all know that an hour can seem an eternity or pass in a flash, according to how we spend it. (*Momo*, 55)

Momo, the main character in Ende's novel, is a homeless, gypsylike street child who makes many friends because she has the marvelous gift of truly listening to others. As the plot thickens we find her resisting a secret army of men in gray suits who are slowly taking over the world. The author reveals later that they live by literally consuming other people's time. They deceive their "clients" by promising them more leisure in the future from their savings accounts in the Time Bank, but in return their victims must save as much time as possible now by speeding up their work, cutting social life, and in the process destroying all joy in life. The mottoes of the gray men (all too familiar to us today) are "Time is precious—Don't waste it!" and "Time is money—Save it!" (67).

At one point Figaro the barber is in a bad mood, feeling he is a failure and doubting the value of his existence. One of the gray men recommends that he save time by eliminating all the activities that in fact give his life meaning: the time he spends with his elderly mother, his social life, his reading, even his daydreaming. Suddenly he becomes future oriented, with disastrous consequences. "The determination to save time now so as to be able to begin a new life sometime in the future had embedded itself in his soul like a poisoned arrow" (65). Yet by changing his lifestyle he becomes increasingly restless and irritable. "People never seemed to notice that, by saving time, they were losing something else. No one cared to admit that life was becoming ever poorer, bleaker and more monotonous . . . [for] time is life itself, and life resides in the human heart, and the more people saved, the less they had" (68).

The story also targets consumerism of material things. Children turn up with new toys that offer nothing to the imagination, leaving them mesmerized but bored. The gray men tempt young Momo with Lola the Living Doll, a talking Barbie-type doll with a never-ending wardrobe of clothes, accessories, and friends to accumulate. It is the perfect toy to teach children a key economic lesson, that "there's always something left to wish for" (85).

Because of their ability to live fully in the present, children are believed to present a greater threat to the gray men's work than anything else. The men persuade adults to legislate against children's free time, arguing that children are the raw material of the future, so they must prepare to be the experts and technicians of tomorrow. In compulsory prisonlike child depots (modern schools and day care centers?), they are allowed only useful, educational games so that "they forgot how to be happy, how to take pleasure in little things, and, last but not least, how to dream" (167–68).

One of Momo's special friends is Beppo, a poor roadsweeper who is deliberately slow and Zen-like in his total attention to the present moment. In order to sweep all day long he had learned that it's no good to hurry. "You must only concentrate on the next step, the next breath, the next stroke of the broom, and the next, and the next. Nothing else. . . . That way you enjoy your work, which is important, because then you make a good job of it. And that's how it ought to be" (36). Because he takes all the time in the world to answer questions—being determined never to say anything untrue—Beppo is widely believed to be "not quite right in the head," and the gray men get him confined to a hospital. When he tries to escape, one of the gray men appears with the lie that Momo has been kidnapped, but she can be ransomed for one hundred thousand hours of Beppo's hard—and hurried—work. Beppo agrees and is released.

In the meantime Momo takes refuge in the magical residence of Professor Secundus Minutus Hora, where "all the time in the world comes from" (142). A sworn enemy of the gray men, the professor helps Momo find and release the gray men's secret hoard of stolen time-lilies. Deprived of sustenance, the gray men evaporate. The lily flowers fly back "to their true home in the hearts of mankind" and suddenly people find they have plenty of time to enjoy flowers and play.

Everyone's sense of time returns to normal—in *Momo*, at least. But have the gray men taken over our own world? Ende wrote this fable before he visited Tokyo, where we write this essay and where Ende must have observed the hordes of gray-suited "salarymen" inflicted with the fatal disease he calls "deadly tedium"—a tedium that motivates much of our escapism into consumerism. As this suggests, the gray men are not a Western or a Japanese problem but a modern problem. What does Buddhism have to say about the source of this problem?

TIME OBJECTIFIED

When asked why his disciples were so radiant, Shakyamuni Buddha replied:

> [My disciples] do not repent of the past, nor do they brood over the future. They live in the present. Therefore they are radiant. By brooding over the future and repenting the past, fools dry up like green reeds cut down.[4]

Mahayana Buddhist teachings can help us understand our present problem with time consumption by tracing it back to the basic dualism that we experience between things (including us) and the time they are "in." This dualism is in fact a fundamental delusion that contributes greatly to our duhkha, or unhappiness. Fortunately for us, this perceived split between things and their time is not something real or objective but something mentally constructed—which means it can be deconstructed.

The problem is not simply that everything dear to us (including—most of all?—ourselves) will pass away; nor is the solution simply to accept that impermanence. Such a response still presupposes the delusive duality between things and time. As Nagarjuna realized, if there is no permanence, then there can be no impermanence either, because the meaning of each is dependent upon the other: "All things are impermanent, which means there is neither permanence nor impermanence."[5] Without the things that are contained in time, time cannot exist as a container. Without nouns there are no referents for temporal predicates. When there are no things that have an existence *in* time, then it makes no sense to describe things as being young or old. "So the young man does not grow old nor does the old man grow old."[6]

Is that clear? Maybe not. If there are no things that exist in time, how are you able to read this book? Isn't it because you bought (or borrowed) it last

week? Nagarjuna's argument is, typically, too abstract to connect easily
with our everyday experience. Here Dogen's more concrete images can help
us. Dogen deconstructs the dualism between things and time by reducing
each term to the other. On the one hand, he demonstrates that *objects are*
time. Objects have no self-existence because they are necessarily temporal,
in which case they are not objects as we usually understand them. On the
other hand, he also demonstrates that *time is objects*. Time is not an objective container but manifests itself *as* the ephemeral processes we call objects, in which case time, too, is different from how it's usually understood.
"The time we call spring blossoms directly expresses an existence called
flowers. The flowers, in turn, express the time called spring. This is not existence within time; existence itself is time."[7] In his *Shobogenzo* Dogen
combines subject and predicate in the neologism *uji*, which is usually
translated as "being-time":

> "Being-time" here means that time itself is being ... and all being
> is time. . . . Time is not separate from you, and as you are present,
> time does not go away. . . .
>
> Do not think that time merely flies away. Do not see flying
> away as the only function of time. If time merely flies away, you
> would be separated from time. The reason you do not clearly un-
> derstand time-being is that you think of time as only passing. . . .
> People only see time's coming and going, and do not thoroughly
> understand that time-being abides in each moment. . . .
>
> Time-being has the quality of flowing. . . . Because flowing is
> a quality of time, moments of past and present do not overlap or
> line up side by side. . . . Do not think flowing is like wind and rain
> moving from east to west. The entire world is not unchangeable,
> is not immovable. It flows. Flowing is like spring. Spring with all
> its numerous aspects is called flowing. When spring flows there is
> nothing outside of spring.[8]

When time flows, there is nothing—*no thing*—outside of time. To treat
time as a commodity, then, is to be caught up in a delusion that makes us
hurry up in order to gain the time to slow down. This is just the trap that the
gray-suited time thieves encourage people to fall for. The commodifying
attitude that tries to save time cannot help but carry over into the rest of our

lives. Understanding time as a resource, to be used like any other resource, means we lose the ability to *be* time. Having become habituated to hurrying, it becomes difficult for us to slow down, even in situations when hurrying is inappropriate. How many people take their laptops and cell phones with them when they go on vacation? During a quiet afternoon lying on the beach, we still remember all those things we need to do.

Like Nagarjuna, Dogen also emphasizes that the relativity of objects and time implies that objective time-as-a-container-for-things is a delusion. If there is only time, then there is no time. I am being-time when I no longer situate my activities within another, constructed time understood as external to me. In place of the present as a thin, moving line between the immensities of past and future, I live *in* the "eternal now" when I nondually *become* whatever I am doing.

Dogen makes this point using the image of firewood and ashes:

> Firewood becomes ash, and it does not become firewood again. Yet, do not suppose that the ash is future and the firewood past. You should understand that firewood abides in the phenomenal expression of firewood, which fully includes past and future and is independent of past and future. Ash abides in the phenomenal expression of ash, which fully includes future and past. Just as firewood does not become firewood again after it is ash, you do not return to birth after death.
>
> This being so, it is an established way in buddha-dharma to deny that birth turns into death. Accordingly, birth is understood as no-birth. It is an unshakeable teaching in Buddha's discourse that death does not turn into birth. Accordingly, death is understood as no-death.
>
> Birth is an expression complete this moment. Death is an expression complete this moment. They are like winter and spring. You do not call winter the beginning of spring, nor summer the end of spring.[9]

Because our life and death, like spring and summer, are not *in* time, they are timeless. If there is no nontemporal being who is born at a certain time and dies at another time, then there are only the *being-time* events of birth and death. But if there are only those events, with no one that they happen *to*, then there is really no birth or death, because our notions of birth and death are dependent upon a person that they happen to. Instead, there is "just *this!*"—*tada* in Japanese. Shakyamuni Buddha is sometimes called the tathagata, literally "the one who just comes/just goes." Or we may say that there is birth-and-death in every moment, with the arising and passing away of each thought and act. Then there is nothing lacking in the present that needs to be fulfilled in the future, and spring is not an anticipation of summer. Each moment, each event, is whole and complete in itself.

In other words, the Buddhist solution to this aspect of our suffering involves realizing that I am not *in* time, because I *am* time. What I do and what happens to me are not events in time; they are the forms that time takes right here and now. If I *am* time, though, I cannot be trapped *by* time. Paradoxically, then, to *be* time is to be *free from* time. Momo is free because she lives in such a timeless world. It is not that she always *has* time for her friends. Rather, her way of listening to them is loving and nourishing because her being-time is open to their being-time. Figaro overlooks this, trying to save something that cannot be saved because time is not something we can ever *have*.

Momo also shows us that being-time is not only what we *are*, it is what *we* are. In individualistic cultures such as most Western consumerist societies, my time is *mine*. I protect and cherish it. I may need to sell a certain amount of it for money every week, but the rest belongs to me. I can spend it however I like; it is part of my disposable income. Today we take this for granted and base all our business and recreational planning on this premise. But premodern cultures show us that such an attitude is not natural or inevitable. Unfortunately, our possessive attitude toward time often encourages an indifference to civic concern, a lack of devotion to the collective that is necessary to address the enormous social and ecological issues we face. Without such collaborative participation, these problems are unlikely to be successfully resolved.

That Nagarjuna and Dogen both emphasize the problematical nature of this duality shows that our problem with time is neither modern nor Western. Contemporary time compression merely aggravates the split further, trapping us more deeply in delusion. Does this mean that objectifying and commodifying time as something we are *in* is a basic tendency of the human condition? Is this habit common to all cultures? Apparently not. In contrast to Western society, some premodern tribal societies lack awareness of objective time as an abstract reference point outside events. E. E. Evans-Pritchard's classic study on the Nuer of central Africa rather wistfully concludes:

> I do not think that they ever experience the same feeling of fighting against time or having to coordinate activities with an abstract passage of time, because their points of reference are mainly the activities themselves, which are generally of a leisurely character. Events follow in a logical order, but they are not controlled by an abstract system, there being no autonomous points of reference to which activities have to conform with precision.[10]

What is new today is modern technologies and forms of social organization that enable us to quantify time much more precisely. Commodification of time was made possible, and perhaps inevitable, by the clock. As clock time became central to social organization, life became "centered around the emptying out of time (and space) and the development of an abstract, divisible and universally measurable calculation of time."[11] The collective objectification of clock time means that now, insofar as we are social beings, we all must live according to this universal standard. The complexities of our social interactions require such a mechanism for their coordination, even though such a lifeless way of patterning time has led to an experience of it that is completely alien to the real world. Alien or not, most of the time we have no choice but to pay attention to the fact that in order to make that 10:00 A.M. class we have to catch the 9:16 bus.

In other words, time today *is* an objective container for us, for that is the way it has been socially constructed. But to live *only* according to that collective construct is to "bind ourselves without a rope," to use the Zen metaphor. With clock time, time is objectified and consumed as outside the activity and regulating it. With Dogen's being-time, in contrast, the temporality of an activity is integral to the activity itself. We can sometimes notice this difference in the way music is played. Either the notes march along precisely following the time signature, or we are so absorbed in those notes that we do not notice the time signature at all because the music nondually embodies its own time. The musical example is a good one because it reminds us that the solution is not always to slow down. Some music sounds better played fast. Many sports wouldn't be as much fun if you couldn't run. The point is to find the pace that is appropriate for the activity—or, stated even less dualistically, to let events generate their own temporality. Most of us know better than to make love watching the clock. Can we learn to "make love" to the whole world, in all our activities?

THE LACK OF TIME

If time commodification and consumption have become such a problem for us, why do we distinguish so sharply between clock (absolute) time and the events that happen "in" it? For Anthony Aveni, an anthropologist who studies different time systems, the common drive behind our temporal schemas is a quest for order, which is necessary to secure the cosmos and the self that inhabits it. "Temporally speaking, we desire the capacity to anticipate where things are going, to relieve our anxiety by peeking around nature's corner as far as it will follow."[12] Deeper than the desire for order, however, is what Damian Thompson describes in *The End of Time* as our "deep-seated human urge to escape from time which, in the earliest societies, was usually met by dreams of a return to a golden past."[13] Christianity changed that by situating us toward the end rather than the beginning of time, thereby promoting a golden future instead. In a crucial step toward modernity, the Italian hermit Joachim of Fiore (1135–1202) conceived of a coming golden age not outside of this world (in heaven) but *within* this world. This shift eventually gave birth to our modern preoccupation with progress.

Perhaps the difference between a golden past and a golden future is less important than the shared impulse to transcend time as we know it experientially, because its ineluctable course carries us all to a final destination we dread. In a poignant passage, Momo asks Professor Hora if he is Death, and he replies: "If people knew the nature of death, . . . they'd cease to be afraid of it. And if they ceased to be afraid of it, no one could rob them of their time any more" (144). Thompson sums up his study of apocalyptic time by concluding that the human understanding of time is always distorted by death: "The belief that mankind has reached the crucial moment in its history reflects an unwillingness to come to terms with the transience of human life and achievements. Our urge to celebrate the passing of time fails to conceal an even deeper urge to escape from it."[14]

In contrast, the Buddhist tradition begins with Shakyamuni's willingness to come to terms with the transience of human life and achievements. According to the traditional myth, it was Shakyamuni's encounter with an old man, an ill man, and a corpse that motivated his spiritual quest. Zen satori, for example, is sometimes called "the great death" because it involves ego death, "letting go" of the sense of self. From a Buddhist perspective, however, an explanation of time compression and commodification that focuses *solely* on death denial and symbolic immortality is inadequate.

That brings us back to the Buddhist emphasis on *anatta*—"no self" in modern terms—the claim that my sense of self is not something that exists independently but is rather a conditioned and ungrounded mental construct. Repression of this uncomfortable fact returns continually as a sense of *lack*: the feeling that "something is wrong with me."[15] We all experience this but understand it in different ways (I'm not rich enough, famous enough, loved enough . . .). Consumerism plays on this very effectively by offering to fill up our sense of lack with commodities. The implication is always that the *next* thing we buy will end our lack. Advertising surrounds us with images of attractive, smiling people who obviously feel no lack, and we too can be happy like them if we use the same products.

Another way to describe this sense of lack is that we don't feel "real" enough. If I feel ungrounded, the solution is to (try to) become more grounded, which is where religion traditionally comes in. It usually offers us this answer: Do this or that, and you will be saved. But what solutions are possible in a secular society focused on the individual? Now becoming real depends upon my own efforts—*which require me to use my time well.*

For Buddhism, then, the self is better understood not as a thing but as an ongoing *process* that seeks perpetually, although in vain, to feel secure by making itself more real. Since the modern, more individualized ego self is even more of a delusion, it is all the more unsatisfied with itself; and then on top of that, it must explain the dissatisfaction. The reason must be that I have not attained my goals. Since the goals I do accomplish bring no satisfaction, I need more and more ambitious projects . . . leading to more and more time compression.

In psychoanalytic terms, the pressure we feel to accomplish something is an internalization of the intentions we project outward into the world. Psychoanalyst Neil Altman noticed his compulsion to accomplish something during his years as a Peace Corps volunteer in southern India. Raised in an individualistic culture emphasizing achievement more than affiliation, Altman, like most of us, had been trained to use his time *efficiently*:

> It took a year for me to shed my American, culturally based feeling that I had to make something happen. . . . Being an American, and a relatively obsessional American, my first strategy was to find security through getting something done, through feeling worthwhile accomplishing something. My time was something that had to be filled up with progress toward that goal.[16]

The more we experience time as objective, the more alienated is the sense of self that is *in* time and therefore more desperate to *use* time in order to try to gain something from it. Greater, too, is our awareness of the always-threatening end of our own time through death. Our own sense of separation from time motivates us to try to secure ourselves within it. Yet according to Buddhism, the only satisfying solution is the essentially spiritual realization that *we are not other than time.*

Unfortunately, this self-defeating dynamic has taken on a collective social life that supports our modern preoccupation with economic expansion and technological development. As sociologist Max Weber pointed out, this historical process has become all the more obsessive because it has no particular goal except more and more. Ende also understood this. In a talk given in Japan in July 1985 and later published in the *Asahi Journal,* he spoke to his urgent concern to set human beings free from the obsession of economic growth.[17] Unfortunately, this obsession is now intrinsic to our economic system, which must keep growing if it is to avoid collapse. The technological challenge of how to produce things has more or less been solved, so the greater economic challenge for the developed or "economized" countries is how to stimulate ever more consumption among those who have the money to buy things.

But is our fascination with that game declining? I wonder if the attraction of the future is collapsing, if we are now psychologically "disinvesting" from both the individual and the collective projects—always future oriented—that we hope will make us real. Without faith in any spiritual alternative, however, we remain trapped in the future because that provides the only way we can think of to address our sense of *lack.* We try to "progress" faster and faster because we do not know what else to do, what other game to play. The more we suspect that we are headed nowhere, the faster we need to run. Fewer and fewer of us still believe that economics or technology will solve our world's problems and lead to a better life. The collective *lack* project of technological development is questioned by an increasing number of people. For those who still control the dominant institutions of government and corporations, however, the final stage of "progress" has become quantified into a one-dimensional game of economic growth as measured numerically by GNP and GDP.

How else can we deal with this pervasive sense of *lack*? If we accept the Buddhist denial of a substantial self, we open up the possibility of a this-worldly transcendence of self, realizing the nondual interdependence of a no-longer-alienated subject with a no-longer-objectified world. Buddhist awakening occurs when I realize that I am not other than that world. One way to express this is that I am what the world is doing right here, right now. This is liberating because it frees me from the self-preoccupation of always trying to ground myself in constructed reality. If *I* am not inside *my* body, looking out at the world outside, then *I* do not need to secure myself. Once *I* have realized this by letting go of *my self* there is nothing that needs to be made *real.*

So the final irony of my struggle to ground myself—to make myself feel real by filling up my sense of *lack*—is that it cannot succeed because I am already grounded in the totality. It turns out that my lack is a *lack* only as long as I dread it and attempt to fill it up. When I cease doing that, my lack transforms into the source of my creative energy, welling up from a fathomless source. Consumerism is so addictive because it seems to offer a this-worldly, commodified solution to what is basically a spiritual problem. Insofar as we are transformed spiritually, consumerism is revealed as a delusive way of thinking and acting that can never give us the secular salvation or happiness that it promises.

We cannot just ignore collective clock time as a social construction, but we do not need to be trapped within it. We become free of objectified, commodified time insofar as life becomes more playful. That is because play is what we are doing when we do not need to gain something *from* a situation. When we do not devalue the here-and-now in order to efficiently extract something from it, then there will be the time—the being-time—to smell the roses as we do our work with pride and loving care, as happens at the end of *Momo*:

People stood around chatting with the friendliness of those who take a genuine interest in their neighbors' welfare. Other people, on their way to work, had time to stop and admire the flowers in a window-box or feed the birds. Doctors, too, had time to devote themselves properly to their patients, and workers of all kinds did their jobs with pride and loving care, now that they were no longer expected to turn out as much work as possible in the shortest possible time. (235)

PART THREE

Buddhist Ethics of Consumption

13

Three Robes Is Enough

Ajahn Amaro

WHEN INDIVIDUALS ASK to take up the life of a Buddhist monastic, at the time of their ordination ceremony they make an agreement with their preceptor, the mentor responsible for their training. This elder says to the candidate: "Those who have gone forth from the household life should be prepared to robe themselves in scraps of thrown-away cloth, to eat whatever food is given to them as alms, to live at the root of a tree as their only shelter, and to use naturally occurring remedies as medicine for sickness. Do you agree to live by this standard for as long as you are a monastic?" The candidate answers: "Yes, I do."

Thus, at the very beginning of intensely focused spiritual training, one commits to train the heart to be content with the simplest standard of living. Of course, life often provides food, clothing, and shelter of a considerably higher standard and one can be very glad of that. Nonetheless, it is quite significant that this opening agreement explicitly links spiritual life and contentment with having little. In so doing, it demonstrates that contentment is a natural expression of spiritual practice.

Furthermore, this agreement is not just made once and then quietly shelved and forgotten. Monastics are encouraged to reflect daily on how they are relating to the use of their dwelling place, their clothing, food, and medical concerns. One is constantly refreshing one's attention to that

domain: "What am I taking for granted?" "Do I feel hard done by if someone else gets the better food?" "Am I fussy about which dentist I see?" "Do
I choose to wear patchy robes so that I can look more like a genuine ascetic than the others?" And so forth.

Each day Theravada monks in training recite these reflections:

> Wisely reflecting, I use the robes: only to ward off cold, to ward
> off heat, to ward off the touch of flies, mosquitoes, wind, burning
> and creeping things, only for the sake of modesty.
>
> Wisely reflecting, I use almsfood: not for distraction or for
> vanity . . . only for the maintenance and nourishment of this
> body, for keeping it healthy, for helping with the spiritual life;
> thinking thus, "I will allay hunger without overeating, so that I
> may continue to live blamelessly and at ease."
>
> Wisely reflecting, I use the lodging: only to ward off cold, to
> ward off heat, to ward off the touch of flies, mosquitoes, wind,
> burning and creeping things, only to remove the danger from
> weather, and for living in seclusion.
>
> Wisely reflecting, I use supports for the sick and medicinal
> requisites: only to ward off painful feelings that have arisen, for
> the maximum freedom from disease.[1]

Buddhist monastics are also subject to limits placed on the quantity or
quality of their material possessions. In the origin story for the first rule in
the discipline that deals with relinquishing inappropriate possessions, the
Buddha recounts how he was inspired to set such a limit:

> As I was walking on the road from Rajagaha to Vesali, I saw many
> monks coming along buried in robe cloth—with great wads of
> extra cloth piled on their heads, on their backs and on their hips.
> Seeing them I thought, "All too soon these foolish men have
> come under the spell of over-indulgence with respect to robe
> cloth. What if I were to set a limit, lay down a restriction on how
> much in the way of robes a monk should have?"
>
> Then traveling by stages I came to Vesali. There I stayed at
> the Gotamaka Temple. Now that time was the coldest part of
> the winter, and I sat outside wearing one robe and was not cold.

Towards the end of the first watch I became cold so I put on a second robe and the cold feeling abated. Towards the end of the middle watch I became cold so I put on a third robe and the cold feeling abated. Towards the end of the final watch, as dawn arose putting joy on the face of the night, I became cold so I put on a fourth robe and the cold feeling abated.

I thought, "Those who have gone forth as monastics, even those delicately brought up who might be afraid of the cold, are certainly able to get by with this amount in the way of robes. Suppose I were to set a limit and were to allow just three robes." So, monks, I allow you three robes: a double-layered outer robe, a single-layer upper robe and a single-layer inner robe—thus four layers of cloth.[2]

These basic standards of renunciation, simplicity, and frugality are contained within the code of conduct for all Buddhist monastics. In addition, the Buddha also allowed the possibility of refining this element of spiritual training even further for those who wished and for whom such greater austerities might be useful. This refinement is embodied in the thirteen *dhutanga*, or optional ascetic practices that the Buddha considered appropriate for his students.

As most people are probably aware, India in the Buddha's time as now was replete with yogis engaging in all kinds of austerities: standing on one leg for forty years, eating only cow dung, letting the fingernails grow until they pierce the flesh . . . the list is gruesome and infinite. Having once been just such an ascetic, the Buddha criticized self-mortification as an end in itself. So when allowing his disciples to take up more austere practices, he was very specific as to what was suitable and what was not. The list of things he allowed included eating only once a day, not lying down to sleep, living only on the food offered on the morning almsround and refusing extra food from the monastery kitchen, living at the foot of a tree rather than in a hut. By this small sample it can be seen that these austerities were designed to challenge the instinctual urges in the realms of food, sleep, and shelter, but they were not physically damaging or repulsive by the standards of general society.

Perhaps the most significant attributes of these austere practices were the stipulations that the Buddha placed around their use. He said that there were five reasons why someone might engage in such forms of spiritual training: (1) in the belief that by experiencing pain and difficulty they are burning up bad karma; (2) in the belief that by experiencing pain and difficulty they are creating good karma; (3) because everyone else does them and one doesn't want to be seen as a weakling; (4) because people praise those who follow such practices and one wants the praise; (5) for the sake of simplicity of living. Of all these reasons, the Buddha said only the fifth was noble and worthy; the other four were based on superstition, wrong view, or foolishness.

SIMPLICITY, MODERATION, AND CONTENTMENT

Although these guidelines are mostly derived from monastic training and lifestyle, it has always been the case that the broader Buddhist community of lay practitioners has taken its lead from and followed the spirit of the example set by the monastics. "Austere practices" and "renunciation" might seem far removed from the lives of ordinary folk holding down jobs, raising children, engaged in the ten thousand dimensions of worldly responsibility, but they embody a spirit of contentment and voluntary simplicity that is of inestimable worth to all.

Two of the most well-known and oft-recited teachings of the Theravadan Buddhist scriptures extol the virtue of *santutthi* or contentment. These verses, learned by every child in Southeast Asia from an early age, have guided the lives and cultures of Buddhist nations for centuries.

> *Avoiding those of foolish ways;*
> *Associating with the wise*
> *And honoring those worthy of honor. . .*
> *Providing for mother and father's support*
> *And cherishing spouse and child*
> *And ways of work that harm no being . . .*
> *Respectfulness and of humble ways,*
> *Contentment and gratitude: . . .*
> *These are the highest blessings.*[3]

This is what should be done
By one who is skilled in goodness,
And who knows the path of peace:
Let them be able and upright,
Straightforward and gentle in speech.
Humble and not conceited,
Contented and easily satisfied,
Unburdened with duties and frugal in their ways.
Peaceful and calm, and wise and skillful,
Not proud and demanding in nature.
Let them not do the slightest thing
That the wise would later reprove.
Wishing: In gladness and in safety,
May all beings be at ease![4]

There is a gentleness of spirit that is carried by these words, an encouragement to live lightly and respectfully with all beings. Central to these qualities is the principle of the Middle Way. This is the way of balance: neither neglecting one's own needs nor overinflating them, taking into account the environment we live in and the needs of our fellow beings as much as our own immediate concerns.

Another Buddhist term that is used frequently in reference to this principle is *matannuta*: moderation, or knowing the right amount. In his illuminating text *Buddhist Economics*, the contemporary Thai philosopher and social commentator Ven. P. A. Payutto suggests:

Matannuta is the defining characteristic of Buddhist economics. Knowing moderation means knowing the optimum amount, how much is "just right." It is an awareness of that optimum point where the enhancement of true well-being coincides with the experience of satisfaction. The optimum point, or point of balance, is attained when we experience satisfaction at having answered the need for quality of life or well-being. Consumption, for example, which is attuned to the Middle Way, must be balanced to an amount appropriate to the attainment of well-being rather than to the satisfaction of desires. *Thus, in contrast*

to the classical economic equation of maximum consumption lead-
ing to maximum satisfaction, we have moderate, or wise consump-
tion, leading to well-being. [author's emphasis] [5]

This principle of "knowing the right amount" may seem very simple, but as Ven. Payutto points out, it is very broad and deep in its application to our lives. It is as relevant to the marketplace and to the world of household-ers as it is in the lives of the monastic community. Our need as humans to give our hearts fully to the development of this quality was outlined by the Buddha in the *Ovada Patimokkha*. The Buddha gave this discourse shortly after his enlightenment, when the monastic community was growing and in need of some guidelines for the monks and nuns:

> *Patient endurance is the supreme practice*
> *for burning up unwholesome states . . .*
> *Restraining all harmful speech, hurting none,*
> *Being self-possessed in the way of virtue,*
> *Knowing the right amount in taking food,*
> *Having a secluded place for sleeping and meditation,*
> *Making efforts to practice with a pure heart:*
> *These are the teachings of all the Buddhas.*[6]

Perhaps the most significant aspect of this teaching was that every single person listening to this discourse was known by the Buddha to be already fully enlightened. That the Buddha felt it necessary to pass on this advice indicates the depth of the human habit of *not* knowing that subtle, perfect balancing point. It is as if he were saying, "Just because you are fully enlightened doesn't preclude the possibility of over- or underestimating your needs, or overlooking what might be appropriate to time and place." If it is difficult for an arahat, a fully enlightened person, not to overeat oc-casionally, it should come as no surprise that we also miss the mark from time to time.

The qualities of moderation and contentment have recently come under challenge in Southeast Asia. In the late 1950s and 1960s, as Thailand launched itself into the international marketplace, the Thai government of the time made the extraordinary move of specifically requesting that the leading abbots and teachers of the Thai Buddhist community not encourage *santutthi* and *matannuta* in the population.

In their drive to encourage productivity and consumerism, the political powers regarded moderation and contentment as obstacles to their program. Sad to say, most of the monastic community acquiesced to this request, being culturally conditioned to not cause conflict and to maintain the status quo. However, one prominent teacher, Ajahn Buddhadasa, had no fear of those in power. Although he had official ranks and titles, he was not at all worried about losing them if he spoke up. He came right out and openly challenged the politicians, asking them if they felt they were wiser than the Buddha: "Surely the Buddha would never have extolled qualities so highly and universally regarded if they were something that could possibly be harmful?"

Ajahn Buddhadasa showed how greed, selfishness, and wastefulness were actually the more harmful qualities, and that a healthy economy would need to be based on wholesome rather than unwholesome principles. Buddhadasa drew on the early Buddhist scriptures, warning that if the government pursued its chosen policies, it was likely to do more harm than good in the long run. Needless to say, he was heavily criticized for getting involved with politics and rocking the boat, but it was hard for anyone to fault him on his scholarship, his reasoning, or his straightforwardness. His voice was heard, and eventually the government ban on contentment was lifted.[7]

RENUNCIATION IN THE WORLD

Although many of the teachings quoted here come from the distant past, and even in their more recent translations still carry an aura of remoteness and antiquated religiosity, they nonetheless are talking about timeless qualities of the human heart. The greed, love, and wisdom of today are indistinguishable from those qualities as they occurred at the time of the Buddha. We might not habitually think in the language of "seeking sense pleasures" or "renunciation," but try substituting "material dependencies," "addictions," and "voluntary simplicity" and we suddenly find ourselves in familiar terrain.

Perhaps we can see that the spirit of renunciation and letting go of the compulsive pursuit of sense pleasure and material gain are indeed identical with today's aspirations to break free from the dictates of the consumer culture and the anxieties generated by advertising, peer pressure, and complacency. Thus these teachings can carry very useful messages for us here and now.

Raimundo Panikkar, in his book *Blessed Simplicity*, stated: "Not everyone has the inclination to take up the vocation of monasticism, but all of us have some part of us which is a monk or a nun, and that should be cultivated." This "inner monastic" describes that dimension of our being that is already utterly free, independent, whole—that does not need anything to complete it or for anything to be subtracted from it—and that is full of a radiant love for all beings. The formal outer life of a monastic—peaceful, respectful, unselfish, humble, nonpersonal, nonsexual, nonviolent—is designed to resonate with and support the realization and fulfillment of inner wholeness and self-sufficiency. As Martin Heidegger wrote: "Renunciation doesn't take; renunciation gives; it gives the inexhaustible strength of simplicity." Likewise in the words of Simone Weil, the highly regarded Christian philosopher: "We only possess what we renounce; what we do not renounce escapes us. . . . In general we must not wish for the disappearance of any of our troubles, but instead for the grace to transform them."

Renunciation and contentment were widely extolled in the Buddha's teachings. He realized that even though the majority of his students had no desire to pursue a lifelong monastic vocation, nevertheless the regular employment of renunciate principles would certainly help everyone to overcome the burdens of fussiness and neediness that exhaust so much of our energy and financial resources. The Buddha upheld basic moral standards encapsulated in the Five Precepts. On the lunar quarters he instituted a "one-day-a-week ordination" for those who felt a particular commitment to his teaching and wanted to deepen their insight and broaden their freedom of heart. Observance of the following eight factors forms a foundation for the practice of renunciation, and thus the capacity to choose simplicity.

When the Uposatha observance is complete in eight factors, it is of great fruit and benefit, radiant and pervasive.

1. Here a noble disciple reflects thus: "As long as they live, the enlightened ones abandon the destruction of life and abstain

from it; with club and weapon laid aside, they are conscientious and kindly, and dwell compassionate towards all living beings. Today I too, for this day and night, will do likewise. I will imitate the arahats in this respect, and the Uposatha observance will be fulfilled by me."

2. "As long as they live, the enlightened ones abandon the taking of what is not given and abstain from it; they accept only what is given, expect only what is given, and dwell with honest hearts devoid of the inclination towards theft. Today I too, for this day and night, will do likewise."

3. "As long as they live, the enlightened ones abandon sexual activity and live the celibate life, remote from sexuality, refraining from the practice of sexual intercourse. Today I too, for this day and night, will do likewise."

4. "As long as they live, the enlightened ones abandon false speech and abstain from it; they are speakers of truth, adherents to truth, trustworthy and reliable, no deceivers of the world. Today I too, for this day and night, will do likewise."

5. "As long as they live, the enlightened ones abandon wines, liquors and intoxicants, which are the basis of negligence, and abstain from them. Today I too, for this day and night, will do likewise."

6. "As long as they live, the enlightened ones eat only once a day and refrain from eating at night, from untimely meals. Today I too, for this day and night, will do likewise."

7. "As long as they live, the enlightened ones abstain from dancing, singing, musical performances and unsuitable shows, and from adorning themselves by wearing jewelry and applying scents and makeup. Today I too, for this day and night, will do likewise."

8. "As long as they live, the enlightened ones abandon the use of high and luxurious beds and seats and abstain from them; they make use of a low resting place, either a small bed or a straw mat. Today I too, for this day and night, will do likewise."

When, monks, the Uposatha observance is complete in these eight factors, it is of great fruit and benefit, radiant and pervasive. [8]

To his aunt and stepmother, Mahapajapati Gotami (also the former queen of the Sakyan people), the Buddha gave specific advice shortly after her ordination as the very first of his female monastic disciples. He urged her to renounce things that "lead (1) to passion, not to dispassion; (2) to bondage, not to detachment; (3) to accumulation, not to diminution; (4) to having many wishes, not to having few wishes; (5) to discontent, not to contentment; (6) to gregariousness, not to seclusion; (7) to indolence, not to the arousing of energy; (8) to luxurious living, not to frugality." Of such elements arising from material comfort, status, and wealth one should see: "This is not the Dharma; this is not the Discipline; this is not the Buddha's Teaching."[9]

Renouncing excess, appreciating what one has, monastics develop the capacity to render the heart supremely content with whatever the world has to offer.

GENEROSITY, WEALTH, AND FRUGALITY

As a counterpoint to his critiques of greed and materialism, the Buddha praised highly the qualities of unselfishness, generosity, and frugality. In a notable exposition on qualities conducive to harmonious communal living, he taught:

> As long as you show lovingkindness to your fellows in the spiritual life, openly and in private, in acts of body, speech and mind;
> ... share with your virtuous companions whatever you have received as a rightful gift, even down to the food you are eating; ... you may be expected to prosper and not to decline.[10]

Regarding the accumulation of capital, the Buddha did not praise or criticize wealth; he was much more concerned with people's actions. Ven. Payutto engaged the Buddha's ideas on wealth to support an alternative model of Buddhist economics.

> According to the Buddhist teachings, wealth should be used for the purpose of helping others; it should support a life of good conduct and human development. According to this principle,

when wealth arises for one person, the whole society benefits, and although it belongs to one person, it is just as if it belonged to the whole community. A wealthy person who uses wealth in this manner is likened to a fertile field in which rice grows abundantly for the benefit of all. Such people generate great benefit for all those around them. Without them the wealth they create would not come to be, and neither would the benefit resulting from it.[11]

According to early texts, the Buddha taught that the householder who shares his or her wealth with others is following the path of the Noble Ones. "If you have little, give a little; if you have a middling amount, give a middling amount; if you have much, give much. It is not fitting not to give at all. Kosiya, I say to you, 'Share your wealth, use it. Tread the path of the Noble Ones. One who eats alone eats not happily.'"[12] Some people make it a daily practice not to eat until they have given something to others. This practice was taken up by a reformed miser in the time of the Buddha, who said, "As long as I have not first given to others each day, I will not even drink water."[13]

As Ven. Payutto points out, when the wealth of a virtuous person grows, other people stand to gain. But when the wealth of a mean person increases, it is at the expense of those around him. People who grow more and more wealthy while society degenerates and poverty spreads are using their assets wrongly. Here wealth is not fulfilling its true function. It is only a matter of time before something in the system breaks down. If people use wealth wrongly, it no longer benefits others and instead becomes a hindrance, destroying human dignity, welfare, and community. In short, Buddhist teachings stress that our relationship with wealth be guided by wisdom and understanding of its true value and limitations. It is important that we not be burdened or enslaved by wealth. Instead we should be masters of our wealth and use it to benefit others.

The Buddha outlined four kinds of wholesome happiness that come from wealth:

(1) The happiness of ownership—so that one can reflect: "This wealth has been rightly acquired through my own honest efforts"; (2) the happiness of enjoyment—so one can reflect: "I

have derived benefit from this wealth and have been able to perform good works"; (3) the happiness of freedom from debt—so
one can reflect: "I experience pleasure and happiness as I owe no
debts, large or small, to anyone at all"; and (4) the happiness of
blamelessness—so one can reflect: "My actions of body, speech
and mind have all been innocent and blameless." The wise person, comparing the first three kinds of happiness with the last,
sees that they are not worth a sixteenth part of the happiness that
arises from blameless behavior.[14]

In another teaching the Buddha listed the benefits of wealth as (1) the
capacity to support one's family; (2) the capacity to support friends and peers;
(3) the capacity to safeguard one's possessions from thieves, confiscation, fire
or flood; (4 and 5) the capacity to support individual religious seekers.[15]

As one might deduce from these teachings, the Buddha was critical of
miserliness for being a waste of resources for the community, but also for
the individuals who were making themselves miserable, when they could
be bringing joy into their lives. There is an early story describing a rich old
miser who had recently died, leaving no heir to his huge fortune. The king
of Kosala pointed out that the old miser had lived on broken rice and vinegar and had worn the simplest clothing.

> The Buddha remarked: "That is how it is, Your Majesty. The fool-
> ish man ... supports neither himself nor his dependents. ... He
> does not make offerings. .... His wealth, accumulated but not
> used, disappears to no purpose. His wealth is like a forest pool,
> clear, cool and fresh, with good approaches and shady setting, in
> a forest of ogres. No one can drink, bathe in or make use of that
> water."[16]

Even though the Buddha criticized miserliness, he praised highly its
wholesome relative, frugality. Once again he considered the *attitude* behind what we do to be vastly more important than precisely *what* we
do. One of the best illustrations of the skillful employment of frugality
comes from an incident that occurred shortly after the Buddha's passing
away. Ananda, formerly his attendant for twenty-five years, had gone to

the city of Kosambi, arriving near the local king's pleasure garden. When the palace women saw Ananda, they went over to pay their respects and he heartened them with spiritual teachings. They were so inspired that they donated many lengths of cloth—enough for five hundred robes—to their beloved teacher. The king was indignant over the matter and went to see Ananda.

"But what can you, Honorable Ananda, do with so many robes?"

"I will share them with those monks whose robes are worn thin."

"But what will you do with those old robes that are worn thin?"

"We will make them into dust cloths, to line thatched roofs with."

"But what will you do with those dust cloths that are old?"

"We will make them into mattress coverings."

"But what will you do with those mattress coverings that are old?"

"We will make them into ground coverings."

"But what will you do with those ground coverings that are old?"

"We will make them into foot wipers."

"But what will you do with those foot wipers that are old?"

"We will make them into dusters."

"But what will you do with those dusters that are old?"

"Having torn them into shreds, Your Majesty, having kneaded them with mud, we will use them to patch any cracks there might be in the plastering."

Then King Udena thought: "These disciples of the Buddha use everything in a very proper, frugal way, they do not let things go to waste." And with that he bestowed yet another five hundred lengths of robe cloth on the Venerable Ananda.[17]

So, in contradistinction to miserliness, even though one might not be endeavoring to be acquisitive, our skillful relationship with the material world can end up attracting more abundance to us, and the result can be joyfulness rather than misery.

APPLYING THE TEACHINGS TODAY

There are many ways in which the values outlined in all these teachings can be usefully applied to the lives of people today. The principles point to specific ways we can guide our actions and attitudes to lead to the welfare and happiness of ourselves and the world. As we engage issues of wealth, generosity, moderation, and simplicity in the contemporary context of consumerism, we can consider these basic ethical principles taught by the Buddha.

In a discourse given to a layman called Tiger Paw, the Buddha taught that there are four things that lead to the welfare and happiness of family people.[18] First, whatever may be the means by which we earn our living—whether by farming, business, practicing therapy or teaching school, or by some other craft—we need to practice *persistent effort*: to be skillful and diligent, investigating the appropriate means to succeed at our work. Second, we need to practice *protection*, to guard the wealth acquired by our efforts and the strength of our faculties. This is taking proper care of righteous wealth righteously gained. It is wise to consider how we can invest or save our resources so that neither thieves nor the government can unjustly rob us, unloved heirs cannot make false claims, and the vagaries of the stock market cannot undercut our gains. Then we will be able to use our earnings to invest in wholesome alternatives to destructive materialism. Third, we should learn the value of *good friendship*, associating with people who are of mature virtue, accomplished in faith, generosity, and wisdom. This will help stabilize our community and support the ongoing flow of resources. Fourth, it is wise to lead a *balanced life*, neither extravagant nor miserly, so that our income exceeds our expenditures rather than the reverse. This means reducing debt and managing household and civic budgets wisely.

Further on in this discourse, the Buddha taught that there are four spiritual accomplishments that support a layperson's welfare and happiness. First, we should take up the cultivation of *faith*, developing confidence in the worth of a spiritual practice. This means trusting in the merits of the teachings and practices that point beyond pursuing self-centered needs. Second, it is important to establish a standard of beautiful *conduct* based on the Five Precepts. Such moral integrity is a great source of peace and happiness for us as individuals, as well as being a blessing and helpful example to those around us. Third, we should cultivate the practice of *generosity*. With a heart free of the stain of stinginess, one can be generous, open-handed, delighting in giving and sharing, bringing great joy to others. Fourth, we should make conscious efforts to calm the mind and develop *wisdom* through meditation. The Buddha's understanding of "wisdom" meant seeing into the transiency of experience, the arising and passing away of all phenomena. This insight is noble and liberating and can lead to the cessation of suffering.

As we can see from the many scriptural selections in this essay, the Buddha did not shirk from the world of economics and the use of wealth. But he did drive a clear line down the Middle Way between need and greed. These discourses may seem only tangentially related to the themes of simplicity, consumerism, and greed, but they are nonetheless of deep significance. Such a pattern of living described by the Buddha is the result of the efforts of the person who has truly escaped the cycles of self-centered consumption and who has the genuine welfare of all at heart. Although the appropriate use of the material world can be a skillful means to a well-balanced life, *true* happiness cannot come from any outside source but ultimately *only* from within our own hearts. A simple and wholesome lifestyle is certainly conducive to personal happiness, but it needs to be always backed up by genuine attunement of our hearts to nature.

Perhaps this point is best illustrated by the verse that is traditionally recited after one renews one's commitment to the core practice of *sila*, beautiful, wholesome conduct, as summarized in the Five Precepts. It speaks not just of the rules as outwardly observed but also (and more important) to those modes of conduct as simply the natural disposition of the pure heart.

> *Sila, the pure heart, is the source of happiness,*
> *sila is the source of true wealth,*
> *sila is the cause of peacefulness—*
> *therefore, let sila be perfected.*

For if our hearts are truly attuned to The Way Things Are, then from moment to moment we experience a deep contentment; there is nothing whatsoever that we are lacking.

Practicing Generosity in a Consumer World

Santikaro

Good is giving, dear sir!
Even when there's little, giving is good.
When done with faith too, giving is good;
The gift of the righteous gain is also good.
And further: Giving discriminately too is good.

—*Samyutta Nikaya,*
Sagathavagga, Devatasamyutta

THIS CABIN, this frozen river, this breathing in and out, this ever-changing consciousness, and much, much more are the natural gifts reminding me of the sources of dana. Out this sunlit window, the Arrow River still flows under more than a foot of ice, joining the Pigeon, which forms the border between Ontario and Minnesota before emptying into Lake Superior. I hear the Arrow rushing as I walk upon it, following animal tracks and an otter's belly slide—what playful joy! Bundled up roly-poly against the cold, I run in sympathetic happiness through the cold biting air, kicking up puffs of snow with my clumsy boots. Winter stillness highlights coarse breathing. Stinging cold on the face deepens appreciation for the warm safety of clothes, cabin, and fire. Eyes feast on the stark beauty of crystalline snow, rusty lichens on cracked cliff rock, leafless birches and aspens, snow-catching firs, river grass adding mellow gold—nothing in me deserves this beauty and wonder, yet it is given, provided, shared.

The sun is a gift of warmth and light even as it sets. The snug cabin was built by nameless others, these days given for my use by Ven. Punnadhammo, the abbot. Paul the steward cooks daily meals and tends to other needs quietly, kindly. Propane gas, candles, and other goods are provided by the community's support network. Trees have given their wood that I may stay warm, even toasty, and survive the minus-fifteen-degree nights. I am clothed in the offerings of Thai, Chinese, Sri Lankan, and American donors. It is all gift. What isn't? Given by others, by nature, by Dhamma.[1]

These gifts lift me out of my little habits and petty concerns, revealing how the gift of Dhamma is so much more than teachings, meditation advice, words. The gift of Dhamma is life, well-being, freedom, and more. It is everything because everything is Dhamma. And Dhamma is all gift, can only be given, never taken. Its nature is to share, recycle, circulate in a mandala of generosity rather than the *samsara-vattha* of desire.

Dhamma, too, is the greatest gift of my life. May it be a gift for all of society as we struggle for meaning in a world of dollars, logos, oil, and military spectacle. The Dhamma of giving is a disinfectant, a gunk dissolver, an antidote for the monetary values, brand names, and "it's the economy, stupid" that clutch at our hearts and swirl in our brains and taint our blood. Reflecting on dana amid such troubling forces on one hand, and the wonders of Dhamma and nature on the other, I am challenged to increase my own giving and transform my life into something that can be a gift for others.

I write as an American monastic recently returned to Chicago (and now disrobed) after twenty years in Siam. I find myself grappling with the challenges of integrating my Thai experience with the complex American cultural mix of healthy (that is, democratic) and unhealthy (worship of profit) elements. For many years I was supported by poor Thai farm families, middle-class supporters of Suan Mokkh, and kind people in the cities I visited. Their generosity pervades Thai culture, yet often I failed to appreciate the power of the dana they modeled all around me. This essay is part of my own coming to terms with the deeper implications of dana that escaped me for too long.

That money has a big place in the American consciousness is beyond question. That money and wealth play a disruptive and corrupting role in religion is widely acknowledged. The growing accumulation of wealth by the plutocracy foretells increasing polarization and violence in an already violent society. Even middle-class Americans, rich by the standards of most of the world's people, spend much of their money on indulgences, entertainment, and addictions. Consequently, money and its uses, how we think about giving and receiving, how we define our roles as Buddhists within a consumer culture, and how Buddhist groups and centers fund themselves are among the most important moral and practical issues facing American Buddhism in the coming decades.

Dana (giving, generosity) plays a central role in these issues and thus deserves careful examination, especially today, when a capitalist distortion of dana may already be setting in. Here I will consider dana as a core Buddhist value and practice, and examine how it mitigates, redeems, and undermines consumerism. I will also consider how consumerism can undermine and corrupt dana. American Buddhists are keen to adapt Buddhism to their own culture. To the extent that U.S. culture is capitalist, consumerist, and forgetful of history—which I believe is largely the case—adapting Buddhism to U.S. culture will be fraught with peril. This danger may be unique in the history of Buddhism, unlike its earlier adaptations to animist, Brahman, Confucian, Taoist, and Bon cultures. The problem isn't so much adapting to Judeo-Christian culture as to the consumerism-capitalist culture that has apparently taken over the religious culture.

I suggest that dana—in all its wonderful, profound simplicity—is a necessary and significant part of what Dr. Buddha would prescribe for our times. It can be understood without hours of study. It liberates us from acquisitive and protectionist habits. It mitigates individualism and nourishes community. Its meaning spans the most basic levels of practice through to the ultimate. It challenges "me" and "mine," fostering letting go. A reinvigorated and updated understanding and practice of dana can serve as a powerful antidote to consumerism's ills. I see this as essential for Buddhism to stay on course as we navigate this bizarre postmodern world seeking genuine peace and liberation.

DANA IN BUDDHIST TEACHINGS

Dana means "gift, offering, giving, generosity." Dana involves sharing the gifts, benefits, and resources that have come to us—material, intellectual, artistic, social, spiritual—with those worthy of them. Dana means giving things of value where they are needed and when they will be of benefit. Dana involves things worth giving; it is not merely the convenient sort of donation that gets rid of unwanted junk. Nor is it the proud charity superiors give to their supposed inferiors.

Recipients qualify as worthy in various ways. One is genuine need, such as experienced by victims of famine, war, and natural disasters. Orphans, the ill, the indigent, and the poor are also deserving of dana, for their needs are real. They deserve our help, not pity. A special case should be made also for inmates, addicts, and other social outcasts; their needs are profound in many ways. Those who live committed, unselfish lives based in Dhamma are also worthy of support, for example, a doctor serving the homeless or a serious Dhamma student. Most worthy are those who understand that everything is a gift to be passed on, who commit themselves to a renunciate style of life and strive to drop all self-centeredness. With nothing retained as "mine," they keep dana in active circulation and elevate or increase its value spiritually.

The Buddha's own story is marked throughout by generous giving and receiving. His great awakening depends on the dana of Sujata, a serving girl, and Sotthiya, a grass cutter. Her sweet milk-rice and his fresh-cut grass sheaves give the Buddha-about-to-be strength and comfort for the supreme final effort. To these are added gifts of nature—a cool river for washing away accumulated ascetic grime, a friendly forest in which to meditate, the shade of trees, and the copacetic sounds of birds. Finally, the Naga king provides his great hood for protection from weather and malevolent forces. Thus the Buddha's supreme human effort was not entirely individual; it was based on the collective circulating charity of many beings. In return, liberated from personal concerns, the Buddha gave his entire life in service of the Dhamma.

The teaching of dana continued through the sangha founded by the Buddha.[2] Monks and nuns walked nobly out of forests and ashrams, along village paths and city streets, stopping at houses to beg silently. A village child, housewife, or old man offers a spoon of rice, a dollop of curry, or piece of fruit into the bowl of the begging monastic. Not merely a stereotype, the practice still survives today in Southeast Asia, helping to sustain Buddhism as a living reality. The early lay exemplars practiced dana along with meditation and discussion, completing the Four Assemblies of practice (bhikkhus, bhikkhunis, lay men and women) needed for Buddhism to be whole and sustainable.

The Buddha praised gifts given to communities of serious practitioners (*sanghadana*) over gifts given to individuals, even the most exalted of all. Giving to the Thus-Gone-One who needs nothing was valued less than giving to those training in the way, their guides, and the community that keeps this noble way alive. Such dana keeps up the centers of tradition, learning, and cultivation that support all who follow the way, whether home leavers or householders. As individuals, only buddhas can fulfill the highest ideal of practice; with noble community, even struggling members are uplifted so that they can contribute too.

> *This is the Sangha of upright conduct*
> *endowed with wisdom and virtue.*
> *For those people who bestow alms,*
> *for living beings in quest of merit,*
> *performing merit of the mundane type,*
> *a gift to the Sangha bears great fruit.*[3]

Dana is described as the first of three bases of good, meritorious activity (*punnakiriyavatthu*). Besides dana, the other two are ethics and virtue (*sila*) and cultivation (*bhavana*). These nonmeditation aspects are believed more accessible and suitable for householders. The practical effect of this is that dana is seen as a householder practice, while study, practice, and meditation, as well as keeping a more refined ethical discipline, are the realm of monastics. Nonetheless, the three bases of good action apply equally to monastics living with middle-class consumer trappings where meditation is an optional, frequently nonexistent, part of their lives. For today's monastics with more material resources than society's poor, the practice of dana is an act of honesty, humility, and necessity.

Dana is also found among the *parami*, perfections (*paramitas*). Giving is listed first among the virtues for crossing over, both among the ten parami of Theravada and the six of Mahayana. A remarkable passage in the Venerable Buddhaghosa's *Visuddhimagga*, a Theravada classic, presages the Mahayana in its explanation of the perfections:

> For the Great Beings' minds retain their balance by giving preference to beings' welfare, by dislike of beings' suffering, by desire for the various successes achieved by beings to last, and by impartiality towards all beings. [In other words, the four brahmaviharas, or divine abidings.] And to all beings they give gifts, which are a source of pleasure, without discriminating thus: "It must be given to this one; it must not be given to this one." And to avoid doing harm to beings they undertake the precepts of virtue. . . . Through equanimity they expect no reward. Having thus fulfilled the Perfections, these then perfect all the good states . . . and the Eighteen States of the Awakened One. This is how they bring to perfection all the good states beginning with giving.[4]

The final parami perfected is also the first—dana. What is often portrayed as the most basic virtue also turns out to be the culmination, the last fulfilled before the bodhisattva is ready for a final birth. I take this to show that the spirit of dana runs throughout and perfects all the parami. For the bodhisattva, there is no tolerance, wisdom, and compassion without wholehearted unlimited giving. One must give completely of oneself for compassion and the other perfections to be realized.

DANA AS ANTITHESIS AND ANTIDOTE TO CONSUMERISM

Consumerism is the current dominant form of capitalism, a system that biases capital over labor and money values over other values. Thus it biases the things that make money over things that make meaning, happiness, wisdom, compassion, and other virtues. In our world, consumerism is more than an economic system, more than political economy. It increasingly functions as substitute religion, debased, shallow, and unable to liberate. As the dominant value system, way of thinking, and way of life, consumerism has a powerful influence even on those of us who struggle against its seductive tentacles. Many Western Buddhists disdain the retention of "Asian cultural baggage" but may be unconscious of the consumerist baggage of their own cultures.

Though I view consumerism as a generally harmful ideology, I do not intend to demonize commodities, trade, and markets, as they are necessary parts of any economy. Yet this form of capitalism takes many things (such as acquisitiveness, individualism, frivolity, and waste) to extremes. The purpose of this discussion is to restore healthy values to the systems of trade and finance, that is, to find and recover healthy boundaries between commodities, private property, market value, and money on one hand, and voluntary gifts, circulating communal property, cultural value, and virtue on the other.

In such a context, how can dana retain its proper meaning and place? How is dana central among wise responses to consumerism that foster Dhamma understanding and practice both individually and communally? Further, let's turn this antagonism around. Vice cannot flourish where virtue is strong. By reinvigorating and strengthening the practice of dana, consumerism can be neutralized. We can identify a number of ways that consumerism has an impact on us that also concern how we understand and practice dana. Here I will discuss three: the impact on social values, on community, and on monasticism. Concurrently, I will suggest some ways the practice of dana can counteract consumerism's influence.

Dana as Primary Value

How, then, is the virtue and practice of dana confused and corrupted by consumerism?

The meaning of my life
buying and owning things
then throwing them away.[5]

I use this sort-of haiku as a working summary of consumerism. In it, money and market value are the measure of everything. Meaning and value are derived and abstracted from things that can be bought, that is, commodities. Once abstracted, such value can be distorted, exaggerated, and concocted through advertising. With most media and much education performing this function, we end up in the consumerist society of today. In this particular construction of values, our lives center on what we own, rather than what we are, our character and virtue. Everything becomes commodity, even family and love are mediated by market mechanisms. But how can the market value suffering, compassion, good health, community, loneliness, a peaceful heart, spiritual insight, and liberation?

Generosity is expressed under the influence of other cultural and religious values. Unhealthy value systems obstruct, distort, or pervert it. Consumerism, for example, turns upside down the ethos of a dana-honoring culture. Wherever consumerism is strong, its values dominate and can even colonize religious values. Values of profit, individual pleasure, and egocentric freedom push aside socially cohesive values such as dana. For example, many of the problems in modern Thai Buddhism can be understood by analyzing how consumerist values have been insinuated into customs and practices that were previously Buddhist.

As increasing areas of life are mediated by price-tagged goods and services, the sphere of voluntary giving shrinks. Despite the mantra of "free trade," price tags limit freedom and gratitude. They value things according to one narrow set of criteria and ignore others. Exchanges within the domain of markets are dominated by those with capital and come with the legal backing of contracts, courts, and lawsuits, none of which inspire gratitude. Gratitude, a voluntary response of heart and action that occurs naturally toward generosity, is rare in trades and deals. When economic benefit becomes the primary "good," generosity is marginalized.

In consumerism, economic or trade value is hegemonic. Values constructed out of aesthetic appreciation, love of nature, friendship, solidarity, and spiritual practice are secondary, if not marginal, for these are precisely what the logic of consumerism undermines. Appreciation of and gratitude for these values cannot arise when we are focused on getting the next thing. When we lose track of giving, even Dhamma can come with a price tag, whether for retreats asking hefty fees or for Dhamma books that spin profits for truth-constraining megamedia corporations. Buddhism becomes a growth business and fundraising becomes a major focus of group energies.

True dana is given and received freely as favor, out of kindness. Societies in which generosity is operative, gracious, and strong are motivated by a web of healthy, mutually supportive values. Dana makes an excellent indicator of social health and cohesion. Are we generous in the care and resources we give our children, elderly, poor, and each other? Are we generous with those who appear different because of race, class, religion, or ethnicity? The practice of dana is a direct antidote to the calculations of the market that permeate consumerist lifestyles. Rather than figuring what we can get from an exchange, we focus on what others need and what we can give. When both recipient and giver value the gift in terms of friendship, shared meaning, and Dhamma, we step outside the market's confines. That wins some space for other values to take hold as well.

As we practice valuing things (material and immaterial) without the price tags, we are more able to discern what is truly Dhamma and what is not. We may even learn that the old cliché is true: the best things in life are free. When we donate at a teaching, it helps us listen better, reflect more freely, and feel happy by helping. The donation doesn't earn us anything; it begins the necessary shift from self-centeredness to unselfishness that Dhamma requires. We still must investigate and practice within ourselves, but this can now be less weighed down by calculation.

We moderns tend to mistake complexity for sophistication and intelligence, forgetting the origins of the word *simple*. Dana is simple both in terms of being comprehended easily (children understand it without any trouble) and in its coherence. It need not be complicated; it can unify rather than fragment. Something so simple as generosity allows all to participate regardless of degrees, professional credentials, class, and wealth. Thus it supports democracy and promotes equality. When we put generosity at the center of our lives, we are much more immune to the tricks of consumerism. Dana's simple pleasure reminds us that technoflashiness and endless pseudovariety are fleeting, confusing, and tiring. Giving frees us from seeking, obtaining, owning, protecting, ensuring, and from the violence these activities can foster, allowing space for appreciation and gratitude.[6] We find more lasting value and happiness in kindness, sharing, and understanding.

Perhaps we in the West have a special service to offer the buddha-dhamma in these times. In America, Europe, Japan, and the other bastions of pervasive consumerism, we have more experience with modernity than those in emerging markets. We have been swimming in increasing complexity, commodification, and individualism for some time. On one hand, we may be more submerged in the fragmentation and dishonesty needed to sustain the illusion that consumer products bring happiness and meaning. On the other hand, these very dilemmas may situate us better to understand and mitigate them. Since dana and consumerism represent opposite values, we postmoderns will have a hard time with the simplicity of giving if we insist on hi-tech, fragmented complexity. Conversely, we can enjoy the benefits of dana if we simply relax the grip of buying, consuming, and owning. How we work our way through these challenges will profoundly influence the future of Buddhism in the West as well as in the Asian source countries that are bombarded with our consumerist culture whether they like it or not.

Dana for the Sake of Community

As understood in early Buddhist cultures, community naturally involved layers of dana. However, consumerism and other modern forces have made the old approach to community precarious. The Thai experience illustrates this well. Recovering sangha is one way that people have found to create nonconsumerist breathing space.[7]

Traditional Buddhism in Thailand and elsewhere has had an agrarian village base. There, doing good or "making *boon*" (from *punna*, goodness) has been the central community value.[8] Back when the lines between family, economics, community, politics, and religion were tenuous, *boon* circulated as the main currency within the religious economy of Thai life. The most prominent practice of "doing good" consisted of giving food to the monks and making other donations to the wat (temple). Before capitalism took over, such dana was almost always in kind, there not being much actual cash in village economies. Dana supplied the material goods needed by the monks personally and for the daily running of the temple. Villagers gave what they had to give and considered "good" or worthy of giving: their best food, cloth, tools, labor, craft skills, and knowledge. As the wat served as community center, clinic, counseling center, news exchange, entertainment stage, and market, in addition to its religious and spiritual functions, support for the wat meant support for the entire community. In fact, until modernization, wats were communal property more than monastic property, sustained by generosity.

For their part, the monks were expected to live simply and unselfishly, to look after the wat and guard traditions. When somebody wanted to talk about a problem or the weather, the monks would listen. When someone needed a ritual, blessing, or chant, the monks would go. They were available 24-7, as we now say, as country doctors used to be in the United States. Actually, many of the monks *were* country doctors. Being available and helpful was central to the life of village monks, including the itinerant meditators who would come and go.[9] Most important, the participation of monks gave religious meaning to daily acts of generosity and kindness, elevating these from the realm of mutual obligations to spiritual significance.

Boon circulated within fairly large loops connecting infants with grandparents, rich and poor, women and men, temple dwellers, ancestors, spirits, even honored water buffalo. The giving was seldom binary and tended to circulate widely as the blood of the community so long as its members understood goodness mutually. The money economy gradually changed most of that as capitalism shifted the operative principle away from goodness and onto money, from boon to baht (the Thai currency). Increasingly, donors gave baht, or food purchased with baht, rather than preparing food and other offerings themselves. Village skills and handicrafts suffered, partly because they were not volunteered and learned at the wat. Time spent in the fields working for cash crops increased, economic migration increased, and children saw less of their parents. Communal work and shared labor disappeared; even the wats had to start paying for labor. Things that did not earn money were devalued. Eventually Buddhism was expected to aid economic survival, magically if not concretely.

In many Thai towns today, monks queue up at dawn markets before stalls at which entrepreneurs sell ready-made food offerings. Donors queue up on the other side, pay their baht, pick up a tray, and turn to put the food in the bowls of waiting monks or buckets carried by temple boys. Then donors and donees go on their way. All very efficient, in the wonderful way of consumer capitalism, with donors putting less time and care into their offering and monks appreciating them less.[10]

Rather than food offered as *boon* in promise of better karmic fruits, baht is given in hope of more baht—successful business ventures, passing exams for career advancement, winning the lottery. The monks, too, are more money minded. Monastic titles and positions are linked to funds raised and spent on temple buildings. Stories are told of people getting rich after donating to a certain monk (for example, Luang Por Khoon) or wat (for example, the infamous Wat Phra Thammakai).[11] Temple services such as the large funeral industry are treated as investments by temple committees, complete with outsourcing of flowers, coffins, and catering. City monks indirectly probe how much dana will be given before deciding which meal invitations to accept. Monks travel, study, and live in the same consumer economy as everyone else. As nothing is free anymore, they also need money. And they struggle, too, with the temptations of consumerism.

For Buddhists who see community as refuge and a priceless gem, anything that saps the lifeblood of community is threatening. The logic of consumerism includes increasing consumer "goods," maximizing market share, and eliminating inefficiencies. More consumers means more sales. Thus, sharing is out, individualism is in. Communal property is out, private property is in. Consumerism undercuts community by encouraging personal consumption patterns: focusing on what "I" want, how "I" want to look and feel. It's all about "me" and not much about "us." The word *community* is now used loosely, often without any connection to shared physical place or face-to-face relationships.

Rejuvenating true dana means engaging in aspects of practice that take place off-cushion. Practicing dana within community can take many forms: bringing food to share with each other and the needy, offering skills and labor to community tasks, caring for teachers and guests, visiting the sick, helping with child rearing and elder care, mending cushions, endowing retreat scholarships, contributing to schools, attending peace rallies, building civil society—the possibilities are numberless. When Buddhist teachers and leaders depend on offerings and gifts, they accept a role that is more than professional. By connecting with students in this way, they promote the practice of generosity and gratitude, their own openness facilitating the sharing of dhamma.

Each time a gift is given, the nurturing bonds of community strengthen as gratitude for each other and the group deepens. The activity of physically handing something to another puts us in direct contact and relationship.

Communal property balances private property and vibrant commons—parks, libraries, places of worship—which provide the space to do things together, gratis. When community is anchored in solid meditation practice and supported by such giving, emotional and relational needs can be taken care of more openly. For example, we notice somebody has missed a regular sitting a few times. We call up and find there's been a death in her family. Word is passed and offers appear to babysit, cook meals, and drive kids to school. Most of all, the expressions of friendship make a difficult time easier. The external support provides time for the bereaved member to meditate, which can help her accept her feelings of loss. The unhealthy need for "consumer therapies" such as eating, drinking, and shopping are mitigated by such sangha support.

Among the Six Dhammas for Harmonious Living Together, sharing resources has a central place.[12] Sharing is an antidote to individualism and thus to consumer ego building. Gifts are the tangible signs of friendships that weave us into larger wholes. Unlike cash and plastic, direct dana makes us more concretely and consciously interdependent with others, which generally makes us more open to them. Circulating gifts keep this alive, which in turn nurtures all of us. The basic goodness of our giving nurtures us, as does the refuge of community.

Dana and Monasticism

Buddhism began as a mendicant movement, and monastic training has provided most of its teaching, scholarship, and leadership. In Asia, monasticism is now in a period of decline, owing to its own inability to adapt to rapid social change and because so much of the change is inimical to it. In the West, whose own monastic tradition was marginalized with the onset of modernity, various forces exclude monasticism. Consumerism is one of these. As a committed monastic myself for many years, I hope for Buddhist monasticism to find its proper role in modernity and expect that role to be a vital part of modern Buddhism's capacity to avoid the seductions of consumerism. This role will require monastics to adapt to modernity but not surrender to it, and to share leadership equally with other sincere practitioners.

Buddhist monasticism, as I understand it, is a lifestyle choice that gives primacy to dhamma study, practice, and service. Along with spiritual practice, monastic life recasts and purifies the ordinary work we perform each day through daily training based in simplicity, renunciation, and generosity. Buddhadasa Bhikkhu, with whom I lived for almost a decade, integrated the so-called spiritual and worldly by teaching that work is dhamma practice and dhamma practice is work. Dhamma practice is the inner spiritual work that transforms our lives, which is then integrated with the ordinary duties of daily life. While monastics are traditional exemplars of this, the principle applies to all Buddhists.

Work is Dhamma practice when we work for the sake of the work, out of compassion, to lessen our own selfishness. We lose the capacity for such spiritual work—work as service and letting go—when we debase its meaning to something done primarily in exchange for money to buy and consume. Professionalizing livelihood into careers further isolates vocation from other dimensions of life. The more we define ourselves through careers and material goods, the more we become *Homo consumerus* without a clue how to live an integrated, spiritually grounded life. Such trends buffet everyone under consumerism, monastics included.

Nuns and monks, as human beings living in the same world as everyone else, are susceptible to modern temptations. As they conform to the cultural imperatives of consumerism, monasticism and teaching as vocations (in the old sense of the special lifework to which we are summoned) become professions (in the modern sense of occupations through which one earns a living). Consequently, they grow concerned with incomes and budgets, thinking certain bottom lines are needed to survive. When monastics succumb to pressures to build big, beautiful monasteries and centers, with all the modern amenities, their focus wanders from Dhamma. The spirit of dana leaks out and money-mindedness creeps in.

With shifting values, monastics and other spiritually committed people come to see themselves as needing to be relevant and productive. What do they have to offer people, they wonder? Are they "marketable?" As such thinking takes hold, the subtle qualities of Dhamma escape the productivity radar. Production compulsion pressures them to give up the old, simple, renunciate ways. No longer supported just because they live a noble life, they must now earn their keep, which is judged more by market standards than dhammic ones. If both monastics and the laity are colonized by consumerism, how can Buddhism flourish?

The monastic life as calling, not career,[13] is a lifestyle honorable in itself, challenging us all to a way of life that supports dhamma practice more fully and deeply. Renouncing the means to generate income, monastics need dana to survive. Simple and upright, with clear basic needs, monasticism inspires support. Simultaneously, it is a vehicle for giving on successively more noble levels, thus embodying dana. The monastic way expresses life as gift both in receiving and offering. As a bonus, this lifestyle also produces art, architecture, poetry, historical records, social services, and community cohesion, all of which are free-flowing antidotes to consumerism.

As a further bonus, this lifestyle naturally produces teachers and teaching capable of questioning consumerism. Though most monastics need not be teachers, teachers arise as long as the integrity of the lifestyle is maintained. In India and traditional Buddhist cultures, householders have supported monasticism because they saw it as beneficial to themselves, their families, and society. As laity shared the fruits of their material production, monastics reciprocated with instruction. By facilitating householder participation in dhamma-centered life, monastics were known as a "field of goodness" (*punnakheta*). When monastics give openly, they are like bees collecting pollen from flowers and producing honey. The rice of householders is then converted into *punna* and dhamma. This is truly Dhammadana when monetary and economic considerations are absent.

With monasticism under assault by consumerism, the task today is to rejuvenate what remains of healthy monastic-lay relationships in Asia and adapt these creatively to modern realities. In the West we are growing Buddhist monasticism from scratch and must do so against the consumerist flow. As a former bhikkhu, I wonder how I can remain true to the alms mendicant lifestyle when there is little chance of collecting enough to eat through traditional methods (not to mention frostbite in winter). There seems to be little social space for noble begging and not much "windfall" to be gleaned when all lands have owners. If we keep to the traditional praxis of not accepting and using money, whatever the form, we must find lay people to provide everything we need. Or should we avoid troubling lay supporters by accepting the conveniences of credit cards and Internet shopping? The appearance of personal self-sufficiency facilitated by consumerism (within the limits of credit lines) comes at the cost of greatly reduced flow of dana, without which Buddhist monasticism cannot survive.

PRACTICING GENEROSITY

While consumerism preys on the alienated ego of modernity, generosity offers a way of loosening the grip of egoism on the heart. By practicing dana genuinely, we undermine the psychological structure of consumerism as we liberate ourselves from its selfishness. We will always be consumers, eaters, materially auto-producing "selves"; consumption is how biological life is recycled and therefore is not an evil in itself. Rather, it is the ideology of consumerism that is destructive because it destroys gift, generosity, decency, life, dhamma. In the Buddha's time, this would have been considered a form of *miccha-ditthi* (wrong understanding). Buddhist practice requires integrating our physical needs and realities within a larger spiritual view that sees beyond ordinary ego needs, let alone the pettiness of consumerism. Honoring and practicing generosity can help us recover and stick to that way of wisdom, compassion, and liberation.

As I finish this piece, I'm halfway around the planet in Siam while the hot season awaits the collecting of the monsoons. Rains aren't daily yet, but enough have already come to scare away fears of El Niño dryness. The air is warm, thick, pungent here. The vegetation is lush, vibrant, full. Brilliant yellow butterflies flutter through the treetops in front of me. Below, the brown, turbid Pasak River winds around this cozy retreat past craggy limestone hills. The mango trees planted along the roads and pathways have dropped fruits too numerous for workers to harvest and guests to eat. Friends, colleagues, and students here also give kindness, food, support, and companionship in the study of life and Dhamma. Once again I am blessed by abundant natural and human generosity. Here the same sense of life, beauty, and gift flows through me and fills the heart just as a few months ago in Canada. Different seasons, different continents, different latitudes, yet life, nature, and Dhamma are everywhere. The Gift is beyond me as it embraces me. I surrender once more to all these gifts and great joy. May such surrender become as natural as breathing in and out.

Wash Your Bowls

Norman Fischer

THERE'S AN OLD ZEN STORY that I like very much. A monk comes to the monastery of the acclaimed Master Zhaozho. Diligent and serious, he asks for instruction, hoping for some esoteric teaching, some deep Buddhist wisdom, or, at the very least, a colorful response that will spur him on in his practice. Instead, the master asks him, "Have you had your breakfast yet?" The monk says that he has. "Then wash your bowls," the master replies, the only instruction he is willing to offer.

Although this story might seem merely to illustrate the gruff, odd, and cryptic style of the Zen master, it actually makes a fundamental point. Zhaozho wants to bring the monk down to the immediate present of his training. "Don't look for some profound Zen instructions here. That's too heady and abstract. Open your eyes!" he seems to be indicating. "Just be present with the actual stuff of your ordinary everyday life—in this case, bowls." A commentary to the story, as it appears in one of the koan collections, says, "When food comes, you open your mouth; when sleep comes, you close your eyes. As you wash your face you find your nose; when you take off your shoes, you feel your feet."[1] Another commentary simply says, "It is so clear it is hard to see."[2]

I have always appreciated the Zen emphasis on the material, practical aspects of our lives. Like the monk in the story, I came to San Francisco Zen Center years ago with huge metaphysical concerns. A student of literature, philosophy, and religion, and a product of the sixties drug and anti-Vietnam War culture, I was full of questions about what was real, what was right, what was enlightenment, what was consciousness. The world that I had inherited from my parents, in which so much was taken for granted, seemed no longer tenable. Everything was up for grabs; reality, apparently, needed to be reconstructed. I came to Zen Center propelled by this spirit, and I was willing to go to almost any length to meditate, read texts, practice austerities, listen to lectures—anything to answer my all-consuming questions.

But my questions weren't answered at all. They seemed to have very little to do with the Zen enterprise as it was presented to me. Instead of study and discussion (the only modes of truth discovery I knew at the time), I was taught how to mop the floor, wash the dishes, and tend the garden. Actually it was very good training for me. It was exactly what I needed. And out of the grounding that this training gave me, my metaphysical concerns began to be slowly and soulfully settled. As it turned out, the answers I was looking for were not propositional. Nor were they to be found in spiritual experiences, enlightenment flashes, or meditative states—although there were enough of these over the years to keep me going. Little by little, through tending to the daily life of the temple in the context of regular, disciplined meditation practice and just enough Buddhist instruction, I began to live my answers instead of talk them, to breathe and feel them bodily instead of intellectually.

Sometimes the Buddhist instruction I received had to do with the religious teachings of the tradition. I did hear a certain amount about impermanence, about emptiness, about nirvana. But more often I heard about being present, simply being present with body and mind fully engaged. Once, in the middle of a long silent retreat, I remember hearing my teacher begin speaking during a meal in a grave tone, as if he were about to explain the secrets of the universe. "When you eat the three-bowl meal during retreat," he intoned, "you should eat out of the first bowl first, and then eat some food from the second bowl, and then the third bowl, and then go back to the first bowl. This is the best way to eat."

This kind of instruction, this style of training, is quite in line with the classical Zen approach. Master Zhaozho was not unique. Over and over again throughout Zen literature you read of students approaching their masters with many complicated matters, only to be brought back down to earth directly. "What is Buddha?" a student asks. "The cypress tree in the courtyard!" the master replies. "What is the Way?" "A seven-pound shirt!" Like the teachers of old who saw that their students' existential concerns could best be met here on earth rather than high up in the clouds, my teachers grounded me and helped me keep my balance. "It's right here—in front of your nose," they told me over and over again.

The word *zen* means meditation, and meditation is certainly the most well-known of all Zen practices. But the meditation practice this tradition emphasizes is not exactly spiritual contemplation. In the Soto Zen that I practice, meditation is called *shikantaza*, which means "just sitting." Soto Zen teachers continually stress the actual mechanics of sitting as sitting. When you receive meditation instruction, you are not given lofty objectives, mantras, or deep koans to meditate on. Instead the instructor will talk to you about many details of physical posture: the alignment of your ears and shoulders, the correct position of your hands and arms, the placement of hips and knees, and how to pay attention to your breathing. The instruction will be so physical, so concrete and specific, that you might well wonder when the "Zen" part begins. But this *is* the Zen part: the meditation practice is in fact quite physical. To pay attention intensely to the body in all its details, to be present with the body in its physical immediacy—*this* is the practice, and the depth of the practice derives from this.

In Soto Zen monasticism the emphasis on the physical as the fountainhead of the spiritual extends through and past the body to all aspects of monastic life. "Careful attention to detail," is the motto of the school. As Zhaozho instructs, monks are to be quite present with and careful of their bowls, their robes, their shoes. The temple work is considered not a necessary and unfortunate series of chores but rather an opportunity to realize the deepest truths of the tradition. Zen monastics take on the daily job of cleaning the temple inside and out, rushing up and down to wet-wipe the wood of the pillars and floors, raking leaves, cutting wood, drawing water. All these immediate physical tasks are seen as essential spiritual practices. The monks are continually taught that none of these physical maintenance jobs differ in any way from sutra chanting, text contemplation, or meditation itself. All is physical, all is immediate, all is the stuff of enlightenment. Meaning comes not so much from what you understand as simply through the way you do whatever it is you are doing.

Following a key text by Japanese Soto founder Dogen Kigen, called "Instructions to the Head Cook,"[3] Soto Zen temples, both in America and Japan, are especially devoted to kitchen work. Monks carefully wash, chop, and combine ingredients, clean pots and pans, mop floors, serve meals with dignity and beauty. Workers in Zen kitchens are instructed to approach their tasks, however menial or repetitive, with full religious attention, giving themselves fully to what they are doing. In Zen centers, "kitchen practice" is a revered undertaking with detailed procedures for the mindful care of food and tools. In our center, for instance, there is a "knife practice": knives are always washed immediately after use rather than being placed in a sink for washing later on (someone might be cut). There is also a "counter-cleaning practice" (wiping down with vinegar at the end of each work period), a "cutting-board practice" (different boards carefully stacked in different locations for fruit, onions, and other foods), and a "chopping practice" (specific ways of holding the knife and the food to be cut for various styles of chop). All of these teach the practitioner that the manner in which something is accomplished, its proper "dharma," as well as the way in which the cleaning up is done, is just as much a part of the work practice (if not much more!) as the result.

Careful attention to detail is not confined to kitchen work. The daily schedule usually calls for a period of mindful silent cleaning immediately following meditation. Even the maintenance shop has a Buddhist altar in it. Tools are to be handled with respect and put away in their proper places, not *after* work is done but as an integral part of the work. Monks and laypeople ordained in the tradition sew their own Buddhist robes and are enjoined to care for them as sacred vestments. Bowls used for eating in the meditation hall are to be handled "as if they were Buddha's own head."[4] Being present with and respectful of all material things, as if each and every one of them were a sacred object, is a primary practice and a primary value. The head monk in a monastic training period not only gives lectures and meets privately with students; he or she is also in charge of taking out the garbage and cleaning toilets. These traditional assignments are seen as holy tasks to be undertaken with full respect and honor (remembering an old koan: "What is Buddha?" "A shitstick!"). For students in training, the sight of the head monk diligently carrying garbage pails or wielding a toilet brush with full attention is as much a part of his or her teaching as the words uttered in the dharma hall.

In training period, too, Zhaozho's words about bowls are taken quite literally in the practice of *oryoki* (formal Zen eating practice). Monastics take all of their meals with full formality in the meditation hall, eating out of a set of three bowls, which are wrapped ceremonially in a set of cloths, often hand sewn by the practitioner. The choreography of managing the cloths, laying out the chopsticks and spoons, receiving the formally served food, chanting, eating, and, yes, washing out the bowls with the hot water offered with bows and tender care is truly prodigious. It takes years to master and feel comfortable with the practice, but when you do, you find the movements enjoyable and beautiful. What at one point seemed fussy, complicated, and arbitrary, now having fully entered into the fingers and palms of the hands seems simply lovely in its quiet grace. Like playing the piano, which requires much clumsy exercise before fluency is achieved, the physical acuity of simply eating a meal is transformed through oryoki into a profound religious act. Such a practice of quiet physical carefulness—to the point where it becomes deep almost beyond speaking of it—has been extended from Zen into Japanese culture. Here the acts of making and drinking a cup of tea, arranging flowers, or writing a simple phrase with a brush on a piece of paper have become high forms of religious art.

Far from offering a path to transcend the material world, then, the process of Zen practice deepens and opens the material world, revealing its inner richness. This is accomplished not by making the physical world symbolic or filling it up with explanations or complications but simply by entering the physical world wholeheartedly, on its own terms. When you do that, you see that the material world is not just the material world, something flat and dumb, as we might have thought. The way we have always, unimaginatively, understood the material world to be is not in fact what it is. As the Zen masters show us, the material world is not superficial or mundane. What is superficial and mundane is our habitual view of the material world, which we have so long insisted on reducing to a single dimension. Dissatisfied with that, we look elsewhere for some relief, some depth. Zen master Yanguan knew this and tried to illustrate it for his attendant. "Bring me my rhinoceros fan," he said one day. "The fan is broken," the attendant said. "Then bring me the rhinoceros," Yanguan said.[5]

To see the material world as it really is is to recognize its nondifference from the highest spiritual reality. For where is spiritual reality if it isn't right here in the middle of our lives in the material realm, bleeding through space and time at every point? Zen training is the effort to learn to enter the material world at such a depth and to appreciate it. As the story of Zhaozho indicates, the way to see the material world as it really is in its fullness is to be present with it and to take care of it. Thus, "Wash your bowls!"

All this is to say that Zen is quite a materialistic tradition. Far from proposing a spiritual alternative to materialistic life, Zen affirms the materialistic realm as nondifferent from the spiritual. In other words, Zen spirituality is not achieved through avoiding, bypassing, or transcending the material realm: it is achieved by entering the material realm in a mindful and thoroughgoing way.

Once many years ago, not long after I was ordained as a Zen priest, I visited my cousin in Miami. An oral surgeon, good at what he does and consequently rather wealthy, my cousin is quite enamored with cars. When he takes a fancy to a particular kind of car (once it was a Mercedes Benz sports convertible, later a Ford Bronco), he buys several versions of it, so that he typically has a small fleet of cars, all the same model, in different colors and with slightly different features. On this particular visit, he was quite taken with the Chevrolet Corvette. Quite tentatively he asked me whether I'd like to have a ride in one, and I said sure. He rolled the convertible top down, and we went out onto the highway, speeding along at a good clip and stirring a wonderful warm south Florida breeze as we went. I was impressed with the automobile's smooth handling and considerable power, and I enjoyed the ride thoroughly.

On our return I expressed my enthusiasm for the car. My cousin was surprised at my reaction. Clearly he'd expected that as a religious person I'd have disapproved of his conspicuous consumption. Maybe I did. But apart from any ideas I may have had about that, I could appreciate the actual experience of the automobile and enjoy it. He asked me how that was. "In experiencing the material world," I explained to him, with all the didactic authority of a newly ordained priest, "there are always two elements in play, the material object—in this case a car, the highway, the scenery going by—and the sense organs and mind that apprehend that object. You need both object and organ to have an experience of the material world. We all have bodies, we all eat food. So we are all materialists. So-called materialists emphasize the object; so-called nonmaterialists, or religious people, emphasize the sense organs and the mind. But we all always need both. The fact is, though, if the mind and the sense organs are acute enough, even a fairly humble object can bring a great deal of satisfaction. Think of how much money I save by practicing Zen! I can get a lot of good out of just one ride; I don't have to buy the car!" He saw my point. Just as he spent long hours working on teeth and jaws, and more hours studying the cars he wanted to purchase, I spent long hours on my meditation cushion cultivating my mind and perceptions, each of us working from his own angle on the question of being alive in this material world.

Honing the sense organs and mind (which includes the heart and spirit) does take cultivation. It takes mindfulness, the skill of quieting the mind so it can be present with what actually is, rather than with received, knee-jerk ideas about what is. The truth is, what we call "materialism" isn't really materialistic—it is idealistic. In other words, it is not the objects that we are after in our consuming—it is what those objects mean to us and to the people in our world. If you don't think this is true, just consider advertising. While advertising may once have had a mostly informative purpose, now its function is to create an aura of emotion and ideology around an object, so as to make it seem much more desirable than it actually is. A friend pointed this out to me in a magazine ad for a van. In the photo the van was parked on a gorgeous beach, with its doors wide open on both sides. On one side of the van was a man reclining. On the other side was a beautiful woman in a bathing suit, lying on the sand with her feet in the sea. A luminous, almost ethereal, shaft of sunlight shone down from the sky, right through the open doors of the van and onto the woman's sensuous face. The photo, digitally touched up with rich colors and smooth surfaces, suggested something delightful, which had nothing whatsoever to do with the actual van it was depicting.

This is a far cry from "wash your bowls," which emphasizes taking a very humble object and making it magnificent—not by applying images of desire but by simply and repeatedly taking care of it mindfully. Once, the twentieth-century Japanese Zen master Nakagawa Soen Roshi gave a retreat in America. The retreat took place in a rented school building, so there wasn't much kitchenware available for serving meals. The daily schedule included a tea service, and since there were no teacups, paper cups had to be used. On the first day of the retreat, after the initial serving of tea, the retreatants began to wad their cups to throw them away, but the Roshi stopped them. "No!" he scolded. "We need to use these same cups each day, so you have to save them." For seven days the retreatants used the same paper cups for tea. When the retreat was over, Soen Roshi said, "Okay, now we can throw away the paper cups." But the students wouldn't hear of it. "Throw them away?! These are our cups that we have used mindfully every day. How could we possibly throw them away? They are precious to us!"

My friends are always astonished when I tell them how much I enjoy shopping malls, especially at Christmastime when they are full of shoppers. I enjoy the feeling of joining together with other people who are out looking for gifts for their loved ones, anticipating a festive meal with them, happy to be spending lots of money in a celebration of life. I am, of course, aware of all the waste and misery that also accompanies the holiday season, but mostly that is not what I focus on. Yes, the parking lot is too crowded, and yes, the amount of merchandise in the stores is overwhelming. But I can't help it, I still enjoy myself.

The contemporary American shopping mall may seem like a recent blight on social life, but the truth is shopping malls are as old as human civilization. I have visited Jerusalem several times and walked through the narrow streets of the Old City. They are now, as they have been for millennia, crowded with shops overflowing with merchandise, jammed in cheek by jowl with each other, shopkeepers shouting at passers-by to get their attention. I have also spent many happy hours at the great Indian market in Oaxaca, Mexico, where you see women selling tamales, butchers displaying sides of beef, and all manner of clothing, jewelry, liquor, and food, including the Oaxacan specialty, peppered grasshoppers. Although I don't buy much at any of these places, I enjoy the spectacle. I especially enjoy the feeling of being with the people, shoppers and shopkeepers alike—all of us brought together in one teeming location by the simple human need for material goods that we hope will bring pleasure, comfort, and sustenance into our lives.

In the end, commerce is communication, a way of being together, transacting, each of us helping the other to fulfill our human needs. Thirteenth-century Japanese Zen master Dogen says in his essay "Bodhisattva's Four Methods of Guidance": "To launch a boat or build a bridge is an act of giving. . . . Making a living and producing things can be nothing other than giving."[6] I know that it is possible for us to engage in commerce as an act of participation and compassion—to buy and sell in that spirit. Through the process of spiritual practice, we can cultivate a view of material things that appreciates them for what they are in themselves and recognizes in them an opportunity for meeting each other on the ground of our shared human needs.

When you do business with someone, you are cementing a relationship with that person. You could see the relationship as adversarial (who will get the best of whom?), but you could just as easily see it as mutual, each of you providing as fairly and as pleasantly as possible what the other needs. It is within the power of any of us to cultivate an attitude of mutuality in our economic transactions. In doing so, we come to see our customer, our supplier, our dealer, our banker, as friends, people who, like us, want to be happy, want to take care of their families and earn a living. To look at commercial life like this and to conduct ourselves as if it were so takes sensitivity and mindful awareness. This we need to develop over time, working with our thoughts and responses just as we work with our breath on the cushion. Part of that work is to be honest and realistic about our own greed, our own fear, our own confusion. But if we can do this with enough clarity and patience, then it may be possible for us to conduct our economic lives with some peacefulness and enjoyment.

For instance, we could pay attention to our thoughts and feelings as we engage in the acts of purchasing or selling to examine honestly our attitudes about money. To what extent is our feeling about money connected to our sense of self-worth—our sense of being powerful and important, or weak and unimportant? Clearly money, in and of itself, has very little to do with these feelings. Whatever feelings of high or low self-esteem we may have, they probably exist independently of money. We have only projected these feelings onto money and are very likely conducting our financial lives in a distorted or at the least an unconscious way. Perhaps our ingrained, habitual, and unexamined attitudes about money are just the playing out of childhood conditioning. Having grown up deprived we may be worried that there won't be enough; or, having grown up with plenty, we may feel guilty that there is too much or be constantly expecting more. Reflecting on this—not so much by thinking about it in the abstract as by observing in detail what we do, say, and feel as we deal with money—we can find a way to clarify how money actually functions in our private world. If its function is not reasonable or healthy for us, we can find, based on our honest investigations, the relief that always comes when something unconscious and dysfunctional comes to conscious awareness. Eventually we might be able to view money more clearly as a means of exchange between people, a convenient device for the distribution of the material things necessary for living. We might come to see money less as a source of worry, pride, or guilt and more as a way for us to share life together.

Contemporary commerce is characterized by its immense complexity. There is very little about it that is local. Goods we buy and sell involve unknown and unseen participants from all over the globe, many of whom may be exploited or exploiting others in the process of fulfilling our needs. To conduct our economic lives mindfully requires us not only to be mindful of our attitudes, the goods we buy, and our relationships to the people who supply us these goods but also to be as informed as we can be about the possible exploitation involved in our purchases, and to use our purchasing power to reinforce goodness and weaken greed and exploitation. When we know that a company or product is harmful to its workers, competitors, or the environment, we simply don't buy that product. When we know that a company or product is making a conscious effort to offer something useful in as harmless a way as possible, we go out of our way to buy it. When this is our consideration, price or convenience becomes less important than relationship. We want to give our business to people we can really support, and whose efforts we are interested in encouraging.

I suppose the effort to keep informed about companies we do business with (whose policies change constantly, and who seem these days to be bought and sold with alarming and tremendous frequency) could become crazy-making in the midst of the complicated lives we are all leading. Still, knowing that it is impossible to do it perfectly, we can nevertheless do it as perfectly as possible, trusting our intention more than our information. Information in the present age is powerful, but it goes out of date almost as soon as it's gathered. Intention, on the other hand, can remain firm and can help keep us on a wholesome course. While it is shortsighted to be uninformed, trusting to intention alone, intention's power to transform the world should never be underestimated.

It seems to me that the world is in need of a new economic theory to replace the one that is now in effect—unrestrained free-market capitalism. This system operates on the faith that an "unseen hand," as Adam Smith called it, will see to it that things don't go out of bounds. That free-market capitalism is, in this sense, fundamentally based on religious or mystical foundations has been more or less lost on us. There is, as we all know, plenty of greed, injustice, and gross manipulation in our economic system. Yet the world's capitalistic movers and shakers apparently believe in the mystical rightness of "the market," that somehow the market (which often seems to take on the proportions of a deity) will in the end serve us all as well as anything else could, and is less subject to corruption and disaster than other, more rational systems. In fact, the unseen hand has been relatively reliable. Although our world economy is in fairly terrible shape (especially when you consider its ecological costs), it is also miraculous that it is in as good a shape as it is (considering its complexity and the fact that it is ruled by people who are not as well-meaning as one would like). Many people starve, but more people are being fed every day. And little by little some of the more enlightened nations are joining together to cooperate for the collective good not only of each other but of the planet.

I don't know if Adam Smith ever proposed a definition of the "unseen hand," but here's mine: it is the sum total of human goodness, of our love for ourselves and each other, and of our hopes for a future that will be more humane than the present or the past. Perhaps we can trust the unseen hand to inspire us to more mindful consumption and production as time goes on, and to discover, eventually, some new organizing principles for our economic life. Until then—and long after!—we have our spiritual practice to guide our daily conduct as we go forth into the world, earning and spending as we must.

Green Power in
Contemporary Japan

Duncan Ryuken Williams

SEVERAL YEARS AGO the Japanese Soto Zen environmental division produced a CD of songs encouraging sect members to avoid disposable chopsticks. The message was to carry around "my *ohashi*" (chopsticks) as a way to save forests. Upset by this anticonsumerist message, the national chopstick manufacturer's association pressured sect headquarters to block the CD release. The project ground to a halt. In Japan, when competing interests of labor/industry and environment come to a head, Buddhist organizations almost always side with industry. Institutional Buddhism in Japan not only tends to support the establishment but is perhaps the most conservative pillar in contemporary Japanese society.

Buddhist temples have often served as stewards for much of the natural landscape of Japan since the early medieval period. But explicitly linking Buddhist doctrine with environmental protection is relatively recent. Historically the consumer rights movement in Japan has been driven by local citizens groups and environmental organizations born from the left and labor movements of the 1960s.[1] However, beginning in the late 1970s, a number of Buddhist priests, temples, and lay associations dropped their traditional resistance to what had been perceived as a leftist cause, developing new forms of Buddhist environmentalism that resonated with a more conservative worldview.

This essay takes up Japanese Buddhist initiatives that have addressed two core consumer issues uniting people across the political spectrum: energy and waste.[2] It is well known that postwar Japanese consumers have demanded efficiency, miniaturization, durability, and convenience from manufacturers of every conceivable consumer product from televisions and cell phones to automobiles. This postwar Japanese consumerism fits well with the newly emergent Buddhist environmentalism that focuses on *mottainai*, "not wasting." Rather than being anticapitalist, this environmentalism might be called *hyper*capitalist, since it demands ever more efficient and durable products for the consumer that reduce inefficiency and waste. Difficult questions about long-term nuclear waste have made consumption of nuclear energy problematic for many environmentalists. Given Japan's limited space and resources, waste of all kinds has been under discussion as the government is pressured by the market to develop a zero-emissions society based on recycling. This essay describes three ways Buddhists have become involved in rethinking Japanese consumer ethics through establishment-sect greening initiatives, through engaged Buddhist alternative energy models, and through temple-based recycling education.

THE SOTO ZEN "GREEN PLAN"

In the 1980s Shoei Sugawara, a forward-thinking abbot of the Soto Zen Senryuji Temple in Komae, proposed to his parishioners a way to make the temple more ecological.[3] Even though Buddhism has traditionally advocated friendly relations between humans and nature, he felt the modern world had disrupted this relationship. One of the main characteristics of a Japanese Buddhist temple is the large roof on the main hall (*hondo*), containing the primary image of worship (*honzon*). Sugawara thought that if that broad space were used for solar panels, the temple could be energy self-sufficient. It would be many years before his idea for a "solar temple," using energy friendly to both nature and humans, would be actualized. He persisted in advocating for solar temples to other Soto Zen priests, and finally in the year 2000, a regional meeting of four hundred Soto Zen temples was held in Tokyo. The plenary speaker, Koichi Yasuda (abbot of Eisenji Temple), took up Sugawara's vision, laying out practical steps to install solar paneling at Buddhist temples.

When Senryuji's solar panels were finally hooked up, they produced more than enough energy for the electrical needs of the entire temple complex. Excess energy was sold to Tokyo Electric Power Company at its daytime peak rate, while the temple bought back energy when necessary (on cloudy days and at night) at the cheaper off-peak rates. This arrangement proved to be beneficial to the environment (no pollution), the temple (cheaper energy costs), and the power company (which was in power deficit during peak hours just when the solar panels were producing most energy). There was, however, one problem. Parishioners voiced strong resistance to solar technology because it interfered with the traditional architecture of their temple. Today the temple is working with an architectural firm to develop solar roof tiles made in the traditional Japanese Buddhist temple style. Sugawara sees the solution to this design problem as the key to Buddhist temples' adopting solar energy in the future.

While the energy advocacy of Sugawara stemmed from his personal interests, it was not out of line with his sect. Since 1995 the Soto Zen headquarters has maintained a nationwide campaign for the environment, taking up critical issues of consumer waste and energy use. The earliest of Japanese Buddhist sects to engage these concerns on a sect-wide basis, they developed a comprehensive "green plan" and promoted it to the more than fifteen thousand Japanese temples of Soto Zen Buddhism.

The Green Plan has been part of the official Soto Zen strategy to engage pressing contemporary issues under the slogan "Heiwa, Jinken, Kankyo" (Peace, Human Rights, and the Environment). Through pamphlets, books, and symposia, the sect has encouraged individual priests, temples, and sect organizations to take up the environmental cause as a part of their affiliation with the Soto Zen sect. Educational materials emphasize the teachings of Dogen and Keizan that promote sensitivity to the natural world (such as Dogen's view that grasses, trees, and forests are manifestations of buddha nature). They also point to conservation measures such as monastic rules on not wasting water and food.[4] In the 1998 *Green Plan*, the question is asked, "Why does a Buddhist sect like Sotoshu get involved with environmental issues?" In response, the official doctrine highlights eco-friendly teachings of Shakyamuni Buddha, Dogen, and

Keizan that encourage increasing wisdom and decreasing desire (for example, Keizan's *heijoshin*, "mind of equanimity").

The Plan also draws on teachings from the traditional lay-oriented manual *Shushogi*. Mimicking the traditional five-line verse (*gokun*) used by monasteries before a meal, the sect advocates the following verses for reflecting on the environment:

Green Plan gokun: Save the Earth!
Five Verses to Living the Green Plan in Everyday Life

1) *Let's Protect the Green Earth. The Great Earth Is the Home of All Life.*
2) *Let's Use Water Sparingly. Water Is the Source for All Life.*
3) *Let's Limit Our Use of Heat. Heat Is What Propels All Life.*
4) *Let's Maintain Clean Air. Clean Air Is the Open Space for All Life.*
5) *Let's Live in Harmony with Nature. Nature Is the Buddha in Form.*[5]

The pragmatic character of these verses reflects a general tendency of the Green Plan to focus on everyday acts at the individual or temple level rather than doctrinal justification for its advocacy of green thinking. Green Plan pamphlets for sect households and temples include items such as checklists to monitor the use of TV and other electrical appliances (to meet a sect-wide goal of reducing energy use by 1 percent), information on purchasing "eco-products," warnings on genetically modified foods,[6] and detailed guides on how to properly separate recyclables. As a sign of the times, the sect manufactured and distributed to member households more than one and a half million cell phone straps with the slogan "Soto Zen Buddhism, Green is Life."[7]

To chart progress on these initiatives, the sect established the Sotoshu Green Plan Kikin, or fund, to raise money for nonprofit environmental groups in Japan. To measure carbon emissions output, the sect headquarters distributed a chart to calculate the amount of carbon dioxide (CO_2) each household produces per year. For each activity such as washing dishes, bath use, and aluminum can recycling, the household is encouraged to calculate the amount of CO_2 reduced and to donate the equivalent savings to the Green Plan fund. Based on the Buddhist teachings of using less (*chisoku*) and donating (*fuse*), the fund has been a way to link Buddhist practice, environmental awareness, and fundraising. By focusing on carbon emissions reductions, the Soto Zen Green Plan supports the goals of the Kyoto Protocol, addressing consumption concerns related to global climate change.

ENGAGED BUDDHIST ALTERNATIVES

In contrast to sect-wide activities, a number of individual priests and their temples have developed alternatives outside the sectarian establishment and the mainstream economy. A good example is Okochi Hideto, a Jodo sect priest and leading figure in the Japanese engaged Buddhism movement. As abbot of Jukoin Temple, founded in 1617, with a current parish membership of 250 families, he could easily have settled for the life of a typical parish priest, performing funerary rites and organizing annual services around the temple calendar.[8] But over the years, he has served in all kinds of social and environmental justice movements, including the JVC (Japan Volunteer Center), Kokusai Kodomodomo Kenri Center (JICRC, a children's rights group), and ARYUS (Bukkyo Kokusai Network), and has authored a number of books on small-scale development. Though some of the groups are Buddhist inspired, many are secular nongovernmental organizations working on social welfare issues in Japan and around the world.

The key to Okochi's engaged Buddhism is his interpretation of the Buddhist teaching of suffering. Over the years, he has made numerous trips to Southeast Asia, the Middle East, and Africa. From warfare in Rwanda to genocide in Cambodia, contact with the palpable suffering of people encouraged Okochi to reflect on the relative comfort of Japanese Buddhists. For him, Buddhism is based on feeling the teaching of suffering, not as an abstract concept, but as something in one's guts. In war-torn countries and poverty-stricken regions, Okochi experienced the type of conditions that inspired Honen, founder of the Jodo sect, to develop a Buddhist approach to suffering for the common people. At the time, Honen was responding to the severe socioeconomic conditions of medieval Japan, which left many people starving and impoverished.

Working with suffering, Okochi draws on Buddhist teachings such as the Four Noble Truths for inspiration. In an essay explaining his involvement with a local environmental group, he states:

> When Shakyamuni Buddha (Siddhartha Gautama) gained enlightenment, his first teaching was the Four Noble Truths, that is, first, get a solid grasp of suffering (the problem), second, ascertain its causes and structure, third, form an image of the world to be aimed for, and fourth, act according to correct practices. Then, one gains a sense of the meaning of life in modern society as a citizen with responsibilities in the irreversible course of time. The suffering of the southern peoples and nature, from which we derive support for our lives even as we exploit it, has caused the Edogawa Citizens Network for Thinking about Global Warming to think, and therefore we have achieved concrete results. The problem is structural in nature, so by changing the system and creating measures for improvement, we achieve results.[9]

Okochi interprets suffering as existing not only on a personal level but also at a deep structural level in the modern socioeconomic system. This brings him in line with the analysis of many engaged Buddhists such as Sulak Sivaraksa or A. T. Ariyaratne. For Okochi, Buddhism is a religion not simply for transforming oneself but also for transforming society. As he states, "the 'awakening' sought by the Buddha was an awakening to the entire universe. The Buddha is someone who lives responsibly based on this self-awareness of the universe, that is, as a 'citizen' of the world."[10]

Okochi combines this emphasis on a return to the original teachings of the Buddha with Pure Land Buddhist rhetoric about making *this* world the Pure Land. Many in the Jodo and Jodo Shin traditions interpret Amida's Pure Land to be a heavenly land where believers transfer after death. In contrast, Okochi believes that heavens and hells are manifest in this world and that this world is itself the locus for the development of the Pure Land. This notion is, of course, not original, but it is nevertheless a minority tradition within the Pure Land sects.

Another well-known advocate of this Pure Land approach is Keisuke Aoki, a Jodo Shin priest and the abbot of a temple in Himeji. Aoki was one of the first Buddhist priests to get involved in environmental issues.[11] He has long advocated a Pure Land Buddhist theology in which hell (*jigoku*) can be found in the human mind and in a society based on competition and oppression, while the Pure Land (*jodo*) can be found where the web of life is celebrated and filled with infinite light (*muryo komyo do*). In his 1997 book, *Edo to kokoro: Kankyo hakai kara jodo e* (The Impure Land and One's Mind: From Environmental Destruction to the Creation of a Pure Land), he emphasizes human responsibility in "the destruction of the earth, which is the creation of hell."[12] Well known locally for protecting the sea from overdevelopment, Aoki has energetically campaigned for many years against oil refineries and other industrial production that caused the "red-lake phenomenon" in Harima Bay, ruining the local fishing industry. According to his theology, this hell, which he describes more globally as a "shadow of a society centered on money," can be replaced by an "ecology of the Pure Land," where the Buddha, enlightenment, infinite light, and compassion permeate this world.[13]

In his environmental work, Okochi linked this concept of building a Pure Land on earth with his critique of structural suffering. As an increasing number of Japanese became aware of global warming issues through the 1997 Kyoto conference, Okochi was mobilizing citizens in his locality in Tokyo. He helped establish the Edogawa Citizens Network for Thinking about Global Warming, an offshoot of an earlier organization, Group KIKI, which was dedicated to alternatives to nuclear power and other energy and waste issues. After a study tour to Sarawak, Malaysia, to document the destruction of the rain forest by Japanese multinationals, the group successfully pressured the local council to not use wood from tropical rain forests. The Citizens Network also raised funds for CFC-recovery equipment to donate to car demolition businesses in their local Edogawa Ward, a district responsible for 60 percent of CFC emissions in the twenty-three wards of Tokyo.

By far their most ambitious project was to establish an alternative-energy power plant in the ward to end their neighborhood's dependence on Japanese fossil fuel and nuclear energy. In 1999 the Edogawa People's Power Plant No. 1 was constructed as a citizens' effort to withdraw from the energy companies and the financial institutions that fund them (which engaged in environmentally destructive investments). Its location: on the roof of Jukoin Temple.

The temple name, consisting of the Chinese characters *ju* (life) and *ko* (light), reflected the Jodo tradition's teachings that existence is unlimited life and light of the Buddha. In his rationale for the power plant project, Okochi proclaimed:

> Human life as well as all life existing in nature is mutually inter-
> linked and dependent on each other. This Buddhist concept aims
> at creating a global society of coexistence and co-prosperity.
> Juko-in, in solidarity not only with Buddhists but also with other
> citizens, NGOs and various other groups, is dedicated to ecolog-
> ical development and human rights issues.[14]

This dedication meant that the four-hundred-year-old temple faced a radical rebuilding. After obtaining the understanding of the parishioners, the
temple's architecture was completely modernized using eco-friendly concrete and wood building materials. The traditional roof tiles were replaced
with two sets of fifteen large solar panels that would generate six thousand
kilowatt-hours (kWh). This was enough to receive official recognition
from the local government as the first of several planned People's Power
Plants in Edogawa Ward.

The funding for this project—6 million yen—came from local environmental groups, individual donors, and loans from an independent bank
that the group established: the Mirai Bank, or the Future Bank. Okochi
adapted a temple fundraising strategy from the premodern period, when
donors bought roof tiles for a new temple's construction for a sum above
the actual cost. He asked locals to buy solar panels as a gift to the temple
power plant. The *taiyo kawara,* or "sun tiles," were sold at five thousand yen
per panel and the funds deposited in the new bank.

The model for the Mirai Bank was based on medieval and early Buddhist mutual aid societies (*ko*), with the modern goal of supporting environmental sustainability. Instead of giving their hard-earned money to
the big national banks (which often use people's savings for environmentally destructive projects), the Edogawa citizens chose to invest ethically in
building and protecting the future (*mirai*). Inspired by microcredit bank-
ing in Third World countries, Mirai Bank not only criticized the existing
capitalist system but offered an alternative economic model for a new kind
of sustainable society in Japan. In addition to funding the power plant, the
bank embarked on a consumer campaign to encourage the purchase of
eco-products. Because 60 percent of energy in Japanese households is
consumed by refrigerators, air conditioners, and lighting, the bank began
by focusing on environmentally friendly refrigerators. The bank understood that average families take up new alternatives only if they don't have

to sacrifice comfort or pay exorbitant fees. So, they provided interest-free loans to buy environmentally friendly refrigerators, which reduce energy consumption by four hundred kilowatt-hours per year. This is equivalent to nine thousand yen; thus a bank loan of fifty thousand yen could be paid off in five years.[15]

The solar power plant generated not only alternative energy but also new small-scale economics. Excess energy beyond the temple's energy use was sold to Tokyo Electric Power Company with the income plowed back into paying off the initial investment. The Edogawa Citizens Network for Thinking about Global Warming decided to encourage local citizens to buy this excess energy at a premium with Green Power Certificates. By selling two hundred 30 kHh certificates for one thousand yen each, the power plant could return its initial investment in just nine years. To involve the local community and to build a more mutually dependent society, each Green Power investor also receives Edogawatt bills, a local currency that can be used to pay for babysitting, translation, and other services, "deepening interpersonal relationships and trust."[16] Since solar energy has the lowest maintenance costs associated with energy production (almost zero), the idea is that each People's Power Plant can be profitable within a decade, generating clean, zero-emissions energy, and building a more intimate society at a time when modern Japanese society has grown increasingly impersonal.

Okochi's approach has been very practical and reflects his Jodo sect background and belief that ordinary Japanese citizens can participate in this type of engaged Buddhism without engaging in asceticism or sacrificing comfort. His ideal of "engaged citizenship," or the spirit of volunteerism in society, is active social reform.

> A volunteer, according to Juko-in thinking, is not a person who provides his/her cheap labor to fill in cracks left by the administration, or a person looking for his/her own satisfaction. Volunteers look for the true nature of the problems and promote movements oriented towards social reforms. . . . They should take the side of the weaker (the people) and not the strong side of the system. They begin by experiencing problems of suffering. Then, they move to reflect on the structures and the mechanisms concerning those issues. . . . Those volunteers rich in work

experiences with NGOs show us the face of the Buddha and famous Buddhist saints.[17]

Thus Okochi aligns himself with ordinary citizens, disdaining what some might consider elitist asceticism. His approach differs from the Soto Zen establishment Buddhism because it is based in a critique of the current sociopolitical and capitalist system. With much of mainstream Japanese Buddhism aligned politically with the right and big business, Okochi's leftist rhetoric of siding with the poor and oppressed offers a marginal but important voice in the contemporary Japanese Buddhist landscape.

BUDDHIST CONSUMER EDUCATION

A third approach to reducing waste and changing consumption habits takes place in the context of traditional temple activities. Rinnoji Temple (a Soto Zen temple in Sendai, Miyagi prefecture), whose abbot has been active in volunteer efforts such as AIDS hospice and earthquake relief, is setting an example with its recycling and environmental education programs. Using the idea that the Buddhist spirit of attention to small things and "not wasting" starts at home, the temple looked to its own practices leading to waste and overuse of natural resources.[18]

As a typical, though large, Japanese parish temple, the primary activity of the temple was not Zen meditation but the performance of funerary and memorial services for its parishioners. These services take place at death and in intervals over a period of thirty-three years. Parishioners also visit the temple with flowers and other offerings for the deceased during the annual summer ancestral festival of Obon. At this season the spirits of the deceased are thought to return to the temple graveyard or to the memorial tablet (*ihai*) normally kept in the family altar (*butsudan*). The abbot noticed that an enormous number of flowers were being donated at the temple graveyard—nearly five thousand flower bundles during the Obon season alone—and then were simply discarded into the landfill. The temple conceived of a plan to take these flowers and develop a high-quality composting system, creating fertilizer, which could be donated to local farmers. By 2000 the temple had expanded this recycling project to include the composting of leftover temple food. They also recycled into charcoal the bamboo offering stands used at grave sites.

Environmental education has also become a big part of the temple's activities since 2001. Each year the monks offer a presentation on recycling to the local middle school students using the temple recycling system as a model. In 2003 the temple produced a home video for its parishioners entitled *Kankyo no tame ni* (For the Sake of the Environment) that gave instructions on home composting and how not to waste water used to clean rice. The video targets housewives, who are most responsible for cooking rice and monitoring home recycling. By working with housewives and young teens, the temple reinforced the message that environmental education must begin early and at home.

The Rinnoji example illustrates antiwaste activism that functions within the traditional boundaries of what some have termed "funerary Buddhism based on the parish system." This system, which characterizes mainstream Buddhism in contemporary Japan, tends to emphasize the continuity of tradition and customary/formalistic relationships between priests and parishioners. The fees paid for funerary and memorial services constitute a vast proportion of a temple's income. For the most part, any Buddhist consumer or environmental activities in Japan have had to operate within this system, which has been the mainstay of Japanese Buddhism since the beginning of the Tokugawa period (1603–1867). In contrast to Okochi's engaged Buddhism, temple composting is not a radical departure from social and political norms. However, even within these conservative institutions, Rinnoji Temple provides an example of efforts to raise consumer consciousness.

ETHICAL CONSUMERISM

Whether it be empowering consumers through temple education (Rinnoji), creating energy off the grid through solar roof panels (Jukoin), or making use of sect-wide organizations to promote "green Buddhism" (the Soto Zen Green Plan), Japanese Buddhists are beginning to make structural changes that directly impact consumption patterns. Precisely because establishment Buddhism is a pillar of mainstream Japanese society, even small actions at the more than one hundred thousand Buddhist temples have the potential to make dramatic changes not only at local temples but in the consumption patterns of the millions of lay Buddhist members of those temples.

Transformation of mass consumption patterns often starts with small-scale movements that set trends in the larger society. Buddhist temples in Japan have begun this process of reshaping Japanese society through creating new models of ethical consumerism. If Buddhism can have an impact on a hyperconsumerist culture such as Japan's, it is a testament to the role that Buddhism can play in the global marketplace.

Buddhist temples and centers in America, while still few in number, have a relatively high influence on trends in American popular culture. That influence can be mobilized to rethink consumption patterns and empower consumers to make ethical choices oriented to reduce suffering in the world. These small-scale acts may prove to have enormous impact on American society at large. When Buddhists can transcend borders in these ways—sharing ideas and strategies for a more sustainable society—this can be the beginning of a radical restructuring of the forces of the global economy.

Mutual Correction
Seeing the Pain of Others

David W. Chappell

We must realize that when basic needs have been met,
human development primarily is about being more, not
having more.

—Earth Charter, preamble

FROM THE BEGINNING of human history, human survival has depended on the capacity to consume as much as possible as quickly as possible. Whoever collected and consumed the most food, clothing, shelter, and weapons was the most able to survive. Over time this drive to achieve the utmost diversified and was expressed individually by who had the most cunning and skill, and socially by who had the best strategy and organization. These qualities became further developed through individual achievements in education, technology, sports, and the arts and were accompanied by parallel social achievements in governments, civil society organizations, and corporations.

Today this quest to achieve the utmost is facing new challenges as local cultures disappear into McWorld and as the planet's biological diversity diminishes daily. This challenge will only increase as population grows—from 6 billion to perhaps 9 billion people over the next forty years—and as consumption grows. If we wish excellence in developing the brightest and best, then seeking guidelines and practices that foster global excellence should be our first concern.[1]

What can Buddhism offer to this challenge? What individual and social guidelines are relevant for today's consumerist world? Consumerism lies close to the heart of the Buddha's story, presenting conflicting messages. First there is the exemplary tale "from riches to rags" as Shakyamuni Buddha leaves his sumptuous royal palaces for a life of voluntary poverty. Yet soon after his enlightenment he visited kings and welcomed gifts of valuable parklands and treasures for his Buddhist community. Whereas the Buddha taught individuals to be free from greed and possessions, the early Buddhist social community amassed great wealth. A visit to the Emerald Buddha in Bangkok, or the golden spires of pagodas in Cambodia, demonstrates that in medieval Asia, Buddhist institutions were often the most vivid examples of conspicuous consumption.[2] Religious paths in both East and West have often encouraged a form of "spiritual consumerism" by declaring that spiritual advancement could be won by donations to the religious community. Even today, Buddhism is not exempt from corporate greed.

Certainly in individual practice, Buddhist ethics do offer an antidote to excessive greed through practicing mindfulness, understanding impermanence, and observing the interrelatedness of all things. The peaceful balance and inclusiveness that emerge can support institutional practices that promote equity and harmony. But how to achieve this in our consumer culture? The challenge is to translate Buddhist methods of personal liberation into guidelines for the public sphere. To preserve biological and cultural diversity, liberate people from poverty and disease, and foster social harmony, much more needs to be done at the institutional level to protect the many cultures and forms of life from extinction. Here I suggest five proposals for a Buddhist ethic of consumption that can support institutional evolution in the direction of global excellence.

OPEN DISCLOSURE

In spite of the amazing achievements of modern consumerism, terrible tolls have been paid for its advance. It doesn't take a genius to recognize that our neighborhood shopping centers with their cozy comforts carry a false sense of reality. Not only have they not evolved organically as part of the local neighborhoods—where local dreams, transitions, and interdependence would be part of local observation and memory—but their sources are hidden. No advertisements proclaim who is profiting and by how much. Absent are the connections to the depletion of the earth and the suffering or pride of the workers who fuel the engines of production. There is no trail showing the path from impoverished sweatshop workers to the latest fashions, no pictures of the hands and faces that made the goods, no images in the glitter of jewelry shops of the trails through the forests and into the pits where children dig in the dark for gems.

The most popular form of Buddhism in East Asia is Amida devotionalism, which aims for salvation through rebirth in Amida's Pure Land. This is seen as the best place to hear the dharma and attain enlightenment. Today, however, the setting might seem to resemble an idealized shopping mall. This is how an Amida practitioner is instructed to visualize the Pure Land:

> The rows upon rows of jeweled trees are evenly spaced, and the leaves are in orderly sequence. In between the leaves bloom exquisite flowers, and upon these flowers, fruits made of the seven kinds of jewels appear of their own accord.... This array of exquisite flowers . . . looks like revolving fire-wheels, gently spinning among the leaves.... There is a great ray of light which forms banners, flags, and countless canopies adorned with jewels. Within these jeweled canopies, all the works of the buddhas of the three-thousand-great-thousand worlds appear illuminated.[3]

Doesn't this vision of Amida's Pure Land fulfill our wishes of consumption where all glitters with jewels and gold? Like the shopping mall, the Pure Land is completely available to all, but the currency is trust in the compassionate power of Amida Buddha. The Pure Land, however, is not the final destination but rather a necessary training station to cultivate enlightenment in preparation for returning to save others. While shopping malls actively cultivate attachment, yearning for the Pure Land is said to be neither addictive nor entrapping, safe as a fire built on ice that fizzles in the water created by its own heat. Thus the Pure Land is an enticement that in the end liberates self and benefits others.

Shopping malls, in contrast, deceive by not showing their past, by not showing the source of their goods, by not showing the effort and suffering and skill that produced their goods. They do not point beyond themselves to a higher and more noble purpose. They exist not to help us liberate others but as ends in themselves for consumers, and vehicles of wealth and exploitation for owners. Hardly a source of freedom, the goods of shopping malls become cages that imprison our minds, that conceal the stories of their creation, and that make us indebted to the financial system that generated them.

Buddhist compassion is based on a sense of connection and kinship, but this empathy is thwarted by the privacy walls that corporations construct to avoid responsibility. Nike, the largest garment seller in the world, was exposed for the obscene disparity between Michael Jordan's high endorsement fees and the enslaving wages paid to its Third World workers, usually women and sometimes children. Under enormous pressure, Nike provided the names and addresses of many of its subcontractors to enable human rights groups to investigate the working conditions of its producers. While Nike still remains the center of controversy, it has raised the bar for higher standards of transparency in corporate social responsibility.[4] This may be less true for other firms such as Disney, which subcontracted with the military regime in Burma/Myanmar to produce some of its products.

Instead of privacy walls and concealed stories, Buddhist ethics demand greater mindfulness of corporate-consumer interconnections. More transparency not only is informative but also often transforms the behavior of those being watched, as Amnesty International has shown. Apparently people are less likely to harm others when they know that someone else is watching. From a Buddhist perspective, cultivating compassion depends on direct contact with suffering. Thus it is essential to work toward more *open disclosure* of the sources of production, including the human and ecological costs and the character of the producers. This is my first proposal for a Buddhist ethics of consumption.

MUTUAL CORRECTION

In 1970 the Club of Rome report shook people from their infatuation with endless expansion by showing the limits of growth on our planet. Historically this was the first global-scale confrontation with the limits of the earth. After decades of rapid development, it was quite clear that unrestrained human activity was taking its toll. At Earth Day celebrations around the country, people raised concerns about too much waste, too much stuff, too much apathy. The question was up: Can we make a midcourse correction? Can we restrain human activity to protect the planet?

Buddhist teaching has always emphasized personal restraint in our lives with others. Monastic traditions guard against taking human life, animal life, and even insect life. This precept of *ahimsa* (nonviolence) is concretely illustrated by the traditional monastic allowance of only four possessions: a bowl, a robe, a needle, and a strainer to remove insects from drinking water to protect the lives of these small beings. Monastic ethics are often considered the ideal, and they are elaborated in great detail in Buddhist scriptures. Even in the very early years, the Buddhist monastic community met twice a month on full moon and new moon days to recite together their rules of restraint in front of others. Mahayana rules for monks and laity require that in discrete ways, bodhisattvas must reprove those who are harming others. Even kings were to be modest and to seek guidance from the sangha. So social responsibility via mutual correction pervades Buddhist ethical practice.

Whereas Christians have emphasized that all people are sinners, Buddhists have taught that all of us are imperfect and biased because of our past karma. In both views, individuals are seen as flawed and in need of correction. And in both traditions, emphasis has been placed on ethics for individuals, not institutions. Though individual followers were urged to be nonattached, Buddhist monastic institutions accumulated great wealth.[5] Buddhism has always been expansionistic in the name of altruism, and institutionally it has not developed norms to curb Buddhist growth. Only recently have a few modern Buddhist groups, such as the Tzu-chi Compassion Association of Taiwan, even practiced public bookkeeping. Most Buddhist groups have not. Instead, gifts of dana are slipped into the hands of abbots with no public accounting. Traditional Buddhist groups have been strangely silent on economic matters, suggesting a new age of accountability is needed within Buddhist groups as a method of providing checks and balances.

The Four Bodhisattva Vows offer another expression of mutual correction. First created by Tiantai Zhiyi (538–597), they are still recited daily by contemporary Zen Buddhists:

> *Beings are infinite in number, I vow to save them all.*
> *Compulsive desires are endless, I vow to end them all.*
> *The teachings are innumerable, I vow to learn them all.*
> *Buddhahood is supreme, I vow to embody it fully.*

The first vow, to save all beings, quickly reveals our shortcomings in fulfilling this impossible challenge. It might be called presumptuous, even paternalistic, but at its core, the first vow directs attention to the endless task of serving others. In turn, it is balanced by the second and third vows, which urge Buddhists to correct themselves by ending desire and to learn from others. This correction is needed for both Buddhists and Buddhist institutions to keep greed and consumerism in check at all levels. In fact, it may be those of us who are trying to be helpful to others who are in need of correction ourselves.

Today the money managers of lucrative pension plans and mutual funds are aggressive in monitoring giant corporations and in removing ineffective CEOs. Checks and balances are provided by exposure through media coverage, which can often work more quickly than government regulation. Rather than disparaging these actions as thwarting creativity, we can affirm the need for legal restraints over corporate excess as well as individual harmful behavior. This cultivation of checks and balances, or *mutual correction*, for individuals and institutions is my second suggestion for a Buddhist ethic of consumption.

INCLUSIVE DECISION MAKING

Modern corporations have been given the legal status of persons, based on the 1886 court case of *Santa Clara County v. Southern Pacific Railroad Company*. This ruling invoked the rights of personhood by appealing to the

Fourteenth Amendment, which extended constitutional rights to slaves freed after the U.S. Civil War. But corporations, in fact, are not persons. Single persons do not have access to the golden parachutes for corporate managers that permit escape and exploitation. They are not protected like corporations by the limited liability of stockholders. Furthermore, some research indicates that the courts never did give this status to corporations,[6] a claim that will be tested when the *Kasky v. Nike* case comes to the U.S. Supreme Court.

Though institutions are not biological persons, they impact people and communities in a variety of ways. There is a growing consensus that institutional decision making should follow international guidelines (some of which are not universally supported by Buddhists). The most famous is the Declaration of Human Rights (DHR) now in the process of national ratification. This document protects workers' rights and environmental safety for people impacted by resource exploitation. At their 1992 meeting, the Buddhist Churches of America voted not to support the DHR.[7] Though some writers disagree about how Buddhist metaphysics relates to human rights concerns,[8] Buddhist leaders on the front line, such as the Dalai Lama, Aung San Suu Kyi, and Sulak Sivaraksa, have not been shy about advocating for the DHR as a set of ethical guidelines for humanity in the age of globalization.[9]

Mahayana Buddhist ethics and the Declaration of Human Rights share similar themes. The *Scripture of Brahma's Net*[10] (used by both monastics and laity) and the *Upasaka Sutra*[11] (used only by the laity) are the best-known Mahayana precept texts, though, in fact, there are at least two hundred scriptures containing bodhisattva precepts. The great Japanese *vinaya* scholar Gyonen (1240–1321) summarized Mahayana ethics in his *Risshu Koyo* as: to prevent all evil, to cultivate all good, and to save all beings. Preventing evil includes dissolving false ideologies and attitudes that lead to harm and maintaining the basic five precepts. Cultivating good includes nurturing inner understanding and attitudes of kinship, compassion, and joy toward others. Saving all beings affirms the heroic goal of the bodhisattva—who is dedicated to helping others attain enlightenment; Mahayana texts assert that each and every person is called to be a bodhisattva. The Declaration of Human Rights likewise presents three parallel mandates: to prevent government infringement on the individual (articles 2–21), to affirm social responsibility for human development (articles 22–27), and to visualize and promote a global order of equity and well-being (articles 28–30).

The first of the Buddhist guidelines—preventing evil—is crucial to reducing global suffering related to consumerism. The Buddhist tradition recommends restraining personal behavior to avoid harming others through no killing, lying, stealing, or sexual misconduct. In parallel to this, the first section of the DHR focuses on behavior protecting the integrity of individual life. Whether or not individuals have inalienable legal rights, individuals can be harmed not just by other individuals but also by social organizations, especially the state. The DHR represents a milestone in the evolution of modern institutional ethics in the way it establishes government restraints on harming individuals, and likewise government restraints on corporations from harming individuals and the environment. This moral development in the DHR needs to be more fully embodied by Buddhists in order to make Buddhist ethics relevant to the difficult challenges of global consumerism.

A fundamental principle for consumers and institutions is to avoid harming individuals by being aware of those who will be most affected by their decisions. In meditation one may calmly review the many factors involved in our mental dispositions. Likewise, conscious consumers must also calmly and regularly review a wide range of information from a variety of sources. This principle of inclusive awareness to restrain excess harm applies equally to shoppers and to managers of religious institutions, universities, and nonprofit groups. While those who will bear the costs of decisions may not have the power to determine the decisions, it is important at least that their voices be heard, their advice solicited, and their vote included.

This principle of inclusive decision making—namely, to include in decision making those who are most affected by the decision—has been partially enacted by the World Bank in its projects for listening to the poor and in its World Faiths Development Dialogue. In contrast, the World Trade Organization only reluctantly gave up its efforts to institutionalize a "multilateral agreement on investment."[12] This agreement would have allowed corporations to invest and withdraw themselves from projects anywhere in the world without any feedback from local constituencies or any penalty for local harm that they may have done.

I believe that inclusive decision making reflects the social ethics attributed to the Buddha. The Mahaparinibbana Sutta (Digha Nikaya 16.1) records that the Buddha used seven criteria to evaluate the social strength of the

Vajjian society. The first two are relevant here: holding regular and frequent assemblies, and meeting, dispersing, and conducting meetings in harmony. The Buddha's assumption was that everyone would somehow be involved. Restraining institutional harm by *including in decision making* those who are most affected by the decisions is my third proposal for a Buddhist ethics of consumption.

GLOCALIZATION

A related principle to shared decision making is that "whatever decisions and activities can be undertaken locally should be." This principle is articulated by the International Forum on Globalization (IFG) and given the slogan "Protect the local, globally." The IFG calls this principle "subsidiarity," while others prefer the new term *glocalization.*[13]

Michael Rothschild, president of the Bionomics Institute in San Francisco, has argued that biological systems are successful only when they can decentralize as many functions as possible. He feels that the collapse of centralized planning regimes like the USSR was inevitable because too many decisions were being made by authorities isolated from the work. In a similar way, corporations that favor centralized control by management and lack accountability to stockholders or local communities inevitably become parasites that he calls "corpocracies." Government regulations can encourage or prevent such accountability. The state of Delaware, for example, shields executives from liability by freeing management from accountability to stockholders. It is no surprise that this state alone attracts more than half of the Fortune 500 firms, many of which actively promote consumerism around the world.[14]

Buddhist practice has traditionally been critical of giving false substantiality and heightened value to metaphysical generalizations and personal constructions such as atman and brahman. Applying this practice of critique to social structures can help balance the authority of cultural abstractions such as church, corporation, and nation-state, and the demand to sacrifice life for them. Conservation biologist Jared Diamond suggests that modern state authorities are now so reified that they have been enabled to extract taxes and monopolize violence in what he calls "kleptocracy."[15] While this heightened view of the state has allowed the state to protect strangers and redistribute wealth to the weak and needy, it has also enabled rulers to exploit others and become heedlessly destructive. Economic globalization has fostered a similar aura of power in some corporate circles.

Today moral issues are being framed in economic terms, whether they deal with the environment, health care, or social equity. Increasingly governments are being held hostage to global economic institutions to the detriment of local cultures.[16] In listing the 200 largest financial budgets in the world, Charles Gray found that only 39 were nations, whereas 161 were corporations. The Fortune 500 companies in 1999 consisted of companies that had budgets over U.S. $9 billion, but only 57 national governments had budgets as large as these five hundred corporations.[17] As corporations increasingly "rule the world," citizens and local governments are called to find effective ways to engage these new economic powers.[18]

Buddhist practice emphasizes the constancy of change. Giving special attention to the local need not mean that it should not change. Local traditions have always been in flux. To privilege one way of doing things locally because it is seen as a tradition may sacrifice a vibrant future because of nostalgia, laziness, or attachment. Rather, the values of the past and present, the individual and the collective, need to be explored in their rich potential in a search for more creative ways for life to flourish in the future.

Giving greater attention to the local is one form of critical evaluation of the abstract, whether institutional or intellectual. As such, it is part of traditional analytical practice for Buddhists. Seeing how things come to be in their local details, as well as come apart in their local details, not only informs the mind but also liberates the heart from bondage to limited structures. Calm and critical appraisal of abstractions—whether intellectual or corporate, whether cultural or personal—can uncover the specific and local realities of actual parts and processes. Glocalization— the regular deconstruction of the collective, the imagined, and the abstract in order to privilege the local wherever possible—is my fourth proposal for a Buddhist ethic of consumption.

REGARDING THE PAIN OF OTHERS

Buddhists often invoke "love and compassion" as their motives for action, but these are qualities that must be cultivated through daily practice to be effective. In the earliest Buddhist texts, the most common source of ethical behavior is the generic sympathy that all humans feel. Gautama Buddha told his followers to "go and travel around for the welfare of the multitudes, for the happiness of the multitudes, out of sympathy for the world."[19]

For sympathy to be genuine, it needs to be explicit, to be embodied; it requires links to real people and places. The Dalai Lama explained this basic human response as he reflected on a visit to Auschwitz:

> When I speak of basic human feeling, I am not only thinking of something fleeting and vague, however. I refer to the capacity we all have to empathize with one another, which, in Tibetan we call *shen dug ngal wa la mi so pa*. Translated literally, this means "the inability to bear the sight of another's suffering." Given that this is what enables us to enter into, and to some extent participate in, others' pain, it is one of our most significant characteristics. It is what causes us to start at the sound of a cry for help, to recoil at the sight of harm done to another, to suffer when confronted with others' suffering.[20]

Common human sympathy as the "inability to bear the sight of another's suffering" requires direct contact with suffering. In our consumer society, our material goods often protect us from experiencing such suffering. Even our emotions are being commodified. Advertisers, theme-park operators, and television programmers have learned how to manipulate our emotions to keep our focus on endless desires. Our media-dominated world presents us with infinite imagined communities. In today's TV generation, much of our living and loving is imagined. To invoke sympathy, we must break through media images and make direct contact with living people and those in pain.

Writer Susan Sontag has reflected deeply on the impact of visual images that show the suffering of others. Observing Sebastiano Salgado's moving photographs *Migrations: Humanity in Transition*, taken in thirty-nine countries, she points out that the powerless subjects go unnamed in the captions. While suffering shown on such a scale may prompt sympathy, such photographs can also inhibit action. "Making suffering loom larger, by globalizing it . . . invites them [the viewers] to feel that the sufferings and misfortunes are too vast, too irrevocable, too epic to be much changed by any local political intervention. With a subject conceived on this scale, compassion can only flounder." She goes on to observe that "in a world in which photography is brilliantly at the service of consumerist manipulations, no effect of a photograph of a doleful scene can be taken for granted." [21]

Common human sympathy is the foundation of Buddhist ethics, but it is often manipulated by the media and politicians. Balanced information can help direct our sympathy to where the suffering really is. Herman Daly and John Cobb's Index of Sustainable Economic Welfare and the Genuine Progress Indicator offer more-inclusive gauges of economic impact on people and the environment and illustrate an "economics as if life mattered." [22] We need to require more tools like these to be structured into our media and our social routines. As much as possible we need to know and to experience the impact that complex and distant economic decisions are having on living beings because economics affects the quality of life more than anything else today.

Although measuring the well-being of ecosystems is difficult, it would be helpful if our daily newspapers and weekly news magazines, such as *The Economist* and *Business Week*, provided indexes that measure not just economic growth but the health of the environment as well. Every day the Dow Jones and S&P 500 standings are reported, but only recently has the health of the planet been news. In addition to the growth or decline of the gross domestic product (GDP), we need reports on the growth or decline of vital natural resources, as well as the health and welfare of animals and humans. If there were an international mandate for these status reports, we could keep better track of how well we are caring for the earth, living sustainably, establishing justice, sharing equitably, practicing nonviolence, and so on.

Travel and tourism are another form of consumerism that carries hidden harm. Marveling at the wonders of the world is different from what Gautama Buddha intended when he said to "travel around for the welfare of the multitudes, for the happiness of the multitudes, out of sympathy for the world." While appreciating the wonders of the world, we must also ask on whose backs they were built. While the architecture in the center of Paris is striking, Sulak Sivaraksa reminds us that those impressive buildings were the result of colonization. Though it is good to appreciate beauty and cultural achievements, travel must constantly be balanced and informed by Sulak's advice to "go where the suffering is."

Touching those who live in pain shows us concretely how *harm must be reduced*; this is my fifth proposal for a Buddhist ethic of consumption.

In sum, a first response to consumerism should be to try to reestablish connections between consumers—individual, corporate, and government—and those who are most affected by consumption. And when the actions of consumers are destructive to people or to nature, the Buddhist goal would be to ensure that consumers do not hide from seeing the pain and devastation that their decisions are causing. My argument is not to restrain the "free" market but to enlighten it by increasing the visibility of its activities, its governance, and its costs. By working together in this more open and enlightening arena of checks and balances, I hope that we will naturally develop self-restraints and find a way to evolve a more balanced, humane, and green form of achieving our utmost. As stated in the Earth Charter preamble, "We must realize that when basic needs have been met, human development primarily is about *being* more, not *having* more" (italics added).[23] And being more means finding ways to include the lives of others, in all their differences and pain, in our awareness and decision making.

Notes

Introduction

1. John de Graaf, David Wann, and Thomas Naylor, *Affluenza: The All-Consuming Epidemic* (San Francisco: Berrett-Koehler Publishers, 2001), p. 36.
2. Michael Brower and Warren Leon, *The Consumer's Guide to Effective Environmental Choices* (New York: Three Rivers Press, 1999).
3. Brian Halweil and Lisa Mastny, eds., *State of the World 2004* (New York: W. W. Norton, 2004).
4. David Loy, "The Religion of the Market," *Journal of the American Academy of Religion* 65, no. 2 (Summer 1997): 275–90.
5. Quoted from Raymond Benton, Jr., in Neva Goodwin, "Overview Essay," in *The Consumer Society*, eds. Neva R. Goodwin, Frank Ackerman, and David Kiron (Washington, DC: Island Press, 1997), p. 3.
6. Jonathan Watts, "Concocted Death: A Buddhist Deconstruction of the Religion of Consumerism," in *Santi Pracha Dhamma* (Bangkok: Santi Pracha Dhamma Institute, 2001), p. 126.
7. Yiannis Gabriel and Tim Lang, *The Unmanageable Consumer* (London: SAGE, 1995).
8. Peter N. Stearns, *Consumerism in World History* (New York: Routledge, 2001). See especially chapters 2 to 5.
9. Alan Durning, *How Much Is Enough?* (New York: W. W. Norton, 1992), p. 30.
10. Eric Schlosser, *Fast Food Nation* (Boston: Houghton Mifflin, 2001), p. 4.
11. John C. Ryan and Alan Durning, *Stuff: The Secret Lives of Everyday Things* (Seattle: Northwest Environment Watch, 1997).
12. Hilary French and Brian Halweil, "Microbial Migrations," *Orion* (January 2004).
13. Durning, *How Much Is Enough?* p. 51.

14. Lester Brown et al., eds., *State of the World 1998* (New York: W. W. Norton, 1998), p. 115.
15. Halweil and Mastny, eds., *State of the World 2004*, p. 28.
16. Ibid., pp. 45, 120.
17. Helena Norberg-Hodge, "Buddhism and the Global Economy," *Turning Wheel* (Spring 1997): 13–17.
18. Kalle Lasn, *Culture Jam* (San Francisco: HarperCollins, 1999).
19. Alan D. Kanner and Mary E. Gomes, "The All-Consuming Self," in *Ecopsychology*, eds. Theodore Roszak, Mary E. Gomes, and Allen D. Kanner (San Francisco: Sierra Club Books, 1995).
20. Bill McKibben, *The Age of Missing Information* (New York: Random House, 1992).
21. See for example, Roger Gottlieb, ed., *This Sacred Earth* (New York: Routledge, 1996); J. Ronald Engel and Joan Gibb Engel, eds., *Ethics of Environment and Development* (Tucson, AZ: University of Arizona Press, 1990); Mary Evelyn Tucker and John Grim, eds., *Worldviews and Ecology* (Lewisburg, PA: Bucknell University Press, 1993); Richard Foltz, ed., *Worldviews, Religion, and the Environment,* (Belmont, CA: Wordsworth, 2003). Regarding consumerism, see Paul Knitter and Chandra Muzaffar, eds., *Subverting Greed: Religious Perspectives on the Global Economy* (Maryknoll, NY: Orbis, 2002).
22. Gary Gardner et al., eds., *State of the World 2003* (New York: W. W. Norton, 2003), pp. 152–75.
23. Gabriel and Lang, *Unmanageable Consumer.* See chapter 9.
24. Thich Nhat Hanh, *For a Future to Be Possible: Commentaries on the Five Wonderful Precepts* (Berkeley: Parallax Press, 1993).
25. Rita Gross, "Buddhist Resources for Issues of Population, Consumption, and the Environment," in *Buddhism and Ecology: The Interconnectedness of Dharma and Deeds*, eds. Mary Evelyn Tucker and Duncan Ryuken Williams (Cambridge: Harvard University Press, 1997), pp. 291–312.
26. P. A. Payutto, *Buddhist Economics: A Middle Way for the Marketplace,* (Bangkok: Buddhadhamma Foundation, 1994); Sulak Sivaraksa, *Seeds of Peace* (Berkeley: Parallax Press, 1992).
27. See David Loy, "Pave the Planet or Wear Shoes? A Buddhist Perspective on Globalization," in *Subverting Greed*, eds. Paul Knitter and Chandra Muzaffar (Maryknoll, NY: Orbis, 2002), pp. 58–76; David Loy and Jonathan Watts, "The Religion of Consumption," in *Mindfulness in the Marketplace*, ed. Allan Hunt-Badiner (Berkeley: Parallax Press, 2002), pp. 93–104.
28. Earlier collections include Allan Hunt-Badiner, ed., *Dharma Gaia* (Berkeley: Parallax Press, 1990); Martine Batchelor and Kerry Brown, eds., *Buddhism*

and Ecology (London: Cassell Publishers, Ltd, 1992); Mary Evelyn Tucker and Duncan Ryuken Williams, eds., *Buddhism and Ecology* (Cambridge: Harvard University Press, 1997); and Stephanie Kaza and Kenneth Kraft, eds., *Dharma Rain: Sources of Buddhist Environmentalism* (Boston: Shambhala Publications, 2000).

Chapter 1: Desire, Delusion, and DVDs

1. Buddhadasa Bhikkhu, *Heartwood of the Bodhi Tree* (Boston: Wisdom Publications, 1994), p. 15.

Chapter 3: The Inner Pursuit of Happiness

1. Lisabeth Cohen, *A Consumer's Republic: The Politics of Mass Consumption in Postwar America* (New York: Alfred A. Knopf, 2003).
2. Juliet Schor, *The Overspent American: Why We Want What We Don't Need* (New York: HarperPerennial, 1998), p. 18.
3. Juliet Schor, *The Overworked American: The Unexpected Decline of Leisure* (New York: HarperCollins, 1992).
4. Cohen, *Consumer's Republic*, p. 403.
5. Thomas Hine, *I Want That: How We All Became Shoppers* (New York: HarperCollins, 2002), p. 109.
6. David Loy, *Lack and Transcendence: Existentialism, Buddhism, and Psychoanalysis* (Berkeley: Asian Humanities Press, 1996).
7. See Roger Rosenblatt, ed., *Consuming Desires: Consumption, Culture, and the Pursuit of Happiness* (Washington, DC: Island Press, 1999).
8. Manuel Castells, "The Informational Economy and the New International Division of Labor," in *The New Global Economy in the Information Age: Reflections on Our Changing World*, Martin Carnoy et al. (University Park, PA: Pennsylvania State University Press, 1993), p. 19.
9. Here I use the term *contemplation* in a rather loose way as synonymous and interchangeable with the more widely used term *meditation*, an English rendering of the Sanskrit term *dhyana*. Dhyana leads to and technically can be distinguished from an inner state of unitive awareness, called *samadhi*. The contemplative mode I am describing would include these two realms of dhyana and samadhi. I prefer *contemplation* to *meditation*, as the latter can be associated with use of the discursive intellect, as in Descartes's or Marcus Aurelius's *Meditations*. *To contemplate*, on the other hand, is a Latin-based term that derives from the Greek *theorein*, which means "to behold," or "to see," a state of awareness that more closely corresponds to what takes place in the Buddhist practice of sitting in silence.

10. Dogen, "This Very Mind is Buddha" fascicle, *Shobogenzo* (author's translation). For an alternate translation, see *The Eye and Treasury of the True Law*, vol. 1, translated by Kosen Nishiyama and John Stevens (Tokyo: Nakayama Shobo, 1975), p. 19.
11. This is also known as the *Sutra on Lovingkindness*. See Samuel Bercholz and Sherab Choedzin Koh, eds., *Entering the Stream: An Introduction to the Buddha and His Teachings* (Boston: Shambala Publications, 1993), pp. 141–42.
12. Cited in Alan Clements, *Instinct for Freedom: Finding Liberation through Living* (Novato, CA: New World Library, 2002), pp. 91–92.
13. Ibid., p. 108.

Chapter 4: Young Buddhists in Shopping Shangri-la

1. James Silberstein, personal correspondence, February 9, 2003.
2. Beliefnet.com, Teen Buddhist discussion board, May 17, 2003.
3. Beliefnet.com, Teen Buddhist discussion board, May 16, 2003.
4. Corey Flanders, personal correspondence, February 12, 2003.
5. Dan Fisher, personal correspondence, February 20, 2003.
6. Seunghee Ham, personal correspondence, February 20, 2003.
7. "Convert Zen" is not a lineage but is a shorthand term for the style and culture of Zen that seems to be evolving among the predominantly Euro-American practice groups and centers.
8. Jeff Wilson, personal correspondence, February 9, 2003.
9. Beliefnet.com, Teen Buddhist discussion board, August 11, 2003.
10. Connie Pham, personal correspondence, February 15, 2003.
11. Flanders, personal correspondence, February 12, 2003.
12. Wilson, personal correspondence, February 9, 2003.
13. Beliefnet.com, Teen Buddhist discussion board, Summer 2003.

Chapter 5: Marketing the Dharma

1. *Anguttara Nikaya, Pathamalokadhamma Sutta* (Sutta 5), *Metta Vagga* (ch. 1), *Atthakanipaata.*

Chapter 6: You Are What You Download

1. Thich Nhat Hanh, *For a Future to Be Possible: Commentaries on the Five Wonderful Precepts* (Berkeley: Parallax Press, 1993).

Chapter 7: Cultivating the Wisdom Gaze

1. Khenpo Karthar Rinpoche is the abbot of Karma Triyana Dharmacakra, Woodstock, New York. This quote is from a transcription of a talk given at his center in 2002.

2. José Cabezón, "Singing Bowls and Power Beads: On the Commodification of Tibet" (unpublished paper presented at the symposium "Representing Tibet: A Symposium on the Representation of Tibetan Culture in the U.S.," University of Colorado, Boulder, CO, January 2000), p. 10.

3. Quoted in ibid., p. 11.

4. Chögyam Trungpa, *Cutting Through Spiritual Materialism* (Boulder, CO: Shambhala Publications, 1973).

5. *Materialism* is a gloss of *kla-klo*, which means "barbarian," especially a human being from an uncivilized area unreceptive to the compassionate and wise teachings of the Buddha.

6. Chögyam Trungpa, *The Sadhana of Mahamudra, Which Quells the Mighty Warring of the Three Lords of Materialism and Brings Realization of the Ocean of Siddhas of the Practice Lineage* (Halifax, NS: Nalanda Translation Committee, 1990), p. 6.

7. Frances S. Adeney and Terry C. Muck, "Economic Growth vs. Human Well-Being: An Interview with John Cobb," *Buddhist-Christian Studies Journal* 18 (1998): 77–88.

8. John Cobb has devoted much of the last two decades to the untangling of these issues, and in his work with Herman Daly, former senior economist at the World Bank, has forged a penetrating critique of the economic theories that fuel the international economy. See Herman E. Daly and John B. Cobb Jr., *For the Common Good: Redirecting the Economy toward Community, the Environment, and a Sustainable Future* (Boston: Beacon Press, 1994); and John B. Cobb Jr., *Sustaining the Common Good: A Christian Perspective on the Global Economy* (Cleveland: Pilgrim Press, 1994).

9. Kenneth Kraft, "Prospects of a Socially Engaged Buddhism," in *Inner Peace, World Peace: Essays on Buddhism and Nonviolence*, ed. Kenneth Kraft (Albany: State University of New York Press, 1992), p. 12.

10. Norberg-Hodge, "Buddhism and the Global Economy," *Turning Wheel* (Spring 1997): p. 13.

11. Jamgon Mipham, *Mkhas pa'i tshul la jug pa'i sgo zhes bya ba'i bstan bcos bzhugs so*, published as *Gateway to Knowledge: The Treatise Entitled* The Gate for Entering the Way of a Pandita *by Jamgon Mipham Rinpoche*, vol. 1, trans. Erik Pema Kunsang (Hong Kong: Rangjung Yeshe Publications, 1997). This text is a digest of principal points of the compassionate and wise path of the bodhisattva drawn from the Indian and Tibetan traditions, presented in a systematic and highly condensed manner. My paper draws from the fourth chapter, "Dependent Origination," or *tendrel* in Tibetan.

12. Ibid., 4.1.

13. Quoted in Norberg-Hodge, "Buddhism and the Global Economy," p. 13.

14. Noam Chomsky, "Globalization: The New Face of Capitalism" (address at Boston College, Boston, MA, October 1999). See also Noam Chomsky, *Profit over People: Neoliberalism and Global Order* (New York: Seven Stories Press, 1999).
15. Chomsky, *Profit over People*, pp. 13–15.
16. Norberg-Hodge, "Buddhism and the Global Economy," pp. 13–14.
17. Daly and Cobb, *For the Common Good*, p. 89.
18. Ibid., pt. 1, pp. 25–117.
19. Chomsky, "Globalization" address, 1999. Derrick Jenson, "Driven by Desire: Why the Global Economy Won't Satisfy Us, an Interview with George Draffan," *The Sun* (December 2001): 8.
20. Chomsky, "Globalization" address, 1999.
21. In *Santa Clara County v. Southern Pacific Railroad Company*, the U.S. Supreme Court took it upon itself to rewrite the Constitution, granting to a corporation the rights guaranteed a person of equal protection under the law. A two-sentence assertion by a single judge elevated corporations in this way, laying the foundation for special protections of corporations that have formed the basis of the global economy, changing the course of history. David Korten, *The Post-Corporate World: Life after Capitalism* (Bloomfield, CT: Kumarian Press, 1998), pp. 184–86.
22. Ibid., p. 186.
23. Mipham, *Gateway to Knowledge*, 4.2, 4.7–19.
24. Ju Mipham's text (*Gateway to Knowledge*, 4.2) uses an analysis of the twelve nidanas only for the inner analysis, saying that the outer analysis more appropriately looks at patterns of cause as in the sprouting of a seed or the interaction of the six elements or other cooperating conditions.
25. Ibid., 4.14.
26. Daly and Cobb, *For the Common Good*, p. 88. They use the example of Pimples Carson, John Steinbeck's character in *The Wayward Bus*, who spent half his income on treatments for acne and the other half on candy bars and sweets whose advertisements told him that a working man needed them for quick energy.
27. Mipham, *Gateway to Knowledge*, 4.8.
28. Quoted in Judith Simmer-Brown, "Speaking Truth to Power: The Buddhist Peace Fellowship," in *Engaged Buddhism in the West*, ed. Christopher Queen (Boston: Wisdom Publications, 1999), pp. 80–81.
29. Mipham, *Gateway to Knowledge*, 4.27.
30. Ibid.
31. The term is *anunayadrstikaruna*, or "compassion based on emotionally-tinged views." Robert Thurman, trans., *The Holy Teaching of Vimalakirti* (University Park: Pennsylvania State University Press, 1976), p. 46.

32. Donald Rothberg, "Responding to the Cries of the World: Socially Engaged Buddhism in North America," in *The Faces of American Buddhism*, Charles S. Prebish and Kenneth K. Tanaka, eds. (Los Angeles: University of California Press, 1999), pp. 282–83.

33. Mipham, *Gateway to Knowledge*, 4.43: "The one who perceives dependent origination with the eyes of discriminating knowledge will come to see the *dharmas* possessing the natures of the eightfold noble path, and with the wisdom gaze which comprehends all objects of knowledge will perceive the *dharmakaya* of buddhahood."

Chapter 8: No River Bigger than Tanha

1. Buddhadasa Bhikkhu, *Paramadhama*, vol. 1 (Bangkok: Dhammadana Foundation, 1982), pp. 173–74 (translated from the Thai).

2. We choose to use the old name Siam for the country now known as Thailand because the name Thailand implies authoritarianism, chauvinism, and irredentism. The country was called Siam until 1939, when the name was changed to Thailand. Then it reverted to the original name again in 1946. However, the country has officially been called Thailand ever since the military coup d'état in 1947. This new name signifies the crisis of traditional Siamese Buddhist values. Removing the name the country has carried for all its history has been an important step in the psychic dehumanization of its citizens, especially since the original name was replaced by a hybrid, anglicized word.

3. Helena Norberg-Hodge, *Ancient Futures: Learning from Ladakh* (San Francisco: Sierra Club Books, 1999).

4. P. A. Payutto, *A Dictionary of Buddhism* (Bangkok: Saha Dhammic Co., Ltd.: 2001), p. 211.

5. Sulak Sivaraksa, www.sulak-sivaraksa.org.

6. Buddhadasa Bhikkhu, *Dhammic Socialism*, ed. Donald Swearer, 2nd ed. (Bangkok: Thai Inter-religious Commission for Development), 1993.

7. Ibid.

8. Buddhadasa, "A Notion of Buddhist Ecology," trans. G. Olsan, *Seeds of Peace* (Bangkok) 3, no.2 (May 2530 [1987]).

9. Sulak Sivaraksa, *Seeds of Peace, a Buddhist Vision for Renewing Society* (Berkeley: Parallax Press, 1992), p. 102.

10. Sivaraksa, www.sulak-sivaraksa.org.

11. Payutto, *Dictionary of Buddhism*. These principles include: to hold regular and frequent meetings; to meet together in harmony, disperse in harmony, do business duties in harmony; not to break the agreed principles; to honor and respect the wise elders; to respect and treat women well; to perform proper rituals and spiritual practice; and to support those who practice for enlightenment.

12. For a more detailed story of this monk, see Yano Sherry, "Phra Krusupa-jariyawat—Finding the Middle Path between Modern and Traditional," in *Socially Engaged Buddhism for the New Millennium,* ed. Sulak Sivaraksa (Bangkok: Foundation for Children: 1999), pp. 148–93.
13. Other such organizations are Bandang Tuburan in the Philippines and the Rural Reconstruction Alumni and Friends Association (RRAFA) in Thailand.

Chapter 9: Taming the "I Want" Mind

1. There are six realms of unenlightened existence: devas, humans, and titans in the upper realms, animals, pretas (hungry ghosts), and hells in the lower realms.
2. Translation of the Three Treasures that is used in the lineage of Roshi Philip Kapleau.
3. Zenno Ishigami, ed., *Disciples of the Buddha* (Tokyo: Kosei Publishing, 1989), p. 19.
4. Bassui, *Mud and Water, a Collection of Talks by the Zen Master Bassui,* trans. Arthur Braverman (San Francisco: North Point Press, 1989), p. 22.
5. The Ten Cardinal Precepts, as phrased in the Harada-Yasutani lineage, are
    1. Not to kill but to cherish all life
    2. Not to take what is not given but to respect the things of others
    3. Not to misuse sexuality but to be caring and responsible
    4. Not to lie but to speak the truth
    5. Not to cause others to use substances that confuse the mind or do so oneself but to keep the mind clear
    6. Not to speak of the misdeeds of others but to be understanding and sympathetic
    7. Not to praise oneself nor disparage others but to overcome one's own shortcomings
    8. Not to withhold spiritual or material aid but to give them freely where needed
    9. Not to indulge in anger but to exercise control
    10. Not to revile the Three Treasures (the Buddha, the Dharma, and the Sangha) but to cherish and uphold them
6. Cited in Francis Dojun Cook, *How to Raise an Ox* (Los Angeles: Center Publications, 1978), p. 168.
7. Layman P'ang, *The Recorded Sayings of Layman P'ang,* trans. Ruth Fuller Sasaki, Yoshitake Iriya, and Dana R. Fraser (New York: Weatherhill, 1971), p. 19.
8. Cook, *How to Raise an Ox,* p. 192.

Chapter 10: Penetrating the Tangle

1. Yiannis Gabriel and Tim Lang, *The Unmanageable Consumer* (London: SAGE, 1995), chapter 9.
2. Michael Schudson, "Delectable Materialism: Second Thoughts on Consumer Culture," in *The Ethics of Consumption*, ed. David Crocker and Toby Linden (Lanham, MD: Rowman and Littlefield, 1998), pp. 249–68.
3. Ibid, p. 258.
4. Brian Halweil and Lisa Mastny, eds., *State of the World 2004*, (New York: W. W. Norton), p. 18.
5. Ibid.
6. This paper draws on work developed earlier for the 2003 Buddhism and Ecology conference (Berkeley, CA) hosted by Ryukoku University of Kyoto and the Institute for Buddhist Studies, Berkeley, California.
7. Christopher Chapple, quoted in Hammalawa Saddhatissa, *Buddhist Ethics* (London: Wisdom Books, 1987), p. 75.
8. See Andrew Cockburn, "21st Century Slaves," *National Geographic* 204, no. 3: pp. 2–25.
9. For a detailed review of the four types of clinging, see Watts, "Concocted Death: A Buddhist Deconstruction of the Religion of Consumerism in *Santi Pracha Dhamma*," (Bangkok: Santi Pracha Dhamma Institute, 2001), pp. 126–47.
10. Kazuaki Tanahashi, ed., *Moon in a Dewdrop: Writings of Zen Master Dogen* (San Francisco: North Point Press, 1985), p. 70.
11. Shohaku Okumura, "To Study the Self," in *The Art of Just Sitting*, ed. John Daido Loori (Boston: Wisdom Publications, 2002), p. 105.
12. Ibid., p. 107.
13. Ibid., p. 110.
14. Hammalawa Saddhatissa, *Buddhist Ethics* (London: Wisdom Books, 1987), pp. 73–74.
15. For analysis of the issues facing Buddhists and vegetarian eating, see Kate Lawrence, "Nourishing Ourselves, Nourishing Others: How Mindful Food Choices Reduce Suffering," in *Mindfulness in the Marketplace*, ed. Allan Hunt-Badiner, (Berkeley: Parallax Press, 2002).
16. Quoted in Saddhatissa, *Buddhist Ethics*, p. 77.
17. For an introduction and compilation of the causation texts in the Nidana-samyutta, see Bhikkhu Bodhi, *The Connected Discourses of the Buddha*, vol. 1 (Boston: Wisdom Publications, 2000), pp. 515–661.
18. See Naomi Klein, *No Logo: No Space, No Choice, No Jobs* (Toronto: Knopf Canada, 2000); and Alissa Quart, *Branded: The Buying and Selling of Teenagers* (Cambridge, MA: Perseus, 2003).

19. Green consumers are described as "LOHAS," people who lead Lifestyles of Health and Sustainability. According to *The State of the World 2004*, this group now includes nearly one-third of adult Americans and in the year 2000 accounted for $230 billion in consumer purchases.

Chapter 11: Form and Elegance with Just Enough

1. Shambhala Training is a meditation program that offers training in basic meditation intended for people of all religions or no religion. It is devoid of any specifically religious content so that people who have negative reactions to ritual or religious teachings can experience the benefits of meditation.

2. The Venerable Khandro Rinpoche is one of very few women gurus recognized by the traditional Tibetan religious establishment and perhaps the only such woman teacher who teaches in English and travels internationally. She is considered to be one in the sequence of rebirths of a lineage of important women teachers including Yeshe Tsogyel. She was born in India as the daughter of Mindrolling Trichen Rinpoche, an important Nyingma lineage holder, and was recognized at an early age and trained in the traditional manner for high lamas.

3. Stupas are found universally throughout the Buddhist world, including the so-called "pagodas" of East Asian Buddhism. They began in ancient Buddhist India as reliquary mounds, where the ashes or relics of great teachers were placed. They became places of pilgrimage, and religious institutions often grew up around them. The largest stupa in North America is the Great Stupa of Dharmakaya Which Liberates Upon Seeing at Shambhala Mountain Center in northern Colorado, which enshrines some of the relics of Chögyam Trungpa Rinpoche. For more information, see Adrian Snodgrass, *The Symbolism of the Stupa* (Ithaca, NY: Southeast Asia Program, 1985).

4. David Loy, "The Religion of the Marketplace," in *Visions of a New Earth: Religious Perspectives on Population, Consumption, and Ecology*, eds. Harold Coward and Daniel C. Maguire (Albany: State University of New York Press, 2000), pp. 15–28.

5. I have used this argument in discussing ways to encourage population control. See Rita Gross, "Toward a Buddhist Environmental Ethic," in Coward and Maguire, eds., *Visions of a New Earth*, pp. 147–60.

6. As used in Shambhala Buddhism (and Tibetan Buddhism in general), this stage is called Hinayana, a term that has a precise technical meaning referring to the first stage of the path, understood as a long journey eventually including the Mahayana and perhaps the Vajrayana stage of practice. While the Hinayana teachings of Tibetan Vajrayana Buddhism are similar to those of contemporary Theravada Buddhism, the term is not used to refer to those Buddhist schools.

7. From the daily chant book for Shambhala Buddhism (unpublished source).
8. The Shambhala teachings of Shambhala International refer to the teachings as "the sacred path of the warrior." Many of the teachings draw on the shamanic heritage of Tibet as well as the heritage of Gesar of Ling, the hero of Tibet's national epic. "Warriorship here does not refer to making war on others. Aggression is the source of our problems, not the solution. Here the word 'warrior' is taken from the Tibetan *pawo*, which literally means 'one who is brave.'" Chögyam Trungpa, *Shambhala: The Sacred Path of the Warrior* (Boston: Shambhala Publications, 1988), p. 28.
9. Ju Gampopa, *Gems of Dharma: Jewels of Liberation*, trans. Ken Holmes and Katia Holmes (Forres, Scotland: Altea, 1995), pp. 169–74.
10. Vajrayana Buddhism includes recognition of and practices relating to many beings called protectors. The function of protectors in Vajrayana Buddhism is literally to protect and serve the dharma and dharma practitioners. Some of the protectors are considered to be wrathful manifestations of great buddhas and bodhisattvas. Others are local spirits who obstructed the spread of Buddhism in Tibet but were tamed and converted to become dharma protectors by great teachers such as Padmasambhava. Their appearance is always wrathful and conventionally frightening. Daily practices regarding the protectors include a simple offering, usually of tea and grains, and a series of chants.
11. Shambhala Buddhism daily chant book (unpublished source).

Chapter 12: Consuming Time

1. Joe Robinson, "Four Weeks' Vacation," *Utne Reader* (September–October 2000).
2. Robert Levine, *A Geography of Time* (New York: Basic Books, 1997), p. 107.
3. Perhaps it is no coincidence that Ende later became interested in Buddhism. He visited Japan several times, and his first visit in 1977 included a discussion with a Zen priest.
4. *Samyutta Nikaya* 1.10.
5. Nagarjuna, *Sunyatasaptati*, v. 58 (my version of this famous verse).
6. Nagarjuna, *Mulamadhyamikakarika* 13:5, in Candrakirti, *Lucid Exposition of the Middle Way*, trans. Mervyn Sprung (Boulder, CO: Prajna Press, 1979).
7. Dogen, quoted in Reiho Matsunaga, *The Soto Approach to Zen* (Tokyo: Layman Buddhist Society Press, 1958), p. 68.
8. Dogen, quoted in Kazuaki Tanahashi, ed., *Moon in a Dewdrop: Writings of Zen Master Dogen* (San Francisco: North Point Press, 1985) excerpts from pp. 76–80; trans. altered.
9. Ibid., pp. 70–71.

10. E. E. Evans-Pritchard, *The Nuer* (New York: Oxford University Press, 1969), p. 103.
11. Anthony Aveni, *Empires of Time* (New York: Kodansha, 1995), p. 135.
12. Ibid., p. 331.
13. Damian Thompson, *The End of Time* (London: Minerva, 1996), p. 325.
14. Ibid., p. 332.
15. Developed in depth in David Loy, *Lack and Transcendence: The Problem of Death and Life in Psychotherapy, Existentialism and Buddhism* (New York: Humanities Press, 1996) and David Loy, *A Buddhist History of the West: Studies in Lack* (Albany: State University Press of New York, 2002).
16. Quoted in Levine, *Geography of Time*, pp. 204–5.
17. See a summary of this talk at http://www3.plala.or.jp/mig/talk-uk.html, section IV.

Chapter 13: Three Robes Is Enough

1. *Majjhima Nikaya* 2.13–16, "The Discourse on All the Outflows."
2. *Vinaya* Nis. Pac.1.
3. *Sutta Nipata* 2.4, *Mangala Sutta*, "The Highest Blessings."
4. Ibid., 1.8, *Metta Sutta*, "The Buddha's Words on Loving-Kindness."
5. P. A. Payutto, *Buddhist Economics: A Middle Way for the Marketplace* (Bangkok: Saha Dhammic Co., Ltd., 1994), pp. 69–70.
6. *Dhammapada* 183–85.
7. A number of Ajahn Buddhadasa's teachings on this topic can be found in his book *Dhammic Socialism* and also in Santikaro Bhikkhu, "Buddhadasa Bhikkhu: Life and Society through the Natural Eyes of Voidness," in *Engaged Buddhism: Buddhist Liberation Movements in Asia*, eds. Christopher Queen and Sallie B. King (Albany: State University of New York Press, 1996), pp. 147–94.
8. *Anguttara Nikaya* 8.41, *Uposatha Sutta*.
9. Ibid., 8.53, "The Dhamma in Brief."
10. *Digha Nikaya* 16.1.11, "The Discourse on the Buddha's Last Days."
11. Payutto, *Buddhist Economics*.
12. *Jataka* V 382.
13. Ibid., 393–411.
14. *Anguttara Nikaya* 5.41, abbrev.
15. Ibid., 4.62, abbrev.
16. *Samyutta Nikaya* 3.19.
17. *Cullavagga* 11.13–14.
18. *Anguttara Nikaya* 8.54, "A Layperson's Welfare."

Chapter 14: Practicing Generosity in a Consumer World

1. This essay was begun in a cabin in Ontario, Canada, provided by Arrow River Forest Hermitage. At the time of writing, I was still a practicing monk. While there, along with daily meditation and translation work, I pondered Lewis Hyde's *The Gift: Imagination and the Erotic Life of Property* (New York: Vintage, 1979). As my country banged its war drums in preparation for another invasion of Iraq, it was a gift to dwell for a few weeks in a country more known for its peacekeeping efforts than for making and dropping bombs. All of these inform and move this consideration of dana.

2. Throughout this article, I understand *sangha* in the inclusive sense that includes women and householders, which I believe is in line with the original emphasis—*supatipanno*, those who practice well. As refuge it refers to the "noble ones," those who practice on the highest level and have realized the fruitions of the path. Cf. next note.

3. Sagathavagga, Sakkasmayutta (11), no.15, verses 916–17, in *The Connected Discourses*, trans. Bhikkhu Bodhi (Boston: Wisdom Publications, 2000), p. 333. Here, "Sangha" refers to the four kinds of noble ones, the exemplars of dhammic life and the leaders of the community of the Buddha's disciples.

4. Visuddhimagga ix, 124, Trans. Bhikkhu Nanamoli (Kandy, Sri Lanka: Buddhist Publication Society, 1991), pp. 352–53.

5. Adapted from a haiku proposed by David Loy, Think Sangha colleague and profound elucidator of the lack running through our lives. See David Loy, *A Buddhist History of the West: Studies in Lack* (Albany: State University Press of New York, 2002).

6. See the well-known analysis of violence found in the *Mahanidana Sutta* (D.ii.58–59).

7. The following discussion owes much to the work of Phra Phaisan Visalo, a close friend and colleague whose many excellent writings have yet to be translated into English.

8. Translating *punna* as "merit" tends to distort its meaning, I believe, and may betray a pecuniary spirit that has crept in along with the growing role of money. "Goodness" better conveys the original meaning of *boon*.

9. Kamala Tiyavanich's *The Buddha in the Jungle* (Chiang Mai, Thailand: Silkworm, 2003) provides abundant examples.

10. Such mass produced and poor quality food contributes to the poor health common among monks today.

11. Luang Por Khoon became famous during the 1990s economic boom when rumors spread of people (including royalty) getting rich after making donations

to him. Wat Phra Thammakai has unabashedly embraced capitalism, often distorting the Buddha's teaching to win followers among the merchant and professional classes. In a still unresolved scandal concerning misuse of temple funds, the abbot personally invested in gold mines, which he justified as more efficient in producing devotional objects "marketed" (their own terminology) to devotees.

12. See the *Parinibbana Sutta* (D.ii.80; numerous translations available) and *Kosambiya Sutta* (M.i.322).

13. *Career* originally meant "a course on which horses race" and then "rapid and continuous course of action," especially one involving professional advancement.

Chapter 15: Wash Your Bowls

1. Shoyoroku, *The Book of Serenity*, case 39, trans. Thomas Cleary (Hudson, NY: Lindesfarne Press, 1990), p. 173.

2. Mumonkan, *The Gateless Barrier*, case 7, trans. Robert Aitken (San Francisco: North Point Press, 1990), p. 54.

3. Dogen, "Instructions for the Tenzo," in Kazuaki Tanahashi, ed., *Moon in a Dewdrop: Writings of Zen Master Dogen* (San Francisco: North Point Press, 1985), pp. 53–66.

4. This phrase is used in the priest ordination ceremony at San Francisco Zen Center.

5. Shoyoroku, *Book of Serenity*, case 25, p. 108.

6. Dogen, "Bodhisattva's Four Methods of Guidance," in Tanahashi, ed., *Moon in a Dewdrop*, p. 45.

Chapter 16: Green Power in Contemporary Japan

1. An extensive survey of the origins and development of Japanese consumer and environmental organizations since the 1960s can be found in Margaret A. McKean, *Environmental Protest and Citizen Politics in Japan* (Berkeley: University of California Press, 1981). These organizations include labor unions, consumer buying clubs, associations of housewives, and consumer health organizations.

2. This paper draws on work developed earlier for the 2003 Buddhism and Ecology conference (Berkeley, CA) hosted by Ryukoku University of Kyoto and the Institute for Buddhist Studies, Berkeley, California.

3. The discussion of the Senryuji Temple case comes from an interview with its abbot, Shoei Sugawara, at Senryuji Temple, August 8, 2003.

4. See Sotoshu Shumucho, ed., *Jinken, heiwa, kankyo "Green Plan" no susume* [Human Rights, Peace, and the Environment: Promoting the "Green Plan"]

(Tokyo: Sotoshu shumucho, 1996). The pamphlet highlights Dogen's appreciation of nature.

5. See Sotoshu Shumucho, ed., *Green Plan: Kodo no tame no Q&A* [The Green Plan: Q&A for Action] (Tokyo: Sotoshu shumucho, 1998), questions 3–4, 6–14, 30. These verses can be found on most pamphlets, including Sotoshu Shumucho, ed., *Chikyu o sukue!: Seikatsu ni ikasu Green Plan gokun* (Tokyo: Sotoshu shumucho, n.d.).

6. See editorial, "Idenshi kumikae shokuhin no hyoji gimu settei," *Kyara* 44 (2001): 29–33.

7. See Sotoshu, *Green Plan*, questions 15–30.

8. The biographical data on Okochi comes from his article, "NGO to jiin no tachiba kara," *Bukkyo Times* (May 14, 1998): 7, as well as from interviews I conducted with him in July and August 2003 at Jukoin temple.

9. See the Jukoin Temple Web page http://oa145309.awmi2.jp/page-262.html, "The Citizen's Strategy for Creating a New World," p. 2.

10. Ibid.

11. On Aoki's work protecting Harima Bay, see Keisuke Aoki, *Edo to kokoro: Kankyo hakai kara jodo e* [The Impure Land and One's Mind: From Environmental Destruction to the Creation of a Pure Land] (Tokyo: Fujiwara shobo, 1997), pp. 59, 73.

12. Ibid., in a subsection of chap. 2.

13. Ibid., pp. 146, 229.

14. See the Jukoin Temple Web page http://oa145309.awmi2.jp/page-261.html, p. 1.

15. Many of the details on the solar panel power plant project can be found in Okochi Hideto, "Shimin ga tsukuru taiyoko hatsudensho: Shiminritsu Edogawa daiichi hatsudensho, tada ima kensetsuchu," *Shigen kankyo taisaku* 35, no. 3 (1999): 44–46.

16. See Jukoin Temple Web page http://oa145309.awmi2.jp/page-262.html, "The Citizen's Strategy for Creating a New World," p. 3.

17. See http://oa145309.awmi2.jp/page-261.html, p. 2.

18. See Rinnoji, ed., *Kankyo no tame ni* [For the Sake of the Environment], video (Sendai, Japan: Rinnoji, 2003), and their Web site, http://www.rinno-ji.or.jp.

Chapter 17: Mutual Correction

1. For an accessible overview of the current challenges, see Edward O. Wilson, *The Future of Life* (New York: Alfred A. Knopf, 2002).

2. See Jacques Gernet, *Buddhism in Chinese Society: An Economic History from the Fifth to the Tenth Centuries*, translated and updated by Franciscus Verellen (New York: Columbia University Press, 1998).

3. Ryukoku University Translation Center, trans., *The Sutra of Contemplation on the Buddha of Immeasurable Life as Expounded by Sakyamuni Buddha* (Kyoto: Ryukoku University, 1984), p. 37. Cf. Luis Gomez, trans., *The Land of Bliss: The Paradise of the Buddha of Measureless Light* (Honolulu: University of Hawaii Press, 1996).

4. On May 12, 1998, Nike CEO Philip Knight reported to the National Press Club a plan to improve labor conditions among his company's six hundred subcontractors. While acknowledging Nike's past, which was "synonymous with slave wages, forced overtime and arbitrary abuses," he proposed reforms in health and safety, child labor, workers' education, and independent monitoring. Even though critics remain, such as Naomi Klein in her book *No Logo*, others, such as the consumer watch group Global Alliance, have praised Nike for its efforts.

5. Gernet, *Buddhism in Chinese Society*, trans. and updated by Franciscus Verellen (New York: Columbia University Press, 1998).

6. In his book *Unequal Protection: The Rise of Corporate Dominance and the Theft of Human Rights* (Emmaus, PA: Rodale, 2002), Thom Hartmann found that the claim that corporations were fictive persons did not exist in the ruling made by the judge in the 1886 case but was only a heading that was given to the case by the court reporter.

7. Ironically, this decision was made fifty years to the day after Franklin D. Roosevelt signed Executive Order no. 9066 on February 19, 1942, which led to the detention in prison camps of 35,327 Buddhist Americans of Japanese ancestry. This information was given to me by Alfred Bloom, who participated in the 1992 meeting.

8. See Dameon Keown, Charles Prebish, and Wayne Husted, eds., *Buddhism and Human Rights* (Surrey, UK: Curzon, 1998).

9. See, for example, Aung San Suu Kyi, "In Quest for Democracy," in *Freedom from Fear*, Aung San Suu Kyi et al. (New York: Penguin, 1995), pp. 174–75.

10. See a recent translation of "The Scripture of Brahma's Net" by Hubert Nearman, in *Buddhist Writings on Meditation and Daily Practice* (Mount Shasta, CA: Shasta Abbey, 1994), pp. 49–188.

11. See the English translation of the *Upasaka Sutra* by Heng-ching Shih, *The Sutra on the Upasaka Precepts* (Berkeley: Bukkyo Dendo Kyokai, 1991). Buddhist ethics are designed for two kinds of people: monastics and lay society. Since Buddhism has been dominated by the monastic community more than any other religion, principles of behavior for society are underdeveloped and have tended to urge laity to mimic monastics or to enter the monastery. A very different approach is taken by this important early Mahayana treatise for

lay Buddhists, which elevates the life of the laity above the monastic community, since the laity can give food, medicine, and practical help, whereas the monks can give only words. See also Ono Hodo, *Daijo kaikyo no kenkyu* [Studies on Mahayana Ethics] (Tokyo: Risosha, 1954).

12. The move to include a multilateral agreement on investment (MAI) clause into the charter for the World Trade Organization in the late 1990s was finally withdrawn in the face of opposition, especially by the Council of Canadians and the International Forum on Globalization (IFG), and as demonstrated in the battle in Seattle in 1999.

13. International Forum on Globalization, *Alternatives to Economic Globalization: A Better World is Possible* (San Francisco: Berrett-Koehler, 2002), pp. 60–61; William Lim, "Glocalizing Traditions," in *Socially Engaged Spirituality*, ed. David Chappell (Bangkok: Sathirakoses-Nagapradipa Foundation, 2003), pp. 564–66.

14. Michael Rothschild, *Bionomics: Economy as Ecosystem* (New York: Henry Holt, 1990), p. 303.

15. See the chapter "From Egalitarianism to Kleptocracy," in Jared Diamond, *Guns, Germs and Steel,* (New York: Norton, 1999), pp. 265–92.

16. The decline of democracy because of the global economy is analyzed by Benjamin R. Barber, *Jihad vs. McWorld* (New York: Ballantine, 1996).

17. Charles Gray, "Corporate Goliaths: Sizing Up Corporations and Governments," *Multinational Monitor* (June 1999): 26–27.

18. See the brilliant and timely work by David C. Korten, *When Corporations Rule the World* (San Francisco: Berrett-Koehler, 1995).

19. Harvey B. Aronson, *Love and Sympathy in Theravada Buddhism* (Delhi: Motilal Banarsidass, 1980), chap. 2.

20. Dalai Lama, *Ethics for the New Millennium* (New York: Riverhead, 1999), pp. 63–65.

21. Susan Sontag, *Regarding the Pain of Others* (New York: Farrar, Straus and Giroux, 2002), pp. 78–80.

22. Herman E. Daly and John B. Cobb Jr., *For the Common Good: Redirecting the Economy toward Community, the Environment, and a Sustainable Future* (Boston: Beacon Press, 1994), pp. 443–507.

23. For full Earth Charter text and materials, see www.earthcharterusa.org.

Contributors

Ajahn Amaro studied meditation under Ajahn Chah in Thailand and ordained as a bhikkhu in 1979. After residing for many years at Amaravati Buddhist Centre near London, he helped establish Abhayagiri Monastery in California and is now the co-abbot. His books include *Silent Rain* and *The Pilgrim Kamanita*.

David W. Chappell is Professor of Comparative Religion at Soka University of America and Professor Emeritus, University of Hawaii. He was founding editor (1981–1995) of the *Journal of Buddhist-Christian Studies* and has published many books on Buddhism and its relation to society.

Pema Chödrön is a fully ordained nun and the resident teacher at Gampo Abbey in Cape Breton, Nova Scotia. She is the author of *The Wisdom of No Escape, Start Where You Are, When Things Fall Apart,* and *The Places That Scare You.* Her most recent book is *Comfortable with Uncertainty.*

Thubten Chödrön studied with Ven. Lama Yeshe and Ven. Zopa Rinpoche, receiving full ordination in 1986 in Taiwan. After teaching in Seattle with Dharma Friendship Foundation (DFF) for nine years, she founded Sravasti Abbey in Idaho. Her books include *Open Heart, Clear Mind; Buddhism for Beginners; Working with Anger;* and *Taming the Monkey Mind.*

Norman Fischer is a Zen priest and poet. He is a former abbot of the San Francisco Zen Center and the founder of and teacher at the Everyday Zen Foundation. He is the author of *Taking Our Places: The Buddhist Path to Truly Growing Up;* his latest book of verse is *Slowly but Dearly.*

Joseph Goldstein is a cofounder of the Insight Meditation Society, the Forest Refuge, and the Barre Center for Buddhist Studies. He is the author of *One Dharma: The Emerging Western Buddhism, Insight Meditation: The Practice of Freedom,* and *The Experience of Insight.* He has been teaching insight and lovingkindness meditation retreats worldwide since 1974.

Linda Goodhew is an associate professor in the Department of English Literature and Language, Gakushuin University, Tokyo. A different version of the article on Momo and Dogen is included in the book *Fantastic Dharma: New Buddhist Myth in Modern Fantasy*, forthcoming from Wisdom Publications.

Sunyana Graef, a sanctioned heir of Roshi Philip Kapleau, established the Vermont Zen Center in 1988 and is the head teacher there. She also teaches at the Toronto Zen Center and at the Casa Zen in Costa Rica. She is married, has two grown daughters, and lives in Shelburne, Vermont.

Rita M. Gross is internationally known for her work on Buddhism and gender, including her book *Buddhism after Patriarchy: A Feminist History, Analysis and Reconstruction of Buddhism*. She has also written widely on Buddhism and contemporary social issues and is a senior teacher of Shambhala Buddhism, a network of meditation centers founded by Chögyam Trungpa.

Ruben L. F. Habito was born and raised in the Philippines and lived in Japan for twenty years before coming to the United States in 1989. Author of *Living Zen, Loving God and Healing Breath: Zen Spirituality for a Wounded Earth*, he is resident teacher at Maria Kannon Zen Center in Dallas, Texas, and also teaches at Perkins School of Theology, Southern Methodist University.

Pracha Hutanuwatr is Deputy Director of Santi Pracha Dhamma Institute and Program Director of the Grassroots Leadership Training project in Bangkok, Thailand. He has written a biography of Buddhadasa in Thai and worked closely with Sulak Sivaraksa on many initiatives, including the Spirit in Education Movement and the International Network of Engaged Buddhists.

Stephanie Kaza is Associate Professor of Environmental Studies at the University of Vermont, where she teaches religion and ecology, ecofeminism, and unlearning consumerism. She is a long-time Zen student and the author of *The Attentive Heart* and coeditor (with Kenneth Kraft) of *Dharma Rain: Sources of Buddhist Environmentalism*.

Sumi Loundon is Assistant Director at the Barre Center for Buddhist Studies and editor of *Blue Jean Buddha: Voices of Young Buddhists*. Sumi received a master's degree from Harvard Divinity School, with training in Buddhist studies and Sanskrit. She lives with her husband in Barre, Massachusetts.

David Loy is a professor in the Faculty of International Studies, Bunkyo University, Chigasaki, Japan, and a longtime Zen student. He has written numerous articles on socially-engaged Buddhism in the modern context. His books include *A Buddhist History of the West: Studies in Lack* and *The Great Awakening: A Buddhist Social Theory*.

Jane Rasbash lives in Scotland and works in the field of sustainable development and engaged Buddhism, with extensive involvement in Southeast Asia with the Spirit in Education Movement. She has also served as codirector of the

Grassroots Leadship Training program in Burma and as executive secretary to the Alternatives to Consumerism conferences in Thailand.

Santikaro ordained as a Theravada bhikkhu in 1985 to study under Buddhadasa Bhikkhu in Thailand. He lived at Suan Mokkh Temple until 1999 and spent nineteen years as a bhikkhu. Since disrobing, he continues his work developing Liberation Park, a Dhamma study center in Oak Park, Illinois.

Judith Simmer-Brown is a senior teacher of the lineage of Chögyam Trungpa and professor of Religious Studies at Naropa University in Boulder, Colorado. Her books include *Dakini's Warm Breath: The Feminine Principle in Tibetan Buddhism* and the coedited volume *Benedict's Dharma: Buddhists Reflect on the Rule of Saint Benedict.*

Duncan Ryuken Williams is Assistant Professor of East Asian Buddhism at the University of California–Irvine and an ordained Soto Zen priest. He is the author of a monograph entitled *The Other Side of Zen: A Social History of Soto Zen Buddhism in Tokugawa Japan* and coeditor of *American Buddhism* and *Buddhism and Ecology.*

Diana Winston is a writer, activist, teacher, and the founder of the Buddhist Alliance for Social Engagement (BASE) program. She is the author of *Wide Awake: A Buddhist Guide for Teens.* She served as Associate Director of Buddhist Peace Fellowship though 2002 and is now training as a vipassana teacher with Jack Kornfield.